CW01651176

NEW FORMATIONS

EDITOR:
Judith Squires

CONSULTING EDITORS:
James Donald
Erica Carter

PICTURE EDITOR:
Stephen Johnstone

EDITORIAL BOARD:
Homi Bhabha
Lesley Caldwell
Tony Davies
Jonathan Dollimore
Simon Frith
Jim Grealy
Stuart Hall
Dick Hebdige
Maria Lauret (Reviews)
Graham Murdock
Denise Riley
Jenny Bourne Taylor (Reviews)
Valerie Walkerdine

OVERSEAS EDITORS:
Ien Ang
Tony Bennett
Jody Berland
Victor Burgin
Hazel Carby
Iain Chambers
Joan Copjec
Lidia Curti
Ian Hunter
Cora Kaplan
Noel King
Colin Mercer
Kobena Mercer
Edward Said
Renata Salecl
Gayatri Chakravorty Spivak
John Tagg

New Formations is
published in April,
August and September
by Lawrence & Wishart
144a Old South Lambeth Road
London SW8 1XX
Tel 071–820 9281
Fax 071–587 0469

ADVERTISEMENTS
for enquiries/bookings contact
Lindsay Thomas, Lawrence & Wishart

SUBSCRIPTIONS
For 1992, subscription rates to Lawrence & Wishart are, for 3 issues
UK: Institutions £45, Individuals £28.
North America: Institutions $74; Individuals $50.
Rest of world: Institutions £46; Individuals £30.
Single copies: £12.99

CONTRIBUTIONS, CORRESPONDENCE
should be sent to
The Editor, *New Formations*,
Dept of Politics, University of Bristol,
12 Priory Road, Bristol BS8 1TU

BOOKS FOR REVIEW
should be sent to Maria Lauret,
Dept of English, University of Southampton,
Highfield, Southampton S09 5NH

Prospective writers are encouraged to contact the editors to discuss their ideas and to obtain a copy of our style sheet.
Manuscripts should be sent in triplicate. They will not be returned unless a stamped, self-addressed envelope is enclosed.
Contributors should note that the editorial board cannot take responsibility for any manuscript submitted to *New Formations*.

The collection as a whole © Lawrence & Wishart 1992
Individual articles © the authors 1992

No article may be reproduced or transmitted in any form or by any means, electronic or mechanical, including photocopying, recording, or any information storage and retrieval system without the permission in writing of the publisher, editor or author.

ISSN 0 950-2378
ISBN 0 85315 757 X

Text design by Jan Brown Designs, London
Photoset in North Wales by
Derek Doyle & Associates, Mold, Clwyd
Printed in Great Britain
at the University Press, Cambridge

NOTES ON CONTRIBUTORS

Kobena Mercer has worked at the British Film Institute and is currently teaching at the University of California, Santa Cruz.

Jane M. Gaines is an Assistant Professor of English at Duke University where she is the director of the Program in Film and Video. She is the author of *Contested Culture: The Image, the Voice, and the Law* (University of North Carolina Press, forthcoming).

Couze Venn teaches cultural studies at the Polytechnic of East London, is co-author of *Changing the Subject* (Methuen), and is currently working on a book entitled *Occidentalism and its Discontents.*

Gregory Stephens is currently doing research on multicultural frontiers at the University of California, Davis. He has previously been manager and songwriter for the Ausin, Elouise Burrell and Trickle Down.

Jean-Jacques Lecercle is Professor of English at the University of Paris, Nanterre. He is author of *Philosophy Through the Looking Glass* (Hutchinson), *Frankenstein: mythe et philosophie* (PUF), and *The Violence of Language* (Routledge).

Sandra Kemp lectures in English at Glasgow University, and is author of *Kipling's Hidden Narratives*. She is also a 'Shelf Life' columnist for the *Times Higher Education Supplement*, and has trained previously in both ballet and Graham technique.

Graham Dawson teaches cultural studies at Brighton Polytechnic and has recently completed a PhD on 'Adventure, Masculinity and Empire'.

Daglind Sonolet is a sociologist of culture associated with the *Association pour le Développement des Recherches et Etudes Sociologiques, Economiques et Statistiques*, Paris. More recently she has worked on Sartre's and Kundera's novels and is currently engaged in research on questions of European cultural identity.

David Morley teaches in the Communication Department at Goldsmiths' College, University of London.

Kevin Robins works at the Centre for Urban and Regional Development Studies, University of Newcastle-upon-Tyne. He is co-author of *The Technical Fix* (Macmillan).

CONTENTS

NUMBER 16 SPRING 1992

Competing Glances

EDITORIAL

I

The institutionalization of intellectual debate, coupled with the generational deep-freeze on academic jobs, leaves us with departmentalized, introspective and, frequently, dull intellectual discourse within academia, and little at all outside of it.[1]

1. Thanks to Patrick Wright for discussion of this point.

New Formations, always willfully resistant to categorization, attempts to confront this situation by providing a forum for debates about contemporary cultural issues, in all their diversity, which are multi-disciplinary and forward looking. We seek to reflect and engender new formations of thought.

It is in this context that our 'maverick' journal has found a new 'home'; a home with a publisher not located purely within academic publishing, but nonetheless at the forefront of intellectual debate.

'Competing Glances', our first issue with Lawrence & Wishart, captures this multi-disciplinary critical focus. Articles on 'erotic' photography, rap music, silent movies, postmodern dance, German literature and Japanese culture ... a gloriously diverse agenda drawn together by a shared desire to explore aesthetic ambivalence, strategies of transgression and culturally disruptive forms of resistance.

II

> There is nothing wrong with provocative art. I hope to do something that will shock even myself.'
>
> Andreas Serrano[2]

2. Sarah Kent, 'Mike Bildo, Manuel Ocampo, Andreas Serrano', Saatchi Gallery Catalogue 1992.

When it was declared in US Senate that Serrano's 'Piss Christ' was a 'deplorable, despicable display of vulgarity' and the catalogue of the exhibition torn up to add weight to the rhetoric, the censorship row had just begun. Twenty-five senators signed a letter protesting the funding of the show by the National Endowment of the Arts and the Robert Mapplethorpe retrospective, about to be shown at the Corcoran Gallery, Washington, was cancelled. That summer Jesse Helms, Senator for North Carolina, steered through legislation prohibiting the National Endowment from funding 'obscene or indecent' material. It is in this context that the first two contributors, Kobena Mercer and Jane Gaines, address the work of Robert Mapplethorpe and ask how we are to view these images.

Kobena Mercer addresses the aesthetic ambivalence in visual representation of the black male nude. An ambivalence which exists not inside the text but across the relations between authors, texts and readers. Do photographs like

'Man in a Polyester Suit' reinscribe the fixed beliefs of racist ideology or do they problematize them by foregrounding the intersections of sexuality? Mercer asks this question only to show that an unequivocal answer is impossible. The ambivalent positioning of the reader/viewer coupled with the possibility for contradictory readings derived from the text/image mean that all answers to such a question will be contextual. The photographs are open to a range of contradictory readings whose political character depends on the social identity that different audiences bring to bear on them.

Read contextually, argues Mercer – seen within the realities of contemporary urban gay culture – Mapplethorpe's work can be understood as a 'subversive recoding of the normative aesthetic ideal'. Thus, in the face of the postmodern assertion of the 'death of the author' Mercer claims that it really does matter who is speaking; and it matters because this is itself indicative of where power lies.

Jane Gaines also addresses the issues of whether these photographs are racist and echoes Mercer's argument in asserting that racism (and all other '-isms') lie not in the image, but in the offending social relations which form the interpretive context of the image. Transgression lies not in the image/the act/the text but in its reception. (For further discussion of what it is to transgress see Elizabeth Wilson's review of Jonathan Dollimore's *Sexual Dissidence*.)

In which context I refer to a recent article from the *TLS* entitled '*Viz*: A Qualified Defence'. Arguing for the importance of normality and sanity Robert Grant finds time to be supportive of *Viz*, but states that Gilbert and George, Andreas Serrano and Robert Mapplethorpe (unlike *Viz*) 'are not only utterly humourless, but also purely and gratuitously offensive. They have been defended, moreover, applauded even, by the "progressive" establishment ... Which is worse, the occasional outrageous holiday from good taste, or the self-righteous pomposities which mask a sinister, sustained assault on all taste, all decency and all value?'[3]

3. Robert Grant, '*Viz*: A Qualified Defence', *Times Literary Supplement*, 7 February 1992.

What for one person is a sustained assault on all taste, all decency, all value is for another an anti-canonical, counter-hegemonic form of resistance. Mapplethorpe's representation of taboo couplings, argues Gaines, act as an evocation of a triple transgression (of class, gender and race) and are therefore not surprisingly read as an assault on taste, decency and value for those who locate these within existing white male culture.

Couze Venn, unlike Robert Grant, finds evidence of no such 'sinister, sustained assault' on dominant cultural values. Indeed, he notes that strategies for action and resistance have become as disorganized as capitalism is argued to be. Yet, he argues, in the face of a deep-seated discursive alliance between logocentrism, phallocentrism and ethnocentrism, the need for the production of a 'counter-discourse' is strong. The problem for analysis, argues Venn, is not the existence of texts of oppression, but the development and diffusion of insurgent ways of reading them. This, then, is the claim of Jane Gaines reversed. Just as oppressive relations lie not in the image but in the reading of them, so radical readings can threaten to make any image culturally disruptive.

The desire for the development of 'counter-discourses' articulated within

Venn's piece, is further explored by Gregory Stephens in the context of rap music. Stephens' project is to reveal the extent to which rap music challenges traditional definitions of racial representation; in attempting to define racial boundaries, it simultaneously transgresses them. 'Conscious rap', an artform rooted in the discourse of 'black liberation', is nonetheless being adapted by increasingly multi-ethnic subcultures in order to develop 'imagined communities' that transcend racial and national boundaries. This is not an assimilationist stance but a celebration of hybridity. 'Call-and-response' rap may be a distinctly African American form of discourse but, claims Stephens, it is also well suited to the vernacular culture of an experimental democratic society.

Culturally disruptive forms of resistance need not of course be verbal, as the images of Mapplethorpe reveal so clearly. The next two pieces, by Jean-Jacques Lecercle and Sandra Kemp (the latter originally given at a conference entitled 'Against the Word'), specifically focus on the non-verbal, on non-articulate communication: the silent movie and postmodern dance.

Jean-Jacques Lecercle opens his piece with Walter Benjamin's assertion of the revolutionary primacy of silent movies and dismay at contamination of non-verbal arts by language. Whilst this statement might have appeared, throughout the 1960s and 70s, as simply a nostalgic longing for a past era, the current crisis of logocentrism, claims Lecercle, means that the time has come to think again of the cinema outside linguistic models. So, lest we think that language has conquered the cinema for good, note the recent claim of David Mamet, director of *House of Games* and *Homicide*, that 'the perfect movie does not have any dialogue.'[4]

4. David Mamet, 'Cut to the Bone', in *The Guardian*, 13 February 1992.

This is of relevance to our concern with culturally disruptive forms of resistance in that the silence of silent movies is, according to Lecercle, a locus for the deployment of instinctual drives, and hence likely to generate reactions which are uncontrollable (and, claims Benjamin, revolutionary). There are, argues Lecercle, two levels of language – articulate and general. Silence is the medium of the general language; the script is the intermediacy of articulate language. The way out of logocentrism in the nonverbal arts is to concentrate not on verbal or articulate language, but on the language of the image.

This conclusion left me wondering how one might relate Lecercle's thesis to Stephens' discussion of the radical potential of rap, and drew me to a consideration not of the language of rap, but its rhythm; not the lyrics, but the sounds. Which takes us back to Lecercle and his claim that the 'language of the image, the language of silence ... is ecstatic but static. Articulate language, on the other hand, is garrulous but dynamic, an active process of translation, language bursting into song.' If articulate language represses, as Lecercle claims, rhythmic language, maybe rap allows its expression.

Which moves us onto a discussion of dance and 'expressive arts' which are the focus of Sandra Kemp's piece. As with Lecercle's silent movie one is, Kemp claims, less in control when watching or listening than when turning the pages of a book, which you can do in your own time. Dance, then, is a celebration of 'general language' over 'articulate language'; of the 'polymorphous pleasure of the body' over 'the adult pleasure of the analysis of the text'. Thus Emma Goldmann's celebrated assertion that 'If I can't dance, I don't want to be part of your revolution' takes on, in this context, a new meaning.

In Kemp's piece is also to be found a pursuit of, and celebration of, the 'competing glances' discussed by Gaines. 'As the narrative proceeds,' she says of the dance *Shelf Life*, 'we are forced to relinquish the relative security of a single vision, the desire to see it all.' For Kemp these competing glances are a democratization of the stage-space, just as, for Stephens, the competing voices of rap are the beginnings of a democratic discourse. 'We're talking here about a different kind of viewing, listening or reading, in terms of overlaps and discontinuities – the random aspects of the viewing process, the flickering of attention spans.' (Kemp)

III

If the difficulty of composing a coherent individual identity, given the proliferation of images and versions of the self available, is a common one, it was particularly acute for T.E. Lawrence. Graham Dawson discusses the relationship between the Lawrence of Arabia Legend and the 'real' T.E. Lawrence. The more we read, the more the fantasy hero 'disintegrates into a multiplicity of competing identifications'. His attempt to attain a new identity quitted him of his English self; he dropped one form but could not successfully take on another. This, Lawrence himself recognized, 'let me look at the West and its conventions with new eyes'.

Looking at the West and its conventions with new eyes can, however, be a product not just of individual angst, but also of societal change. A case in point is the re-evaluation of the work of Christa Wolf in particular, and German literary aesthetics in general, in the light of the demise of the communist regime of East Germany. This is the focus of Daglind Sonolet's contribution. Sonolet recounts the controversy over Wolf's work with a view to revealing the deep unease over standards of literary value. For, throughout the entire controversy, Sonolet shows, there has been an evident unwillingness to deal with Wolf's actual writing, to differentiate between personal morality and literary value.

This aesthetic ambivalence takes us back to Mercer's opening discussion of Mapplethorpe. For Sonolet argues that the great insecurity concerning standards of aesthetic judgment can be partially resolved by recognizing that 'literature cannot be reduced either to the varying associations made by the reading public, or to authorial intention, though both aspects are part of its essence. Literature is language, a social instrument of communication, and as such saturated with evaluation.' The novel, she claims, echoing previous arguments, makes this social aspect of language evident, 'where diverse social "voices" confront each other in unresolved dialogue.'

Finally, the West and its conventions are put into renewed focus by Kevin

Robins and Dave Morley in their exploration of Japan, and the ambiguity of its image in the West. For Japan, they argue, is calling Western modernity into question. Japan has come to exist within the Western political and cultural unconscious as a figure of danger, and it has done so because it has destabilized the neat correlation between West/East and modern/premodern. In short, Japan has successfully called into question the supposed centrality of the West as a cultural and geographical locus for the project of modernity. 'The postmodern era,' then, according to Robins and Morley, 'will be the Pacific era. Japan is the future, and it is a future that seems to be transcending and displacing Western modernity.'

Judith Squires
March 1992

THEORY CULTURE & SOCIETY

RECENT & FORTHCOMING CONTENTS:

Anne Bowler and Blaine McBurney *Gentrification of the Avant-Garde*

Rita Felski *Feminist Theory and Social Change*

Pierre Bourdieu *Thinking about Limits*

Nancy Fraser *The Uses and Abuses of French Discourse Theories for Feminist Politics*

Randall Collins *On the Sociology of Intellectual Stagnation: The Late Twentieth Century in Perspective*

Frances Bonner and Paul du Gay *Representing the Enterprising Self: thirtysomething and Contemporary Consumer Culture*

David Frisby *Between the Spheres: Siegfried Kracauer and the Detective Novel*

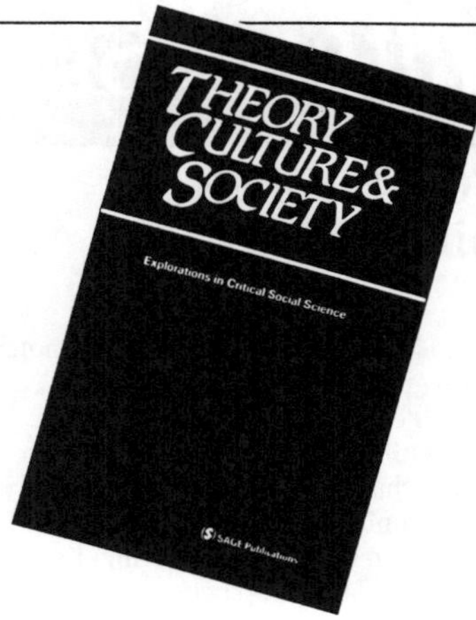

Edited by ***Mike Featherstone***

'It seems to me that Mike Featherstone and his editorial group have done more than any other sociological group to move sociology forward into new terrains of thought and discourse and they have done so with power, grace and insight'.

Professor Norman Denzin, University of Illinois

Published quarterly in February, May, August and November

Make sure you subscribe now!
Use the order form below and save 20%

20% Discount Order Form

Send this order form to:

Sage Publications

6 Bonhill Street, London EC2A 4PU, UK
Tel: 071-374 0645
Or why not fax us your order on **071-374 8741?**

US Orders to:

Sage Publications, PO Box 5096, Newbury Park, CA 91359, USA

❑ Yes! I want to subscribe to *Theory, Culture & Society* at a **20% Discount**

❑ Individual Rate at **£22**(£28*)/ **$36**($46*)
❑ Institutional Rate at **£60**(£75*)/ **$99**($124*)
**Usual 1992 rate*

Name ______________________________

Address ______________________________

____

____

THREE WAYS TO PAY!

❑ **CHEQUE!...** I enclose a cheque (made payable to **Sage Publications**)

❑ **GIRO!...** I have today paid by International Giro to A/c No 548 0353

Date ______________

❑ **CREDIT CARD!...** Please charge my credit card
❑ Mastercard ❑ Access ❑ Visa
❑ Barclaycard ❑ American Express
❑ Diner's Club ❑ Eurocard

Card Number ______________________

Expiry Date __________

Signature ______________________

Date __________

1547

Cultural Studies Books for 1992

TOWNS FOR PEOPLE
Transforming Urban Life
Ken Worpole

Town centres seem to have lost many of their traditional functions – as meeting places, as centres of social, political and cultural life, and as the very focus of the urban 'public realm'. Our civic culture is in crisis with rising street crime, unreliable public transport, inappropriate town planning, the growth of domestic leisure, and social and demographic splintering. Ken Worpole argues that the relationship between citizenship and public space and the values of cultural diversity and cosmopolitanism have been lost in a preoccupation with land-use planning and 'race to the finish' local economic growth. He gives us a new agenda for cultural and civic renewal in our towns and cities.

May 1992 c.112pp 0 335 09964 5 Paperback c.£9.99
0 335 09965 3 Hardback c.£30.00

A CRITICAL AND CULTURAL THEORY READER
Texts and Textuality
Antony Easthope and Kate McGowan (eds.)

There is a growing need for an accessible collection of essays and extracts required for the study of both high and popular culture. This reader, covering Semiology, Ideology, Subjectivity, Difference, Gender and Postmodernism, contains essential writing by Saussure, Barthes, Lacan, Kristeva, Foucault, Derrida and Cixous. It concludes with a section of 'Cultural Documents' with extracts from Leavis, Adorno, Williams and Tzara. With the needs of students in mind, each section is fully introduced and each piece of writing summarized in the notes.

April 1992 c.256pp 0 335 09944 0 Paperback c.£9.99
0 335 09945 9 Hardback c.£35.00

OPEN UNIVERSITY PRESS
CELTIC COURT, 22 BALLMOOR, BUCKINGHAM, MK18 1XW.
TEL: (0280) 823388 FAX: (0280) 823233 TRADE ORDERS: (0280) 822211

new left *review*

NLR 190 THE CLAIMS OF INEQUALITY

Introductory offer—receive this SPECIAL ISSUE free!

NLR PAUL CAMMACK looks at the development of Brazilian capitalism, arguing that the oligarchy's grip on power affords little optimism for the ascendancy of workers' movements.

NLR JERRY COHEN recalls the values of his Communist childhood and questions the current tendency to abandon the pursuit of egalitarian aspirations.

NLR VICTOR KIERNAN and DIMITRIS KYRTATAS on religion: Kiernan explores the relationship between Christianity and Marxism; Kyrtatas considers the social meaning of Revelation.

NLR TONY BENN assesses the evidence of attempts to manipulate and destabilize the Wilson government.

NLR JULIAN STALLABRASS considers the role which tourism, the creation of images and naming play in the transformation of formerly Communist countries.

NLR As an ex-tutor on job-training programmes, ROGER TAYLOR argues that by working from the base we can escape the cul-de-sac of powerlessness.

NLR By its nature, argues TERRY BLOOMFIELD, there is a limit to which the best rock music can be fully subordinated to the logic of the commodity.

NLR Elizabeth Fox-Genovese's *Feminism without Illusions* is reviewed by ELIZABETH WILSON.

NLR BRANKA MAGAŠ comments on Ernest Gellner.

Subscription Address
NEW LEFT REVIEW (190 offer),
120-126 LAVENDER AVENUE, MITCHAM, SURREY CR4 3HP, UK

For a trial subscription to NLR—with this special 144-page issue FREE—please complete the coupon and post it together with your remittance (where applicable) to our Subscription Department—address below.

ANNUAL SUBSCRIPTION
Six issues plus the FREE COPY cost only £22.50 UK; £26/US$42/Can$50 Overseas; £34/US$54/Can$65 Airmail

Please enter my annual subscription to *New Left Review* beginning with NLR 191 and send me NLR 190 FREE

NAME ____________

ADDRESS ____________

____

POSTCODE/ZIPCODE ____________

COUNTRY ____________

☐ I enclose cheque/money order payable to *New Left Review* for £/$______

☐ Please debit my credit-card account:
☐ Visa ☐ Access ☐ Mastercard
☐ Eurocard ☐ AmEx *(please tick)*

Card No.

Expiry date ____________

Or ring our CREDIT CARD HOTLINE: 081-685 0301

Skin Head Sex Thing

Racial Difference and the Homoerotic Imaginary

Kobena Mercer

I

In this article I want to explore the experience of aesthetic ambivalence in visual representations of the black male nude. The photographs of Robert Mapplethorpe provide a salient point of entry into this complex 'structure of feeling' as this is one place where such ambivalence is experienced at its most intense.[1]

My interest in this aspect of Mapplethorpe's work began in 1982, when a friend lent me his copy of *Black Males*. It circulated between us as a kind of illicit object of desire, albeit a highly problematic one. We were fascinated by the beautiful bodies, as we went over the repertoire of images again and again, drawn in by the desire to look and enjoy what was given to be seen. We wanted to look, but we didn't always find what we wanted to see. We were shocked, of course, and disturbed by the racial discourse of the imagery. Above all we were angered by the aesthetic equation that reduced these black male bodies to abstract visual 'things', silenced in their own right as subjects, serving only to enhance the name and reputation of the author in the rarefied world of art photography. But still we were stuck, unable to make sense of our own implication in the emotions brought into play by Mapplethorpe's 'imaginary'.

I've chosen to situate the issue of ambivalence in relation to these experiences because I am now involved in a partial revision of arguments made in an earlier reading of Mapplethorpe's work.[2] This revision arises not because those arguments were wrong, but because I've changed my mind, or rather I should say I still can't make up my mind about Mapplethorpe. In returning to my earlier essay I want to suggest an approach to ambivalence, not as something that occurs 'inside' the text (as if cultural texts were hermetically sealed or self-sufficient), but as something that is experienced across the relations between authors, texts, and readers – in relations that are always contingent, context-bound, and historically specific.

Posing the problem of ambivalence and undecidability in this way not only underlines the role of the reader; it also draws attention to the important, and equally undecidable, role of context in determining the range of different readings that can be produced from the same text. In this respect, it is impossible to ignore the crucial changes in context that frame the readings currently negotiated around Mapplethorpe and his work. Mapplethorpe's death in 1989 from AIDS, a major retrospective of his work at the Whitney Museum in New York, the political 'controversy' over federal arts policy initiated by the fundamentalist Right in response to a second Mapplethorpe exhibition organized by the Institute of Contemporary Art in Philadelphia –

1. References are made primarily to *Black Males* (with introduction by Edmund White), Gallerie Jurka, Amsterdam 1982, and *The Black Book* (with introduction by Ntozake Shange), Schirmer/Mosel, Munich 1986.

2. Kobena Mercer, 'Imaging the Black Man's Sex', in Pat Holland, Jo Spence and Simon Watney (eds), *Photography/Politics: Two*, Comedia/Methuen, London 1986.

these events have irrevocably altered the context in which we perceive, argue about, and evaluate Mapplethorpe's most explicitly homoerotic work.

The context has also changed as a result of another set of contemporary developments: the emergence of new aesthetic practices among black lesbian and gay artists in Britain and the United States. Across a range of media, such work problematizes earlier conceptions of identity in black cultural practices. This is accomplished by entering into the ambivalent and overdetermined spaces where race, class, gender, sexuality, and ethnicity intersect in the social construction and lived experiences of individual and collective subjectivities. Such developments demand acknowledgment of the historical contingency of context and in turn raise significant questions about the universalist character of some of the grand aesthetic and political claims once made in the name of cultural theory. Beginning with a summary of my earlier argument, I want to identify some of the uses and limitations of psychoanalytic concepts in cultural theory before mapping a more historical trajectory within which to examine the constitutive ambivalence of the identifications we actually inhabit in living with difference.

II REVISING

The overriding theme of my earlier reading of Mapplethorpe's photographs was that they inscribe a process of objectification in which individual black male bodies are aestheticized and eroticized as objects of the gaze. Framed within the artistic conventions of the nude, these bodies are sculpted and shaped into aesthetic artefacts that offer an erotic source of pleasure in the act of looking. Insofar as what is represented in the pictorial space of the photograph is a 'look', or a certain 'way of looking', the pictures say more about the white male subject behind the camera than they do about the black men whose beautiful bodies we see depicted. This is because the invisible or absent subject is the actual agent of the look, at the centre and in control of the apparatus of representation, the I/eye at the imaginary origin of the perspective that marks out the empty space to which the viewer is invited as a spectator. This argument was based on a formal analysis of the codes and conventions brought to bear on the pictorial space of the photographs, and, equally importantly, on an analogy with feminist analyses of the erotic objectification of the image of women in Western traditions of visual representation.

Three formal conventions interweave across the photographic text to organize and direct the viewer's gaze into its pictorial space. A sculptural code, concerning the posing and posture of the body in the studio enclosure; a code of portraiture concentrated on the face; and a code of lighting and framing, fragmenting bodies into textured formal abstractions – all of these help to construct the *mise-en-scène* of fantasy and desire which structures the spectator's disposition toward the image. As all references to a social or historical context are effaced by the cool distance of the detached gaze, the text enables the projection of a fantasy which saturates the black male body in sexual predicates.

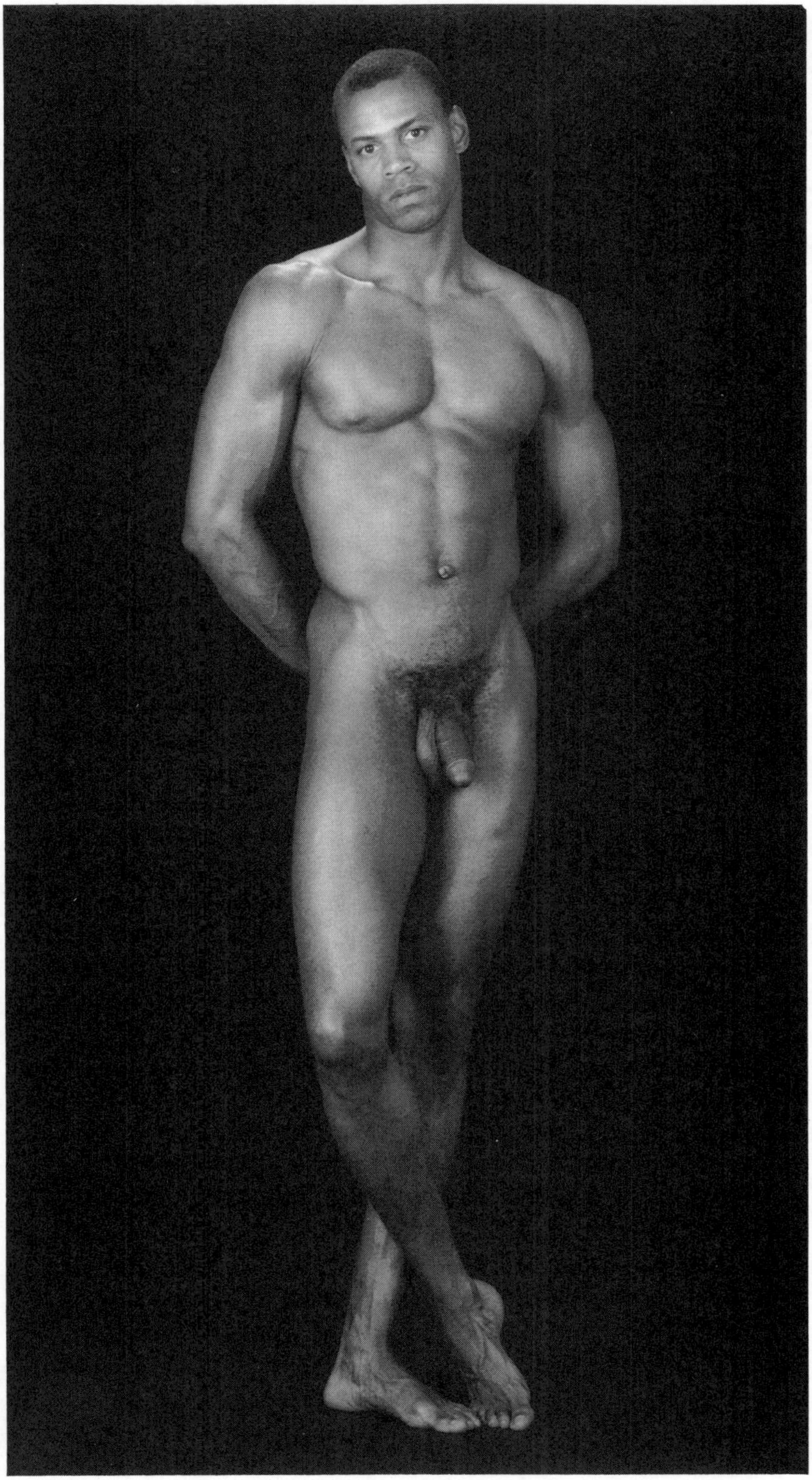

Thomas, 1986. © The Estate of Robert Mapplethorpe, 1986.

These codes draw from aspects of Mapplethorpe's oeuvre as a whole and have become the signs by which we recognize his authorial signature. Their specific combination, moreover, is punctuated by the technical perfection – especially marked in the printing process – that also distinguishes Mapplethorpe's presence as an author. Considering the way in which the glossy allure of the photographic print becomes consubstantial with the shiny texture of black skin, I argued that a significant element in the pleasures the photographs make available consists in the fetishism that they bring into play. Such fetishism not only eroticizes the visible difference that the black male nude embodies, it also lubricates the ideological reproduction of racial otherness as the fascination of the image articulates a fantasy of power and mastery over the Other.

Before introducing a revision of this view of racial fetishism in Mapplethorpe's photographs, I want to emphasize its dependence on the framework of feminist theory initially developed in relation to cinematic representation by Laura Mulvey.[3] Crudely put, Mulvey showed that men look and women are looked at. The position of 'woman' in dominant regimes of visual representation says little or nothing about the historical experiences of women as such, because the female subject functions predominantly as a mirror image of what the masculine subject wants to see. The visual depiction of women in the *mise-en-scène* of heterosexual desire serves to stabilize and reproduce the narcissistic scenario of a phallocentric fantasy in which the omnipotent male gaze sees but is never seen. What is important about this framework of analysis is the way it reveals the symbolic relations of power and subordination at work in the binary relations that structure dominant codes and conventions of visual representations of the body. The field of visibility is thus organized by the subject/object dichotomy that associates masculinity with the activity of looking and femininity with the subordinate, passive role of being that which is looked at.

3. Laura Mulvey, 'Visual Pleasure and Narrative Cinema', *Screen*, Vol 16, no 3, 1975.

In extrapolating such terms to Mapplethorpe's black nudes, I suggested that because both artist and models are male, a tension arises which transfers the *frisson* of difference to the metaphorically polarized terms of racial identity. The black/white duality overdetermines the subject/object dichotomy of seeing and being seen. This metaphorical transfer underlines the erotic investment of the gaze in the most visible element of racial difference – the fetishization of black skin. The dynamics of this tension are apparently stabilized within the pictorial space of the photographs by the ironic appropriation of commonplace stereotypes – the black man as athlete, as savage, as mugger. These stereotypes in turn serve to regulate and fix the representational presence of the black subject, who is thereby 'put in his place' by the power of Mapplethorpe's gaze.

The formal work of the codes essentializes each individual model into the homogenized embodiment of an ideal type. This logic of typification in dominant regimes of racial representation has been emphasized by Homi Bhabha, who argues that 'an important feature of colonial discourse is its dependence on the concept of "fixity" in the ideological construction of otherness.'[4] The scopic fixation on black skin thus implies a kind of 'negrophilia', an aesthetic idealization and eroticized investment in the racial Other that inverts and reverses the binary axis of the fears and anxieties invested in or projected onto the Other in 'negrophobia'. Both positions, whether they devalue or overvalue the signs of racial difference, inhabit the representational space of what Bhabha calls colonial fantasy. While I would now qualify the theoretical analogies on which this analysis of Mapplethorpe was based, I would still want to defend the terms of a psychoanalytic reading of racial fetishism, a fetishism that can be most tangibly grasped in a photograph such as *Man in a Polyester Suit* (1980).

The scale and framing of this picture emphasizes the sheer size of the big black dick. Apart from the hands, the penis and the penis alone identifies the model as a black man. As Frantz Fanon said, diagnosing the figure of 'the Negro' in the fantasies of his white psychiatric patients, 'One is no longer aware of the Negro, but only of a penis: the Negro is eclipsed. He is turned into a penis. He *is* a penis.'[5] The element of scale thus summons up one of the deepest mythological fears and anxieties in the racist imagination, namely that all black men have huge willies. In the fantasmatic space of the supremacist imaginary, the big black phallus is a threat not only to the white master (who shrinks in impotence from the thought that the subordinate black male is more potent and sexually powerful than he), but also to civilization itself, since the 'bad object' represents a danger to white womanhood and therefore the threat of miscegenation and racial degeneration.

The binarisms of classical racial discourse are emphasized in Mapplethorpe's photograph by the jokey irony of the contrast between the black man's private parts and the public respectability signified by the business suit. The oppositions hidden/exposed and denuded/clothed play upon the binary oppositions nature/culture and savage/civilized to bring about a condensation of libidinal investment, fear, and wish-fulfilment in the fantasmatic presence of the Other. The binarisms repeat the assumption that sex is the essential 'nature' of black masculinity, while the cheap, tacky polyester suit confirms the black man's failure to gain access to 'culture'. The camouflage of respectability cannot conceal the fact that, in essence, he originates, like his prick, from somewhere anterior to civilization. What is dramatized in the picture is the splitting of levels of belief, which Freud regarded as the key feature of the logic of disavowal in fetishism.[6] Hence the implication: '*I know* it's not true that all black men have big penises, *but still*, in my photographs they do.'

It is precisely at this point, however, that the concept of fetishism threatens to conceal more than it reveals about the ambivalence that the spectator experiences in relation to Mapplethorpe's work as its 'shock effect'. Freud saw the castration anxiety in the little boy's shock at discovering the absence of a penis in the little girl (acknowledged and disavowed in the fetish) as constitutive of sexual difference. The clinical pathology or perversion of the fetishist, like a neurotic symptom, unravels for classical psychoanalysis the 'normal' developmental path of Oedipal heterosexual identity; it is the point at which

4. Homi Bhabha, 'The Other Question: The Stereotype and Colonial Discourse', *Screen*, Vol 24, no 4, 1983.

5. Frantz Fanon, *Black Skin White Masks* (1952), Paladin, London 1970, p120.

6. Sigmund Freud, 'Fetishism' (1927), *Standard Edition* Vol 21 (1961), pp147-57; *Pelican Freud Library*, no 7, 'On Sexuality' (1977), p351-7.

the norm is rendered visible by the pathological. The concept of fetishism was profoundly enabling for feminist film theory because it uncovered the logic of substitution at work in all regimes of representation, which make present for the subject what is absent in the real. But although analogies facilitate cognitive connections which have important cultural and political implications, there is also the risk that they repress and flatten out the messy intermediate space in-between. As Jane Gaines has pointed out concerning feminist film theory, the inadvertent reproduction of the heterosexual presumption in the orthodox theorization of sexual difference also assumed a homogeneous racial and ethnic context, with the result that racial and ethnic differences were erased from or marginalized within the analysis.[7] Analogies between race and gender in representation reveal similar ideological patterns of objectification, exclusion, and 'othering'. In Mapplethorpe's nudes, however, there is a subversive homoerotic dimension in the substitution of the black male subject for the traditional female archetype. This subversive dimension was underplayed or obscured in my earlier analysis. My use of the theoretical analogy minimized the homosexual specificity of Mapplethorpe's eroticism, which rubs against the grain of the generic high art status of the traditional female nude.

7. Jane Gaines, 'White Privilege and the Right to Look', *Screen* Vol 29, no 4, 1988.

8. Michel Foucault, 'What is an Author?', in *Language, Counter-Memory, Practice*, Basil Blackwell, Oxford 1977; see also Roland Barthes, 'The Death of the Author', in *Image-Music-Text*, Fontana, London 1977.

To pose the problem in another way, one could approach the issue of ambivalence by simply asking: do photographs like *Man in a Polyester Suit* reinscribe the fixed beliefs of racist ideology or do they problematize them by foregrounding the intersections of difference where race and gender cut across the representation of sexuality? An unequivocal yes/no answer is impossible, it seems to me, because the image throws the question back at the spectator, for whom it is experienced precisely as the 'shock effect'. What is at issue is not primarily whether the question can be decided by appealing to authorial intentions, but the equally important question of the role of the reader and how he or she attributes intentionality to the author. The elision of homoerotic specificity in my earlier reading thus refracts an ambivalence not so much on the part of Mapplethorpe the author, or on the part of the text, but on my part as a reader. More specifically, it refracted the ambivalent 'structure of feeling' that I inhabit as a black gay male reader in relation to the text. Indeed, I've only recently become aware of the logical slippage in my earlier reading, which assumed an equivalence between Mapplethorpe as the individual agent of the image and the empty, anonymous, and impersonal ideological category I described as 'the white male subject' into which the spectator is interpellated. Paradoxically, this conflation undermined the very distinction between author-function and ideological subject-position that I drew from Michel Foucault's anti-naturalist account of authorship.[8]

In retrospect I feel this logical flaw arose as the result of my own ambivalent positioning as a black gay spectator. To call something fetishistic implies a negative judgment, to say the least. I want to take back the unavoidably moralistic connotations of the term, because I think what was at issue in the rhetoric of my previous argument was the encoding of an ambivalent structure of feeling, in which anger and envy divided the identifications that placed me somewhere always already inside the text. On the one hand, I emphasized objectification because I felt identified with the black male subjects in the field of vision, an identification with the Other that might best be described in Fanon's terms as a feeling that 'I am laid bare. I am overdetermined from without. I am the slave not of the "idea" that others have of me but of my own appearance. I am being dissected under white eyes. I am *fixed*. Look, it's a Negro.'[9] But on the other hand, and more difficult to disclose, I was also implicated in the fantasy scenario as a gay subject. That is to say, I was identified with the author insofar as the objectified black male was also an image of the object chosen by my own fantasies and erotic investments. Thus, sharing the same desire to look as the author-agent of the gaze, I would actually occupy the position that I said was that of the 'white male subject'.

9. Frantz Fanon, *op. cit.*, p82.

10. Jacques Lacan, 'The Mirror Stage as Formative of the Function of the I', in *Ecrits: A Selection*, Tavistock, London 1977.

I now wonder whether the anger in that earlier reading was not also the expression and projection of a certain envy. Was it not, in this sense, an effect of a homosexual identification on the basis of a similar object choice that invoked an aggressive rivalry over the same unattainable object of desire, depicted and represented in the visual field of the Other? According to Jacques Lacan, the mirror-stage constitutes the 'I' in an alienated relation to its own image, as the image of the infant's body is 'unified' by the prior investment that comes from the look of the mother, always already in the field of the Other.[10] In this sense, the element of aggressivity involved in textual analysis – the act of taking things apart – might merely have concealed my own narcissistic participation in the pleasures of Mapplethorpe's text. Taking the two elements together, I would say that my ambivalent positioning as a black gay male reader stemmed from the way in which I inhabited two contradictory identifications at one and the same time. Insofar as the anger and the envy were an effect of my identifications with both object and subject of the gaze, the rhetorical closure of my earlier reading simply displaced the ambivalence onto the text by attributing it to the author.

III REREADING

If this brings us to the threshold of the kind of ambivalence that is historically specific to the context, positions, and experiences of the reader, it also demonstrates the radically polyvocal quality of Mapplethorpe's photographs and the way in which contradictory readings can be derived from the same body of work. I want to suggest, therefore, an alternative reading that demonstrates this textual reversibility by revising the assumption that fetishism is necessarily a bad thing.

By making a 180-degreee turn, I want to suggest that the articulation of ambivalence in Mapplethorpe's work can be seen as a subversive deconstruction of the hidden racial and gendered axioms of the nude in dominant traditions of representation. This alternative reading also arises out of a reconsideration of poststructuralist theories of authorship. Although

Romantic notions of authorial creativity cannot be returned to the central role they once played in criticism and interpretation, the question of agency in cultural practices that contest the canon and its cultural dominance suggests that it really *does* matter who is speaking.

The question of enunciation – who is speaking, who is spoken to, what codes do they share to communicate? – implies a whole range of important political issues about who is empowered and who is disempowered in the representation of difference. It is enunciation that circumscribes the marginalized positions of subjects historically misrepresented or underrepresented in dominant systems of representation. To be marginalized is to have no place from which to speak, since the subject positioned in the margins is silenced and invisible. The contestation of marginality in black, gay, and feminist politics thus inevitably brings the issue of authorship back into play, not as the centered origin that determines or guarantees the aesthetic and political value of a text, but as a question about agency in the cultural struggle to 'find a voice' and 'give voice' to subordinate experiences, identities, and subjectivities. A relativization of authoritative poststructuralist claims about de-centering the subject means making sense of the biographical and autobiographical dimension of the context-bound relations between authors, texts, and readers without falling back on liberal humanist or empiricist commonsense. Quite specifically, the 'death of the author' thesis demands revision because the death of the author in *our* case inevitably makes a difference to the kinds of readings we make.

Comments by Mapplethorpe, and by some of the black models with whom he collaborated, offer a perspective on the questions of authorship, identification, and enunciation. The first of these concerns the specificity of Mapplethorpe's authorial identity as a gay artist and the importance of a metropolitan urban gay male culture as a context for the homoeroticism of the black male nudes.

In a BBC television documentary in 1988, Lynne Franks pointed out that a strong sense of voyeurism is marked by its absence from Mapplethorpe's work. A brief comparison with the avowedly heterosexual scenario in the work of photographers such as Edward Weston or Helmut Newton suggests similar aesthetic conventions at the level of visual fetishization; but it would also highlight the significant differences that arise in Mapplethorpe's homoeroticism. Under Mapplethorpe's authorial gaze there is a tension within the cool distance between subject and object. The gaze certainly involves an element of erotic objectification, but like a point-of-view shot in gay male pornography it is reversible. The gendered hierarchy of seeing/being seen is not so rigidly coded in homoerotic representations, since sexual sameness liquidates the associative opposition between active subject and passive object. This element of reversibility at the level of the gaze is marked elsewhere in Mapplethorpe's oeuvre, most notably in the numerous self-portraits, including the one with a bull-whip up his bum, in which the artist posits himself as the object of the look. In relation to the black nudes and the S/M pictures that precede them, this reversibility creates an ambivalent distance measured by the direct look of the models, which is another salient feature of gay male pornography. In effect,

Mapplethorpe implicates himself in his field of vision by a kind of participatory observation, an ironic ethnography whose descriptive clarity suggests a reversible relation of equivalence, or identification, between the author and the social actors whose world is described. On this view, Mapplethorpe's homoeroticism can be read as a form of stylised reportage which documented aspects of the urban gay subcultural milieu of the 1970s. One can reread Mapplethorpe's homoerotica as a kind of photographic documentary of a world that has profoundly changed as a result of AIDS. This reinterpretation is something Mapplethorpe drew attention to in the BBC television interview:

> I was part of it. And that's where most of the photographers who move in that direction are at a disadvantage, in that they're not part of it. They're voyeurs moving in. With me it was quite different. Often I had experienced some of those experiences which I later recorded, myself, first hand, without a camera
>
> It was a certain moment and I was in a perfect situation in that most of the people in the photographs were friends of mine and they trusted me. I felt almost an obligation to record those things. It was an obligation for me to do it, to make images that nobody's seen before and to do it in a way that's *aesthetic*.

In this respect, especially in the light of the moral and ethical emphasis with which Mapplethorpe locates himself as a member of an elective community, it is important to acknowledge the ambivalence of authorial motivation suggested in his rationale for the black male nude studies:

> At some point I started photographing black men. It was an area that hadn't been explored intensively. If you went through the history of nude male photography, there were very few black subjects. I found that I could take pictures of black men that were so subtle, and the form was so photographical.

On the one hand, this could be interpreted as the discovery and conquest of 'virgin territory' in the field of art history; but alternatively, Mapplethorpe's acknowledgment of the exclusion and absence of the black subject from the canonical realm of the fine art nude can be interpreted as the elementary starting point of an implicit critique of racism and ethnocentrism in Western aesthetics.

Once we consider Mapplethorpe's own marginality as a gay artist, placed in a subordinate relation to the canonical tradition of the nude, his implicitly critical position on the presence/absence of race in dominant regimes of representation enables a reappraisal of the intersubjective collaboration between artist and model. Whereas my previous reading emphasized the apparent inequality between the famous, author-named white artist and the anonymous and interchangeable black models, the biographical dimension reveals an important element of mutuality. In a magazine interview that appeared after his death in 1989, Mapplethorpe's comments about the models suggest an intersubjective relation based on a shared social identity: 'Most of the blacks don't have health insurance and therefore can't afford AZT. They all died quickly, the blacks. If I go through my *Black Book*, half of them are dead.'[11] In his mourning, there is something horribly accurate about the truism that death is the great leveller, because his pictures have now become momento mori, documentary evidence of a style of life and a sexual ethics in the metropolitan gay culture of the 1970s and early 1980s which no longer exists in the way that it used to. As a contribution to the historical formation of urban gay culture, Mapplethorpe's homoeroticism is invested with memory, with the intense emotional residue Barthes described when he wrote about photographs of his mother.[12]

11. 'The Long Goodbye', interview by Dominick Dunne, *Blitz*, London, May 1989, pp67-8.

12. Roland Barthes, *Camera Lucida*, Jonathan Cape, London 1982.

The element of mutual identification between artist and models undermines the view that the relation was necessarily exploitative simply because it was interracial. Comments by Ken Moody, one of the models in the *Black Book*, suggest a degree of reciprocity. When asked in the BBC television interview whether he recognized himself in Mapplethorpe's pictures, he said: 'Not always, not most of the time ... When I look at it as me, and not just as a piece of art, I think I look like a freak. I don't find that person in the photograph necessarily attractive and it's not something I would like to own.' The alienation of not even owning your own image might be taken as evidence of objectification, of being reduced to a 'piece of art'; but at the same time Moody rejects the view that it was a unequivocal relation, suggesting instead a reciprocal gift relationship that further underlines the theme of mutuality:

> I don't honestly think of it as exploitation ... It's almost as if ... and this is the conclusion I've come to now, because I really haven't thought about it up to now – it's almost as if he wants to give a gift to this particular group. He wants to create something very beautiful and give it to them ... And he is actually very giving.

I don't want to over- or underinterpret such evidence, but I do think that this biographical dimension to the issues of authorship and enunciation enables a rereading of the textual ambivalence in Mapplethorpe's artistic practice. Taking the question of identification into account, as that which inscribes ambivalent relations of mutuality and reversibility in the gaze, enables a reconsideration of the cultural politics of Mapplethorpe's black male nudes.

Once grounded in the context of contemporary urban gay male culture in the United States, the shocking modernism that informs the ironic juxtaposition of elements drawn from the repository of high culture – where the nude is indeed one of the most valued genres in Western art history – can be read as a subversive recoding of the normative aesthetic ideal. On this view, it becomes possible to reverse the reading of racial fetishism in Mapplethorpe's work not as a repetition of racist fantasies but as a deconstructive strategy which lays bare psychic and social relations of ambivalence in the representation of race and sexuality. This deconstructive aspect of his homoeroticism is experienced, at the level of audience reception, as the disturbing 'shock effect'.

The Eurocentric character of the liberal humanist values invested in classical Greek sculpture, as the originary model of human beauty in Western aesthetics, is paradoxically revealed by the promiscuous intertextuality whereby the filthy and degraded form of the commonplace racist stereotype is brought into the domain of aesthetic purity circumscribed by the privileged place of the fine art nude. This doubling within the pictorial space of Mapplethorpe's black nudes does not reproduce either term of the binary relation between 'high culture' and 'low culture' as it is: it radically de-centers and destabilizes the hierarchy of racial and sexual difference in dominant systems of representations by folding the two together within the same frame. It is this ambivalent intermixing of textual references, achieved through the appropriation and articulation of elements from the 'purified' realm of the transcendental aesthetic ideal and from the debased and 'polluted' world of the commonplace racist stereotype, that disturbs the fixed positioning of the spectator. One might say that what is staged in Mapplethorpe's black male nudes is the return of the repressed in the ethnocentric imaginary. The psychic/social boundary which separates 'high culture' and 'low culture' is transgressed, crossed and disrupted precisely by the superimposition of two ways of seeing which thus throws the spectator into uncertainty and undecidability – precisely the experience of ambivalence as a structure of feeling in which one's subject-position is called into question.

In my previous argument, I suggested that the regulative function of the stereotype had the upper hand, as it were, and helped to 'fix' the spectator in the ideological subject-position of 'the white male subject'. Now I'm not so sure. Once we recognize the historical and political specificity of Mapplethorpe's practice as a contemporary gay artist, the aesthetic irony that informs the juxtaposition of elements in his work can be seen as the trace of a subversive strategy that disrupts the stability of the binary oppositions into which difference is coded. In social, economic and political terms, black men in the United States constitute one of the 'lowest' social classes: disenfranchised, disadvantaged, and disempowered as a distinct collective subject in the late capitalist underclass. Yet, in Mapplethorpe's photographs, men who in all probability came from this class are elevated onto the pedestal of the transcendental Western aesthetic ideal. Far from reinforcing the fixed beliefs of the white supremacist imaginary, such a deconstructive move begins to undermine the foundational myths of the pedestal itself. The subaltern black social subject who was historically excluded from dominant regimes of representation – 'invisible men' in Ralph Ellison's phrase – is made visible within the codes and conventions of the dominant culture whose ethnocentrism is thereby exposed as a result. The mythological figure of 'the

Negro', who was always excluded from the good, the true, and the beautiful in Western aesthetics on account of his otherness, comes to embody the image of physical perfection and aesthetic idealization in which, in the canonical figure of the nude, Western culture constructed its own self-image. Far from confirming the hegemonic white heterosexual subject in his centered position of mastery and power, the deconstructive aspect of Mapplethorpe's black male nude photographs loosens up and unfixes the commonsense sensibilities of the spectator, who thereby experiences the 'shock effect' precisely as the affective displacement of given ideological subject positions.

To shock was always the key verb of the avant-garde in modernist art history. In Mapplethorpe's work, the shock effected by the promiscuous textual intercourse between elements drawn from opposite ends of the hierarchy of cultural value de-centers and destabilizes the ideological fixity of the spectator. In this sense, his work begins to reveal the political unconscious of white ethnicity. It lays bare the constitutive ambivalence that structures whiteness as a cultural identity whose hegemony lies, as Richard Dyer suggests, precisely in its 'invisibility'.[13] The splitting of the subject in the construction of white identity, entailed in the affirmation and denial of racial difference in Western humanism, is traced in racist perception. Blacks are looked down upon and despised as worthless, ugly, and ultimately unhuman creatures. But in the blink of an eye, whites look up to and revere the black body, lost in awe and envy as the black subject is idolized as the embodiment of its ideal. This schism in white subjectivity is replayed daily in the different ways black men become visible on the front and back pages of tabloid newspapers, seen as undesirable in one frame – the mugger, the terrorist, the rapist – and highly desirable in the other – the athlete, the sports hero, the entertainer. Mapplethorpe undercuts this conventional separation to show the recto/verso relation between these contradictory 'ways of seeing' as constitutive aspects of white identity. Like a mark that is legible on both sides of a sheet of paper, Mapplethorpe's aesthetic strategy places the splitting in white subjectivity under erasure: it is crossed out but still visible. In this sense, the anxieties aroused in the exhibition history of Mapplethorpe's homoerotica not only demonstrate the disturbance and de-centering of dominant versions of white identity, but confronts whiteness with the otherness that enables it to be constituted as an identity as such.

13. Richard Dyer, 'White', *Screen*, Vol 29, no 4, 1988.

In changing my mind like this, suggesting that the ambivalent fetishization of racial difference actually enables a potential deconstruction of whiteness, I think Mapplethorpe's use of irony can be recontextualized in relation to Pop Art practices of the 1960s. The undecidable question that is thrown back onto the spectator – do the images reinforce or undermine racist stereotypes? – can be compared to the highly ambivalent aura of fetishism that frames the female body in the paintings of Allen Jones. Considering the issues of sexism and misogyny at stake, Laura Mulvey's reading, from 1972, suggests a contextual approach to the political analysis of its 'shocking' undecidability:

By revealing the way in which fetishistic images pervade not just specialist

> publications but the whole of the mass media, Allen Jones throws a new light on woman as spectacle. Women are constantly confronted with their own image … yet, in a real sense, women are not there at all. The parade has nothing to do with woman, everything to do with man. The true exhibit is always the phallus … The time has come for us to take over the show and exhibit our own fears and desires.[14]

This has a salutary resonance in the renewal of debates on black aesthetics given that contemporary practices which contest the marginality of the black subject in dominant regimes of representation have gone beyond the unhelpful binarism of so-called positive and negative images. We are now more aware of the identities, fantasies, and desires that are coerced, simplified, and reduced by the rhetorical closure that flows from that kind of critique. But this also entails a clarification of what we need from theory as black artists and intellectuals. The critique of stereotypes was crucial in the women's and gay movements of the 1960s and 1970s, just as it was in the black movements that produced aesthetic-political performative statements such as 'Black is Beautiful'. As the various movements have fragmented politically, however, their combined and uneven development suggests that analogies across race, gender, and sexuality may be useful only insofar as we historicize them and to the extent of what they make possible. Appropriations of psychoanalytic theory arose at a turning point in the cultural politics of feminism, and, in thinking about the enabling possibilities this has opened up for the study of black representation, I feel we also need to acknowledge the other side of ambivalence in contemporary cultural struggles, the dark side of the political predicament that ambivalence engenders.

In contrast to the claims of academic deconstruction, the moment of undecidability is rarely experienced as a purely textual event; rather it is the point where politics and the contestation of power are felt at their most intense. According to V.N. Volosinov, the social multi-accentuality of the ideological sign has an 'inner dialectical quality [which] comes out only in times of social crises or revolutionary changes', because 'in ordinary circumstances … an established dominant ideology … always tries, as it were, to stabilize the dialectical flux.'[15] Indeterminacy means that multi-accentual or polyvalent signs have no necessary belonging and can be articulated and appropriated into the political discourse of the Right as easily as that of the Left. Antagonistic efforts to fix the multiple connotations arising from the ambivalence of the key signs of ideological struggle demonstrate what in Antonio Gramsci's terms would be described as a 'war of position' whose outcome is never guaranteed in advance one way or the other.

We have seen how, despite their emancipatory objectives, certain radical feminist anti-pornography arguments have been taken up and translated into the neo-conservative cultural and political agenda of the Right. For my part, I want to emphasize that I've reversed my reading of racial signification in Mapplethorpe not for the fun of it, but because I do *not* want a black gay

14. Laura Mulvey, 'Fears, Fantasies and the Male Unconscious, or, "You Don't Know What is Happening, Do You Mr Jones?"' (1972), in *Visual and Other Pleasures*, Macmillan, London 1989, p13.

15. V.N. Volosinov, *Marxism and the Philosophy of Language* (1929), Harvard University Press, Harvard 1973, p24.

critique to be appropriated to the purposes of the Right's anti-democratic cultural offensive. Jesse Helms' amendment to public funding policies in the arts – which was orchestrated in relation to Mapplethorpe's homoerotic work – forbids the public funding of art deemed 'obscene or indecent'. But it is crucial to note that a broader remit for censorship was originally articulated on the grounds of a moral objection to art that 'denigrates, debases, or reviles a person, group, or class of citizens on the basis of race, creed, sex, handicap, or national origin'.[16] In other words, the discourse of liberal and social democratic anti-discrimination legislation is being appropriated and rearticulated into a right-wing position that promotes a discriminatory politics of cultural censorship and ideological coercion. Without a degree of self-reflexivity, black critiques of Mapplethorpe's work can be easily assimilated into a politics of homophobia. Which is to say, coming back to the photographs, that precisely on account of their ambivalence, Mapplethorpe's photographs are open to a range of contradictory readings whose political character depends on the social identity that different audiences bring to bear on them. The photographs can confirm a racist reading as easily as they can produce an anti-racist one. Or again, they can elicit a homophobic reading as easily as they can conform a homoerotic one. Once ambivalence and undecidability are situated in the contextual relations between author, text, and readers, a cultural struggle ensues in which antagonistic efforts seek to articulate the meaning and value of Mapplethorpe's work.

16. *New York Times*, 28 September 1989.

What is at issue in this 'politics of enunciation' can be clarified by a linguistic analogy, since certain kinds of performative statements produce different meanings not so much because of what is said but because of who is saying it. As a verbal equivalent of Mapplethorpe's visual image, the statement 'the black man is beautiful' takes on different meanings depending on the identity of the social subject who enunciates it. Does the same statement mean the same thing when uttered by a white woman, a black woman, a white man, or a black man? Does it mean the same thing whether the speaker is straight or gay? In my view, it cannot possibly mean the same thing in each instance because the racial and gendered identity of the enunciator inevitably 'makes a difference' to the social construction of meaning and value.

Today we are adept at the all too familiar concatenation of identity politics, as if by merely rehearsing the mantra of 'race, class, gender' (and all the other intervening variables) we have somehow acknowledged the diversified and pluralized differences at work in contemporary culture, politics, and society. Yet the complexity of what actually happens 'between' the contingent spaces where each variable intersects with the others is something only now coming into view theoretically, and this is partly the result of new antagonistic cultural practices by hitherto marginalized artists. Instead of analogies, which tend to flatten out these intermediate spaces, I think we need to explore theories that enable new forms of dialogue. In this way we might be able to imagine a dialogic or relational conception of the differences we actually inhabit in our lived experiences of identity and identification. The observation that different readers produce different readings of the same cultural texts is not as circular as it seems: I want to suggest that it provides an outlet onto the dialogic character of the political imaginary of difference. To open up this area for theoretical investigation I want to point to two ways in which such relational differences of race, gender, and sexuality do indeed 'make a difference'.

IV DIFFERENT READERS MAKE DIFFERENT READINGS

Here, I simply want to itemize a range of issues concerning readership and authorship that arises across the intertextual field in which Mapplethorpe 'plays'. To return to *Man in a Polyester Suit,* one can see that an anonymous greetings card, produced and marketed in a specifically gay cultural context, works on similar fantasies of black sexuality. The greetings card depicts a black man in a business suit alongside the caption 'Everything you ever heard about black men ... is true', at which point the card unfolds to reveal his penis. The same savage/civilized binarism that I noted in Mapplethorpe's photography is signified here by the contrast between the body clothed in a business suit, then denuded to reveal the penis (with some potted plants in the background to emphasize the point about the nature/culture distinction). Indeed, the card replays the fetishistic splitting of levels of belief as it is opened: the image of the big black penis serves as the punchline of the little joke. But because the card is authorless, the issue of attributing racist or anti-racist intentions is effectively secondary to the context in which it is exchanged and circulated, the context of an urban, commercial, gay male subculture. My point is that gay readers in this vernacular sign-community may share access to a range of intertextual references in Mapplethorpe's work which other readers may not be aware of.

Returning to the 'enigma' of the black models in Mapplethorpe's work: the appearance of black gay video porn star Joe Simmons (referred to as Thomas in *The Black Book*) on magazine covers from *Artscribe* to *Advocate Men* offers a source of intertextual pleasure to 'those in the know' that accentuates and inflects Mapplethorpe's depiction of the same person. Repetition has become one of the salient pleasures of gay male pornography as photographic reproduction and video piracy encourage the accelerated flow by which models and scenarios constantly reappear in new intertextual combinations. By extending this process into 'high art', circulating imagery between the streets and the galleries, Mapplethorpe's promiscuous textuality has a sense of humour that might otherwise escape the sensibilities of non-gay or anti-gay viewers.

The mobility of such intertextual moves cannot be arrested by recourse to binary oppositions. The sculpted pose of Joe Simmons in one frame immediately recalls the celebrated nude studies of Paul Robeson by Nicholas Murray in 1926. Once the photograph is situated in this historical context, which may or may not be familiar to black readers in particular, one might compare Mapplethorpe to Carl van Vetchen, the white photographer of black literati in the Harlem Renaissance. In this context, Richard Dyer has retrieved a revealing instance of overwhelming ambivalence in racial/sexual representations. In the 1920s, wealthy white patrons in the Philadelphia Art Alliance commissioned a sculpture of Robeson by Antonio Salemme. Although they wanted it to embody Robeson's 'pure' beauty in bronze, they rejected the sculpture because its aesthetic sensuality overpowered their moral preconceptions.[17]

17. Richard Dyer, *Heavenly Bodies: Film Stars and Society*, British Film Institute/ Macmillan, London 1987, pp118-23.

The historical specificity of this reference has a particular relevance in the light of renewed interest in the Harlem Renaissance in contemporary black cultural practices. This rediscovery of the past has served to thematize questions of identity and desire in the work of black gay artists such as Isaac Julien. In *Looking for Langston* (1988), Julien undertakes an archaeological inquiry into the enigma of Langston Hughes' sexual identity. Insofar as the aesthetic strategy of the film eschews the conventions of documentary realism in favour of a dialogic combination of poetry, music, and archival imagery, it does not claim to discover an authentic or essential homosexual identity (for Langston Hughes or anyone else). Rather, the issue of authorial identity is invested with fantasy, memory, and desire and serves as an imaginative point of departure for speculation and reflection on the social and historical relations in which black gay male identity is lived and experienced in diaspora societies such as Britain or the United States. In this sense, the criticism that the film is not about Langston Hughes misses the point. By showing the extent to which our identities, as black gay men, are historically constructed in and through representations, Julien's film interrogates aspects of social relations that silence and repress the representability of black gay identities and desires. The search for iconic heroes and heroines has been an important element in lesbian, gay, and feminist cultural politics, and the process of uncovering identities previously 'hidden from history' has had empowering effects in culture and society at large. Julien is involved in a similar project, but his film refuses, through its dialogic strategy, to essentialize Hughes into a black gay cultural icon. This strategy focuses on the question of power at issue in the ability to make and wield representations. Above all, it focuses on who has the 'right to look' by emphasizing both interracial and intraracial looking relations that complicate the subject/object dichotomy of seeing/being seen.

Hence, in one key scene, we see the white male protagonist leisurely leafing through *The Black Book*. Issues of voyeurism, objectification, and fetishization are brought into view not in a didactic confrontation with Mapplethorpe, but through a seductive invitation into the messy spaces in between the binary oppositions that dominate the representation of difference. Alongside visual quotations from Jean Cocteau, Jean Genet, and Derek Jarman, the voices of James Baldwin, Toni Morrison, and Amiri Baraka combine to emphasize the relational conception of 'identity' that Julien's dialogic strategy makes possible. It is through this relational approach that the film reopens the issue of racial fetishism. An exchange of looks between 'Langston' and his mythic object of desire, a black man called 'Beauty,' provokes a hostile glare from Beauty's white partner. In the daydream that follows, Langston imagines himself coupled with

Beauty, their bodies entwined on a bed in an image reappropriated and reaccentuated from the homoerotic photography of George Platt Lynes. It is here that the trope of visual fetishization make a subversive return. Close-up sequences lovingly linger on the sensuous mouth of the actor portraying Beauty, with the rest of his face cast in shadow. As in Mapplethorpe's photographs, the strong emphasis on chiaroscuro lighting invests the fetishized fragment with a powerful erotic charge in which the 'thick lips' of the Negro are hypervalorized as the emblem of Beauty's impossible desirability. In other words, Julien takes the artistic risk of replicating the stereotype of the 'thick lipped Negro' in order to revalorize that which has historically always been devalorized as emblematic of the Other's ugliness. It is only by operating 'in and against' such tropes of racial fetishism that Julien lays bare the ambivalence of the psychic and social relations at stake in the relay of looks between the three men.

Historically, black people have been the objects of representation rather than its subjects and creators because racism often determines who gets access to the means of representation in the first place. Through his dialogic textual strategy, Julien overturns this double-bind as the black subject 'looks back' to ask the audience who or what *they* are looking for. The motif of the 'direct look' appeared in Julien's first film with the Sankofa Collective, *Territories* (1984), which was involved in an 'epistemological break' with the realist documentary tradition in black art. Similarly, what distinguishes current work by black lesbian and gay artists – such as the film and video of Pratibha Parmar, or the photography of Rotimi Fani-Kayode – is the break with static and essentialist conceptions of identity. The salient feature of such work is its hybridity: it operates on the borderlines of race, class, gender, nationality, and sexuality, investigating the complex overdetermination of subjective experiences and desires as they are historically constituted in the ambivalent spaces in between.

Elsewhere, I suggested that, in relation to black British film, such hybridized practices articulated a critical dialogue about the constructed character of black British identities and experiences.[18] Something similar informs the hybridized homoerotica of Nigerian British photographer Rotimi Fani-Kayode. The very title of his first publication, *Black Male/White Male*,[19] suggests an explicitly intertextual relationship with Mapplethorpe. However, salient similarities in Fani-Kayode's construction of pictorial space – the elaborate body postures enclosed within the studio space, the use of visual props to stage theatrical effects, and the glossy monochrome texture of the photographic print – underline the important differences in his refiguration of the black male nude. In contrast to Mapplethorpe's isolation-effect, whereby only one black man occupies the field of vision at any one time, in Fani-Kayode's photographs bodies are coupled and contextualized. In pictures such as *Technique of Ecstasy*, the erotic conjunction between the two black men suggests an Afrocentric imaginary in which the implied power relations of the subject/object dichotomy are complicated by racial sameness. In *Bronze Head*, what looks like a Benin mask appears beneath a black man's splayed buttocks. This shocking

18. Kobena Mercer, 'Diaspora Culture and the Dialogic Imagination: The Aesthetics of Black Independent Film in Britain', in Mbye Cham and Claire Andrade-Watkins (eds), *BlackFrames: Critical Perspectives on Black Independent Cinema*, MIT, 1988, pp50-61.

19. Rotimi Fani-Kayode, *Black Male/ White Male*, Gay Men's Press, London 1987; see also, Rotimi Fani-Kayode, 'Traces of Ecstasy', *Ten-8, no 28, 1988.*

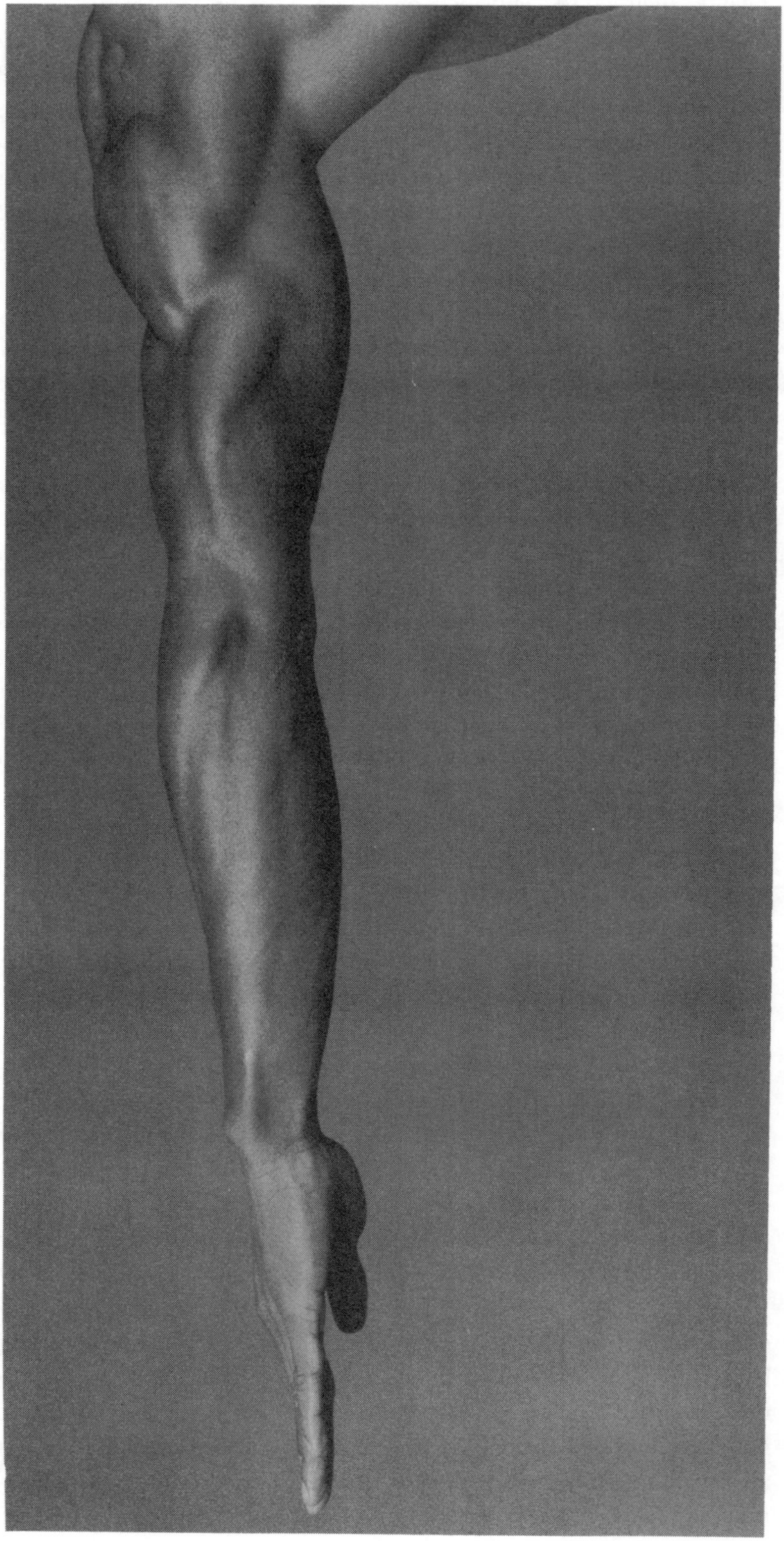

Derrick Cross, 1983. © The Estate of Robert Mapplethorpe, 1983.

contextualization places the image in an ambivalent space, at once an instance of contemporary African art, referring specifically to Yoruba iconography, and an example of homoerotic art photography that recalls Mapplethorpe's portrait of Derrick Cross, in which the black man's bum resembles a Brancusi.

If such dialogic strategies do indeed 'make a difference' to our understanding of the cultural politics of identity and diversity, does this mean the work is different *because* its authors are black? No, not necessarily. What is at issue is not an essentialist argument that the ethnic identity of the artist guarantees the aesthetic or political value of a text, but on the contrary, how commonsense conceptions of authorship and readership are challenged by practices that acknowledge the diversity and heterogeneity of the relations in which identities are socially constructed. Stuart Hall helped to clarify what is at stake in this shift when he argued that such acknowledgment of difference and diversity in black cultural practices has brought the innocent notion of the essential black subject to an end. Once we recognize blackness as a category of social, psychic, and political relations that have no fixed guarantees in nature but only the contingent forms in which they are constructed in culture, then questions of value cannot be decided by recourse to empirical commonsense about 'colour' or melanin. As Stuart Hall put it, 'Films are not necessarily good because black people make them. They are not necessarily "right on" by virtue of the fact that they deal with the black experience.'[20]

20. Stuart Hall, 'New Ethnicities', in *Black Film/British Cinema*, ICA Document 7, Institute of Contemporary Art/British Film Institute, London 1988, p28.

On this view, I would argue that black gay and lesbian artists are producing exciting and important work not because they happen to be black lesbians and gay men but because they have made cultural and political choices out of their experiences of marginality which situate them at the interface between different traditions. Insofar as they speak *from* the specificity of such experiences, they overturn the assumption that minority artists speak *for* the entire community from which they come. This is an important distinction in the relations of enunciation because it bears upon the politics of representation that pertain to all subjects in marginalized or minoritized situations, whether black, feminist, lesbian, or gay. In a material context of restricted access to the means of representation, minoritized subjects are charged with an impossible 'burden of representation'. Where subordinate subjects acquire the right to speak only one at a time, their discourse is circumscribed by the assumption that they speak as 'representatives' of the entire community from which they come. It is logically impossible for any one individual to bear such a burden, not only because it denies variety and heterogeneity within minority communities, but because it demands an intolerable submission to the iron law of the stereotype, namely the view from the majority culture that every minority subject is 'the same'. In the master codes of the dominant culture, the assumption that 'all black people are the same' reinforces the view that black communities are monolothic and homogeneous and that black subjectivity is defined exclusively by race and nothing but race. The dialogic element in contemporary black artistic practices begins to interrupt this restricted economy of representation by making it possible to think of a democratic politics of difference and diversity. The work of black gay and lesbian artists participates in what has been called 'postmodernism' in terms of practices that pluralize available representations in the public sphere. To the extent that their aesthetic of critical dialogism underlines their contribution to the 'new cultural politics of difference', as Cornel West has put it,[21] it seems to me that rather than mere 'celebration', their work calls for a critical response that reopens issues and questions we thought had been closed.

21. Cornel West, 'The New Black Cultural Politics of Difference', British Film Institute Research Fellowship lecture, National Film Theatre, London, 23 June 1989.

22. Gayatri C. Spivak, *In Other Worlds: Essays in Cultural Politics*, Methuen, London 1987.

As I suggested in rereading Mapplethorpe, one of the key questions on the contemporary agenda concerns the cultural construction of whiteness. One of the signs of the times is that we don't really know what 'white' is. The implicitly ethnocentric agenda of cultural criticism, since the proliferation of poststructuralist theories in the 1970s, not only obscured the range of issues concerning black authorship, black spectatorship, and black intertextuality which black artists have been grappling with, but served to render invisible the constructed, and contested, character of 'whiteness' as a racial/ethnic identity. Richard Dyer has shown how difficult it is to theorize whiteness, precisely because it is so thoroughly naturalized in dominant ideologies as to be invisible as an ethnic identity: it simply goes without saying. Paradoxically then, for all our rhetoric about 'making ourselves visible', the real challenge in the new cultural politics of difference is to make 'whiteness' visible for the first time, as a culturally constructed ethnic identity historically contingent upon the disavowal and violent denial of difference. Gayatri Spivak has shown that it was only through the 'epistemic violence' of such denial that the centered subject of Western philosophy posited itself as the universalized subject – 'Man' – in relation to whom the Others were not simply different but somehow less than human, dehumanized objects of oppression. Women, children, savages, slaves, and criminals were all alike insofar as their otherness affirmed 'his' identity as the Subject at the centre of logocentrism and indeed all the other centrisms, ethnocentrism and phallocentrism, in which 'he' constructed his representations of reality.[22] But who is 'he'? The identity of the hegemonic white male subject is an enigma in contemporary cultural politics.

V DIFFERENT DEGREES OF OTHERING

Coming back to Mapplethorpe's photographs, in the light of this task of making 'whiteness' visible as a problem for cultural theory, I want to suggest that the positioning of gay (white) people in the margins of Western culture may serve as a perversely privileged place from which to re-examine the political unconscious of modernity. By negotiating an alternative interpretation of his authorial position, I argued that his aesthetic strategy lays bare and makes visible the 'splitting' in white subjectivity that is anchored, by homology, in the split between 'high culture' and 'low culture'. The perverse interaction between visual elements drawn from both sources begins to subvert the hierarchy of cultural value, and such subversion of fixed categories is experienced precisely as the characteristic 'shock effect'.

Broadening this theme, one can see that representations of race in Western culture entail different degrees of othering. Or, to put it the other way around: different practices of racial representation imply different positions of identification on the part of the white subject. Hollywood's iconic image of the 'nigger minstrel' in cinema history, for example, concerns a deeply ambivalent mixture of othering and identification. The creation of the minstrel mask in cinema, and in popular theatre and the musical hall before it, was really the work of white men in blackface. What is taking place in the psychic structures of such historical representations? What is going on when whites assimilate and introject the degraded and devalorized signifiers of racial otherness into the cultural construction of their own identity? If imitation implies identification, in the psychoanalytic sense of the word, then what is it about whiteness that makes the white subject want to be black?

'I Wanna Be Black', sang Lou Reed on the album *Street Hassle* (1979), which was a parody of a certain attitude in postwar youth culture in which the cultural signs of blackness – in music, clothes, and idioms of speech – were the mark of 'cool'. In the American context, such a sensibility predicated on the ambivalent identification with the Other was enacted in the bohemian beatnik subculture, and became embodied in Norman Mailer's literary image of 'the White Negro' stalking the jazz clubs in search of sex, speed, and psychosis. Like a photographic negative, the white negro was an inverted image of otherness, in which attributes devalorized by the dominant culture were simply revalorized or hypervalorized as emblems of alienation and outsiderness, a kind of strategic self-othering in relation to dominant cultural norms. In the museum without walls, Mailer's white negro, who went in search of the systematic derangement of the senses, merely retraced an imaginary pathway in the cultural history of modernity previously travelled by Arthur Rimbaud and Eugene Delecroix in nineteenth-century Europe. There is a whole modernist tradition of 'racial romanticism' that involves a fundamental ambivalence of identifications. At what point do such identifications result in an imitative masquerade of white ethnicity? At what point do they result in ethical and political alliances? How can we tell the difference?[23]

My point is that white ethnicity constitutes an 'unknown' in contemporary cultural theory – a dark continent that has not yet been explored. One way of opening it up is to look at the ambivalent coexistence of the two types of identification, as they figure in the work of (white) gay artists such as Mapplethorpe and Jean Genet. In *Un Chant D'Amour* (1950), Genet's first and only foray into cinema, there is a great deal of ambivalence, to say the least, about the black man, the frenzied and maniacal negro seen in the masturbatory dance through the scopophilic gaze of the prison guard. In another context, I wrote: 'The black man in Genet's film is fixed like a stereotype in the fetishistic axis of the look ... subjected to a pornographic exercise of colonial power.'[24] Yes, I know ... but. There is something else going on as well, not on the margins but at the very center of Genet's film. The romantic escape into the woods, which is the liberated zone of freedom in which the lover's utopian

23. See Normal Mailer, 'The White Negro: Superficial Reflections on the Hipster', in *Advertisements for Myself*, André Deutsch, London 1959. The fantasy of wanting to be black is discussed as a masculinist fantasy in Suzanne Moore, 'Getting a Bit of the Other: The Pimps of Postmodernism', in Rowena Chapman and Jonathan Rutherford (eds), *Male Order: Unwrapping Masculinity*, Lawrence & Wishart, London 1988.

24. See 'Sexual Identities: Questions of Difference', a panel discussion with Kobena Mercer, Jacqueline Rose, Gayatri Spivak and Angela McRobbie, in *Undercut*, no 17, on Cultural Identities, 1988.

fantasy of coupling is enacted, is organized around the role of the 'dark' actor, the Tunisian, the one who is not quite white. On this view, the ambivalence of ethnicity has a central role to play in the way that Genet uses race to figure the desire for political freedom beyond the prisonhouse of marginality. Once located in relation to his plays, such as *The Balcony* and *The Blacks*, Genet's textual practice must be seen as his mode of participation in the 'liberation' struggles of the postwar era.

The word *liberation* tends to stick in our throats these days because it sounds so deeply unfashionable; but we might also recall that in the 1950s and 1960s it was precisely the connections between movements for liberation from colonialism, and movements for liberation from the dominant sex and gender system, that underlined their radical democratic character. In the contemporary situation, the essentialist rhetoric of categorical identity politics threatens to erase the connectedness of our different struggles. At its worst, such forms of identity politics play into the hands of the Right as the fundamentalist belief in an essential and immutable identity keeps us locked into the prisonhouse of marginality in which oppressions of race, class, and gender would have us live. By historicizing the imaginary identifications that enable democratic agency, we might rather find a way of escaping this ideological bantustan.

Instead of giving an answer to the questions that have been raised about the ambivalence of ethnicity as a site of identification and enunciation, I conclude by recalling Genet's wild and adventurous story about being smuggled across the Canadian border by David Hilliard and other members of the Black Panther Party in 1968. He arrived at Yale University to give a May Day speech, along with Allen Ginsberg and others, in defence of imprisoned activist Bobby Seale. Genet talks about this episode in *Prisoner of Love*, where it appears as a memory brought to consciousness by the narration of another memory, about the beautiful *fedayyin*, in whose desert camps Genet lived between 1969 and 1972. The memory of his participation in the elective community of the Palestinian freedom fighters precipitates the memory of the Black Panther 'brotherhood', into which he was adopted – this wretched orphaned nomadic homosexual thief. I am drawn to the kind of ambivalence, sexual and political, that shows through, like a stain, in his telling:[25]

25. Jean Genet, *Prisoner of Love*, Picador, London 1989, p213.

> In white America the Blacks are the characters in which history is written. They are the ink that gives the white page its meaning ... [The Black Panther Party] built the black race on a white America that was splitting ... The Black Panthers' Party wasn't an isolated phenomenon. It was one of the many revolutionary outcrops. What made it stand out in white America was its black skin, its frizzy hair and, despite a kind of uniform black leather jacket, an extravagant but elegant way of dressing. They wore multi-colored caps only just resting on their springy hair; scraggy moustaches, sometimes beards; blue or pink or gold trousers made of satin or velvet, and cut so that even the most shortsighted passer-by couldn't miss their manly vigour.

Under what conditions does eroticism mingle with political solidarity? When does it produce an effect of empowerment? And when does it produce an effect of disempowerment? When does identification imply objectification and when does it imply equality? I am intrigued by the ambivalent but quite happy coexistence of the fetishized big black dick beneath the satin trousers and the ethical equivalence in the struggle for post-colonial subjectivity. Genet's affective participation in the political construction of imagined communities suggests that the struggle for democratic agency and subjectivity always entails the negotiation of ambivalence. Mapplethorpe worked in a different context, albeit one shaped by the democratic revolutions of the 1960s, but his work similarly draws us back into the difficult questions that Genet chose to explore, on the 'dark side' of the political unconscious of the post-colonial world.

The death of the author doesn't necessarily mean mourning and melancholia, but the mobilizing of a commitment to counter-memory. In the dialogue that black gay and lesbian artists have created in contemporary cultural politics, the exemplary political modernism of Mapplethorpe and Genet, 'niggers with attitude' if ever there were, is certainly worth remembering as we begin thinking about our pitiful 'postmodern' condition.

Competing Glances
Who is Reading Robert Mapplethorpe's *Black Book?*

Jane M. Gaines

I

Can there be anything left to say about Robert Mapplethorpe's notorious black male nudes? There are still two issues stirred up in the debates to which I want to return before the dust settles. One is the delicate question of how critics determine whether or not a work (and by implication its maker) is or is not 'racist'. The other is an obvious question but one which has yet to be framed properly, and that is the issue of the gay community's 'erotic monopoly' on these photographs. On this, I take my cue from Doug Ischar who has referred to the gay subculture as having current 'custody' of Mapplethorpe's work.[1] It's hard to imagine how anyone would begrudge the gay community this honorary custody, yet we wouldn't want to let it blind us to the full diversity of the claims on Mapplethorpe's work, But, one may ask, what other groups would want to claim these images so passionately?

1. Doug Ischar, 'Endangered Alibis', *Afterimage*, vol 17, no 10, May 1990, p8.

2. Kobena Mercer, 'Imaging the Black Man's Sex', in Patricia Holland, Jo Spence, and Simon Watney (eds), *Photography/ Politics: Two*, Comedia, London 1986, p66.

Before answering this question, I want to review some of the arguments that have already been made for seeing Mapplethorpe's imagery in racial terms. In the very early 'Imaging the Black Man's Sex' (a commentary on the 1983 Mapplethorpe retrospective at the London Institute of Contemporary Arts), Kobena Mercer adapted the paradigm of feminist film theory, arguing that the photographs evidenced the white male subject's desire to look at the Other. To summarize his argument in this early essay (the first of four key Mapplethorpe articles Mercer has authored and co-authored): like the white male's aesthetic treatment of the female nude, the white photographer's treatment of the black male nude was an ahistorical idealization; doomed to restage a colonial fantasy, Mapplethorpe had once again reduced the black man to a 'juju doll in the white man's imaginary'.[2] This, then, was the basis upon which one black gay male critic made the case for finding Mapplethorpe's work racist in 1986.

My first response to this argument was enthusiastic agreement – yes, of course, Mapplethorpe's photographs were racist. Furthermore, it seemed to me that his treatment of these bodies *was* analogous to the way the female body has been 'othered' for male contemplation in the history of photographic representation. The white male had orchestrated yet another pleasure scene at the expense of an oppressed group! But the more I considered the comparison, the more I saw problems involved in the attempt to locate 'racism' in the visual image, especially since this seemed to repeat all the errors of the early feminist attempts to locate 'sexism' in images of women. So here I want to consider, first of all, why and how arguments are made for seeing a photographic work as racist (as well as for seeing critical readings as unknowingly racist).

II IS IT OR ISN'T IT RACIST?

To turn, then, to the question of how a critic might interpret an image as 'racist' let me begin by addressing several issues which arise in Thomas Yingling's recent 'How the Eye is Caste', one of the most comprehensive academic essays on Mapplethorpe published after the series of events which thrust the photographer's work into the art world limelight.[3] In this essay, Yingling takes two other critics to task for what he sees as inadvertent racism. Critic David Joselit, for instance, damns Mapplethorpe's work by arguing that it is yet another example of the racism of black stereotypage. But, says Yingling, in his own critique Joselit unwittingly uses cultural clichés about black men, specifically in his reference to the 'suppressed violence' of the models.[4] Yingling's other example, Kay Larson finds, in contrast to Joselit, that the black nudes are not racist. But in her argument against seeing the images as racist depictions, says Yingling, she herself slips into using racial stereotyping, particularly as she defends the 'dignified black' and praises the 'polished bodies' of the subjects. If, as Yingling says, these descriptions 'invoke racist paradigms',[5] they do so with an apparent innocence of having borrowed loaded metaphors and with the intention (in both cases) of doing the opposite – of taking a position against racism. While we would never want to defend white society's 'innocent' obliviousness of its own contribution to the social construction of blackness, we still need to separate well-intended uses from outright slurs. If we're going to submit works of art and criticism to tests of inadvertent 'racism' we probably need to ask more difficult questions than we have been asking. As artist or critic can we use racially-charged signs – whether linguistic or photographic – without again passing on their pejorative history?

Yingling says yes, giving as an example Mapplethorpe's own work which, he says, isn't always consistent in its view of race. *Untitled*, for instance, featuring a nude male subject with his head hooded (an eerie reference to the historical connection between race and lynching), doesn't innocently pass on this history. The photograph appears to the critic to contain a critique of objectification (by which he means the dehumanizing attempt to reduce the black man to nothing more than his large cock). Since the image contains this implicit critique, the critic 'lets it off the hook': this is not so much a racist photograph as a photograph that 'addresses racism', he says.[6]

Is the shroud over the subject's head then an informed sign of African American history which cancels out the uninformed, passive use of the black body as image – the other two-thirds of the photograph? Does this photograph take a deconstructive turn, analogous to the kind of internal critique which feminists stipulated for representations of the female body?

If *Untitled* is a critique of racism, what is there in Mapplethorpe's other work that Yingling finds objectionable, since he says that the black nude photographs 'cannot escape the charge of racism'. It is finally, he says, the 'fetishistic interest' in the black subjects which 'objectifies them and denies them their subjectivity'.[7] Again, the paradigm of racial looking relations is

3. Thomas Yingling, 'How the Eye is Caste: Robert Mapplethorpe and the Limits of Controversy', *Discourse*, Vol 12, no 2, Spring-Summer 1990, pp3-28. These events include Mapplethorpe's death from AIDS in March 1989, the Corcoran Gallery's cancellation of a major retrospective in Washington in May 1989, coincident with the controversy over the NEA funding for museums that had exhibited his work, and the spring 1990 attempt to close down the Mapplethorpe show in Cincinnati. For overviews, see Richard Goldstein, 'The Critic and the Commissar', *Village Voice*, 18 July 1989, pp41-2; Elizabeth Hess, 'Mapplethorpe Goes to Washington', *Village Voice*, 8 August 1989, pp27-30; Grant Kester, 'A Town Called Malice', *Afterimage*, Vol 17, no 10, May 1990, p2; Jayne Merkel, 'Art on Trial', *Art in America*, Vol 78, no 12, December 1990, pp41-51.

4. Yingling, *op. cit.*, pp12-13.

5. *Ibid.*, p11.

6. *Ibid.*, p21.

7. *Ibid.*, p10.

accommodated to the paradigm of gendered looking. Just as feminists often saw women 'pictured' sexually as synonymous with women denied subjecthood, this critique of Mapplethorpe's racism sees black men represented sexually as meaning that blacks are denied subjecthood. But, of course, it is not the fact of their having been photographed nude, it is the *way* in which they are photographed that is crucial.

Generally the case against Mapplethorpe rests on arguments that his models are unable to return the look of the photographer, that they are photographed in parts as opposed to wholes, and that they are unrealistically overvalued and endowed with strange powers (fetishized). These are ways of gauging racism by interpreting telltale signs of an inappropriate relation between the photographer and the subject. And here is where Yingling's indictment of Mapplethorpe might seem to stick – in the key to the attitude of the photographer towards his models revealed not only in the photographs but in the famous *Vanity Fair* interview, the photographer bemoans the fact that over half of the models appearing in the *Black Book* had by then died because they had not been able to afford the health insurance which could have provided them with AZT. 'They all died quickly, the blacks,' he said. But Yingling objects that this way of referring to the models is a king of 'generic categorization'.[8] Is this, then, still the familiar objection to stereotyping which we have met before in feminist critiques? If so, what is its appeal as an argument? Why is it regarded as such a comprehensive and effective critical statement?

While I am in full agreement with the spirit of Yingling's critique, I want now to recall some of the hard lessons of earlier work on the politics of the image which represent possible pitfalls for literary critics and others engaged in this important work on Mapplethorpe. Like this earlier criticism, the Mapplethorpe critique is organized around the two pejorative poles of 'objectification' and 'stereotypage', critical lynchpins which often function interchangeably and synonymously. What is problematic about objectification (even given its more philosophical subject-object relation implications), is that this notion seems always to contain an appeal to a now out-dated humanism and its companion formation of liberal individualism. We find this implicit humanism in such evaluative terms as 'reduced to', 'nothing but', and 'only body', which have often cropped up in feminist work on representation. Strangely, these black bodies which are said to be objectified (not humanly individuated) are actually represented in the classical mode which has historically embodied the ideals of humanism.[10] While this doubleness (denigration/idealization) might seem to be explained with reference to the concept of fetishization, I want to separate that term out from the liberal humanist use of objectification as critique of the image since the fetish has its own different critical implications to which I will later turn.

It is where objectification meets stereotypage that the assumptions behind this humanist critique become manifest, for in the objection to typage (generic categorization) there rests the notion that the individuated is somehow the 'real'. This objection to racial (stereo)typage goes back to the NAACP (National

8. *Ibid.*, p23.

9. Kobena Mercer, in 'Looking for Trouble', *Transition*, no 51, 1980, p192, discusses the contradiction between classical aesthetics and the Englightenment attitude towards the Negro.

10. Thomas Cripps, *Slow Fade to Black: The Negro in American Film, 1900-1942*, Oxford, New York, 1977 pp39-74.

Association for the Advancement of Colored People) campaign against *The Birth of a Nation* which spurred a powerful and just political movement between 1915 and 1920.[11] But this criticism, now absorbed into common sense, is not sufficient to the task which criticism of popular images now needs to accomplish: to show that African Americans are always socially constructed, *not* that they are really and truly better than their depictions in popular forms. For as film critics have been usefully reminded by Steve Neale, stereotypes are alternately held up against an empirical 'real' and an ideological 'ideal', where the positive image is as much a construction as the negative.[12] So this leads us to the question: what would the African American men Mapplethorpe's photographs should have depicted look like? As Isaac Julien and Kobena Mercer have argued, 'it's not as if we could strip away the negative stereotypes of black men, created by western patriarchy, and discover some "natural" black masculinity which is good, pure, and wholesome.'[13] An echo again of feminist film criticism which emphasized the impossibility of 'stripping' the image of woman.[14] How, indeed, do we strip away the connotations of 'suppressed violence' from images of black men?

What I mean to say by pointing out the problems with the ways in which Mapplethorpe's black nudes have been critiqued as 'racist' is not that the images don't bear testimony to a power differential. (I think they do.) I mean to suggest that we need to develop better tools to use when we talk about 'racism' in relation to representation than we devised to speak about photographic representations of women in terms of 'sexism'. In the latter the objectification-stereotypage critique was often in danger of implying that sexism was 'in' the image and not in the offending social relations which form the interpretive context of the image. In giving this impression feminists came close to the Women Against Pornography position of 'blaming the image', a position which always appears to let the society off the hook. To borrow the structure of the AIDS awareness slogan, 'Images don't oppress, people and institutions do', a better theoretical model must make the connection between image and society more manifest. This project requires a thoroughgoing reconsideration of what is meant by 'racism', a term which has recently been turned against African Americans who are now themselves charged with being 'racist'. Here is another place where the parallel between race and gender oppression stops – the reverse 'sexism' charge against women has not stuck as stubbornly.

In 'Rethinking Stereotypes' (perhaps the most comprehensive critique to date of the politics of popular typage), Tessa Perkins has argued that there is a significant difference between 'knowing' racist stereotypes and 'believing' them.[15] I would add to this, third and fourth possibilities – that many people 'hold' stereotypes, and that some of these people sometimes 'act' on the moral assumptions summarized in stereotypes. And here is the difference: whereas one can 'know' and recognize racial stereotypage without believing that it stands for valid information about a social group, when one 'holds' such types in consciousness, one entertains the possibility that the premises informing this

11. Steve Neale, 'The Same Old Story: Stereotypes and Difference', *Screen Education*, nos 32-3, Autumn/Winter 1979-80, pp34-5.

12. Isaac Julien and Kobena Mercer, 'True Confessions', *Ten-8*, no 22, 1986, p6.

13. Mary Ann Doane, 'Woman's Stake: Filming the Female Body', *October*, no 17, 1981, p25; reproduced in Constance Penley (ed.), *Feminism and Film Theory*, Routledge, New York 1988.

14. T.E. Perkins, 'Rethinking Stereotypes', in *Ideology an Cultural Production*, Michèle Barrett, Phillip Corrigan, Annette Kuhn, and Janet Wolff (eds), Croom Helm, London 1979.

15. Stuart Hall, 'The Whites of Their Eyes', in Rosalind Brunt and George Bridges (eds), *Silver Linings*, Lawrence & Wishart, London 1981, pp36-7; reproduced in Manuel Alvarado and John O. Thompson (eds), *The Media Reader*, British Film Institute, London 1990.

typage may be true. Since one might 'believe' the moral implications of perjorative racial typage without 'acting' on such a belief, we would still need a distinction between 'believing' and 'racism in action'. But here, since we're only talking about representations, we want to know at what point people are complicit in passing on constructs which function as commonsense knowledge in a society that is deeply divided along 'racial' lines. Are they complicit when they 'know' and recognize, 'hold', or 'believe' negative stereotypes?

Stuart Hall helps us some more with this problematic by distinguishing *overt* racism (the expression of an openly racist policy or view) from *inferential* racism, the latter the 'apparently naturalized representations of events and situations relating to race' which have 'racist ... propositions inscribed in them as a set of *unquestioned assumptions*'. Of the two, inferential racism is more commonplace but more 'insidious', he says, because of its invisibility.[16] So how do we consider Mapplethorpe's circulation of the commonly, if unconsciously held belief that black men are 'nothing but their cocks', a circulation effected by his choice of nude models whose physical attributes would seem to confirm this belief? His representation may not necessarily be an expression of overt racism, but then it may not be inferential racism either since (as the critics I discuss here agree) it is typage deployed not merely assumed. And like Cindy Sherman's *Film Stills*, some of Mapplethorpe's work (for example, *Man in a Polyester Suit*) depends upon viewers knowing the stereotypage.[17]

To put it another way: is the problem the circulation of the idea *or* the belief in its validity? In his controversial take on the difficulty of using 'race' as a critical category, Anthony Appiah has cautioned about the difference between 'discussing' and 'endorsing' perverse representations of blacks in history, where he says that to fail to make the distinction risks 'shooting the messenger'.[18] Other black critics have raised enough objections to 'racism' as the simple basis of a political critique to make us think twice about our usage. These range from Audre Lorde who compares the diagnostic effectivity of the term 'whiteskin privilege' with the notion of 'racism' (which would seem to have lost its analytic teeth), to Paul Gilroy who has suggested there is no single racism to combat, but rather racisms (plural), that is, historically changing strategies.[19] But finally the most difficult question of all: what should be the position of privileged white critics towards images of blacks in history? Can and should we be the self-appointed critics of the uses of offensive types? Are we the best ones to evaluate images of 'raced' subjects in these terms since we may be oblivious to the subtle signs to which Others are so well tuned – signs we ourselves 'give off'? This is another reason why I shy away from the project of taking the 'racist' temperature of literary, cinematic, and photographic works.

The exhibition history of Mapplethorpe's photographs also demonstrates the limitations of criticizing the photographer exclusively in terms of his 'racism'. Above all, this history demonstrates the importance of the reader, a point made by Kobena Mercer in 'Skin Head Sex Thing' (see ppl-23 in this issue), where he reconsiders his earlier position, motivated by a desire to avoid producing an argument that might be available for appropriation by the New

16. See Judith Williamson, 'Images of Woman', *Screen*, Vol 24, no 6, November-December 1983, pp102-6; reproduced in Judith Williamson, *Consuming Passions: The Dynamics of Popular Culture*, Marion Boyars, London 1986.

17. Kwame Anthony Appiah, 'The Conservation of "Race",' *Black American Literature Forum*, Vol 23, no 1, Spring 1989, p46; see also Kwame Anthony Appiah, 'Racisms', in David Theo Goldberg (ed), *Anatomy of Racism*, University of Minnesota Press, Minneapolis 1990, for the most sophisticated discussion to date of the philosophical implications of the assumptions made about race and the groups that make them, including some review of Appiah's important debate with Houston Baker.

18. Audre Lorde, *Sister Outsider*, The Crossing Press, Trumansburg, New York 1984, p118; Paul Gilroy, 'One Nation Under a Groove: The Cultural Politics of "Race" and Racism in Britain', in Goldberg (ed.), *op. cit.*, p265.

19. Kobena Mercer, 'Skin Head Sex Thing: Racial Difference and the Homoerotic Imaginary', pp 1-23 of this volume. Mercer also makes the point in 'Looking for Trouble', *op. cit.*, p192.

Right. To criticize Mapplethorpe for producing racist images and black bodies as objects is to play into conservative hands, he says, offering the Right a ready-made weapon against the work. Mercer further eludes the New Right by situating himself as an ambivalent reader: he descries the white racial fantasy at the same time as appreciating something else in the image. And what he appreciates is the replacement of the white female with the black male as erotic object. While the same objectionable codification is still in place, the substitution of one body for another is transgressive. Thus the subversive homoeroticism he finds in the nude portrayals leads him to take a new position in relation to Mapplethorpe's photography.[20]

What does it mean to be an ambivalent reader? Mercer suggests that it has something to do with the ability to inhabit more than one position of 'identification'. The ambivalent reader, I would add, is neither conflicted nor undecided, but supremely gifted in the ability to inhabit at least two opposing positions. It may also be that some cultural forms themselves invite an aesthetics of ambivalence, these texts meeting ambivalent readers half way. The Mapplethorpe nudes are particularly prone to evoke ambivalence because of the form-content tension (the body of the underclass Other idealized in classical style). As gay male pornography they are also a low form bathed in high art aestheticism, problematically encouraging bodily arousal in ascetic contexts (the museum, the pages of the art book). But in addition to the conflicts the photographs play on *within* a single viewer, as we know, they themselves have become the center of conflicts *between* disparate groups. While the obvious conflicts involving the advocates of censorship vs free speech and fundamentalist vs liberal groups have been widely discussed, the photographs stir less obvious conflicts between particular 'raced' groups which interest me more.

20. The association of the playright with photography may also have to do with her other dramatic writing. See also Ntozake Shange, 'A Photograph: Lovers in Motion: A Drama', Samuel Freuch, New York 1981.

21. Ntozake Shange, 'Introduction', *Black Book*, St Martin's Press, New York 1986.

22. Thanks to Kobena Mercer for this idea.

III STRANGE BEDFELLOWS

What I want to talk about in this next section is the way Mapplethorpe's nude studies have been claimed by strange bedfellows, and here my point of departure will be his notorious *Black Book*. At Christmas in 1988, I gave a copy of this book to my best friend (a straight white woman), and at the time I quickly read the foreword by black feminist Ntozake Shange, author of the play *For Colored Girls Who Have Committed Suicide/When the Rainbow is Enuf*.[21] In the first short paragraphs she describes her meeting with Mapplethorpe in Houston where together, she says, the two 'flipped through the photographs looking for former lovers we knew were somewhere in the book'. She says to him, 'I can't seem to find him now, but I know he's there somewhere', and Mapplethorpe responds (half smiling), 'I know what you mean, I can't find mine either.'[22]

The image of the black feminist playwright and the white gay male photographer looking for former lovers in the book was still haunting me when, the following Christmas, my best friend gave me the same present I had given her the year before – a copy of *Black Book*. Immediately I reread the foreword. What was it about the dialogue between Shange and Mapplethorpe? Yes, the foreword promises to divulge secrets, but it also offers a way of reading the book – one is invited to look to find the former lovers of the famous playright and the infamous photographer. This is a neat cross-over marketing device, which attempts to reconstruct the icons of an exclusive gay subculture for a wider group of consumers. Taking the invitation to look for lovers literally, the unwary are seduced into the assumption that the models are not all homosexual males, but are both gay and straight, or possibly bisexual. But the beauty of the book is that the actual sexual preference of real models who once existed before the camera doesn't matter. Fantasy finally couldn't care less.[23]

23. Shange, 'irrepressibly bronze, beautiful, and mine', *op. cit.*

24. *Ibid.*

But with Mapplethorpe and Shange's admitted failure to find former lovers (after looking long and hard), we know that their conversation is not really about their own past affairs but is more a kind of shared love of and nostalgia for the black male body. For the reader who takes the cue, this is an even more enticing invitation, a suggestion that one looks to find one's own former lovers, an exercise which could even turn into the fantasy of having future lovers. I do think that with the foreword's subtle reference to sexual scenarios, the book lends itself to such a reading, especially given a title which reminds us of the function of the 'little black book'. But the introduction stops short of acknowledging the ways in which the book is like a soft-core porn magazine by taking an abrupt turn.

After the subtle exchange at the beginning of the book, Shange gives us a four-part poem titled 'irrepressibly bronze, beautiful, and mine'. Surprisingly, it is a 'first love awakening' poem told in the voice of an eight year-old girl who discovers the lure of black maleness in a friend of her father's who gives her a small stone to grasp when he leaves (his heart). Clutching the stone, only 'grasping dreams', she has yet to 'grab holto a man', but later this stone becomes the 'eruption' of 'black volcanoes', stirred by the jazz of Miles Davis and the political imperative of the Blackstone Rangers. These 'black volcanoes ... seep lava *anywhere* there's true love', [my emphasis] but, by the end of the poem, we know that the lovemaking, the 'pulling down of petticoats' and 'lace panties', amidst the 'sweet sweat' is a heterosexual vision.[24]

How are we to reconcile this poem about growing up black and female, about black rural life and African American history, with the idols of the gay urban ghetto represented in the book? The poem tries to retrieve the bodies for the black family and black community life, but they are unwelcome there. The tough torsos, the scarred limbs – testimony to a strange combination of athletic regimen and indulgent risk – cannot be representationally rehabilitated as fathers or husbands. The black porn star can never really go home again.

So the poem and the photographs set up a condition of longing (the black female for a black masculinity which again eludes her), and rivalry (the black male lost to the white male photographer and the lure of the gay scene). But the white male photographer is not the only rival in the scenario. In Shange's poem, the young girl sees the black man bring different white women to St Louis every summer. When one of the women is friendly to the child she thinks, 'why do you like me you're with him & he's mine he's colored/he'll always be like that/like me.'[25] The other rival is the white woman. So three different desiring looks meet over these photographs. What, then, does it mean, for one marginal group to share a secret object of desire with another marginal group?

For straight white women and some gay men (black as well as white), the shared enthusiasm for the black male body is one basis for political solidarity. This meeting over a taboo erotic object is an easy alliance, an 'in-joke' told on white male culture.[26] Note that the reverse doesn't hold true for lesbians and straight white men, that it is seldom acknowledged that the two groups have anything basic in common, although both straight men and lesbians proudly define their identities with reference to the same object, the female body. (Here we find yet another reason why the lesbian object of desire may have been theorized as 'not woman', effectively retrieving this object from male desire.) But in the case of white women and black women, the same comparison on the basis of the preferred object of desire touches a tender nerve. Although we may have solidarity in every other way, our looks cannot meet knowingly over these bodies. Desire goes underground. At this time in history, feminism silently bears this cross in order to hold together an ideal of black and white sisterhood.

So these competing glances set up a looking field not anticipated by contemporary theories of gender and representation. First, the feminist film theory paradigm that has hypothesized looking as endemically male is tripped up by its own premises: the male gaze is not always a 'male gaze', especially when it finds its favorite object in the male rather than the female body. It has already been observed that the notion of patriarchial looking relations can't imagine sexual looking as female.[27] And if the construct hasn't anticipated women looking longingly at women, how can we expect it to fathom that other transgression – white women looking across racial lines? And it is here that I want to digress in order to take the opportunity to consider a problem which contemporary feminist theory has thus far managed to evade. And I say contemporary because some of the issues I want to raise have been visited before (and consequently forgotten) in the first wave of feminism, most notably by African American feminist Ida B. Wells.[28]

IV TABOO COUPLINGS

I want to offer a tentative theory of what might be called taboo couplings – a rough comparison between homosexuality and interracial sexuality, a comparison made strictly in terms of the kind of terror those aberrations strike in the heart of mainstream culture. By taboo couplings I mean sexual relations that confound white male culture, that reject its norm (that is, same race, different gender sexuality). I want to try to think through the different

25. Jonathan Rutherford, 'Who's That Man?', in Rowena Chapman and Jonathan Rutherford (eds), *Male Order: Unwrapping Masculinity*, Lawrence & Wishart, London 1988, p62, was also puzzled by the manner in which the photographs seemed to function as a two-way erotic object: 'They seem to fit into contemporary erotic images of the male body, yet the narcissism is absent. They are the image of a white man's fantasy, on show for the consumption of white men (and women, although the images are homo-erotic rather than hetero-erotic).'

26. For an overview of these issues, see my 'White Privilege and Looking Relations: Race and Gender in Feminist Film Theory', *Screen*, Vol 29, no 4, Autumn 1988; reproduced in Patricia Erens (ed.), *Sexual Stratagems: Issues in Feminist Film Criticism*, Indiana University Press, 1990.

27. See Ida B. Wells-Barnett, *On Lynchings* (1892), Arno Press, New York 1969.

28. This is one of Wells-Barnett's theses, in *In Lynchings, op. cit.* W.J. Cash, in *The Mind of the South*, Vintage, New York 1941), wryly comments that the chances of a Southern woman being raped by a black man were about as great as being hit by lightning.

ways in which these couplings disturb the dominant model: for my hypothesis is that such transgressions don't undermine the cultural dominant in the same way, although I am hesitant to say whether one assault is finally more or less threatening than the other to white male privilege. I have thought this comparison through in terms of race and gender cross-overs, calling attention to the way these acts transgress boundaries, the way they always leave behind one culture and enter into another, either moving from protected straight culture to vulnerable gay and lesbian subcultures or from black skin to white skin (or the reverse), entering through touch into the skin/culture of the other. To help us understand the complexity of these moves, I want to propose three categories of crossing: 1) heterosexual racial cross-over; 2) plain (same race) homosexuality; and 3) homosexual racial cross-over.

One way of thinking about heterosexual racial cross-over (the 'danger' of interracial heterosexual relations) is to consider the way this correct gender but incorrect racial coupling goes 'against nature'. It is an unnatural-natural act which, although said to offend by going 'against nature', should be properly understood as an offence against culture. I should be clear, however, that my usage of 'correct' is meant to indict the intolerance of the Right. (Although in the light of Spike Lee's *Jungle Fever*, it now seems that interracial heterosexuality enjoys the distinction of being politically incorrect on both the Left and the Right.)

In some historical periods, as we know, interracial heterosexual acts which went 'against nature' (albeit by ignoring cultural prohibitions) risked brutal repercussions and even death. Let us not forget, however, how gender has historically crossed race in the United States, so that during Reconstruction the gender factor in clandestine liaisons became telling. From the literature on lynching we know that where the illegal common practice (white men and black women) went unpunished, the illegal uncommon practice was punished by extra-legal vigilantism at the slightest hint of an alliance. By alliance here I mean consensual relations between black males and white females rather than forced relations (mythical rape), negligible in numbers during this period.[29]

In my second category, what I call plain (same race) homosexuality, I want to 'control for race'. Here, homosexuality without racial cross-over is a correct racial but an incorrect gender coupling. But as we know, same race gay and lesbian couples get no credit from the dominant culture for their compliance with racial norms: we might say that their wrong gender choice is overdetermining. Does this suggest that splitting sexuality and procreation is any more troublesome to white male culture than 'spilling' blood in such a way that racial lines become confused? Recent history may have invalidated this question since it now seems that taboos against homosexuality are based less and less on rejection of a procreative mandate and more and more on the threat of death and disease.[30]

We need to turn to our third category, the homosexual racial cross-over to see how these old taboos function in different combinations. In this category, whether we are talking about black men loving white men or white women

29. The best discussion of the heterosexual mandate is still Adrienne Rich, 'Compulsory Heterosexuality and Lesbian Existence', in Ann Snito, Christine Stansell, and Sharon Thompson (eds), *Powers of Desire: The Politics of Sexuality* Monthly Review Press, New York 1983.

30. Hilton Als, in 'The Color Line: Christopher Street and the Road Not Taken', *Village Voice*, 2 July 1991, pp35-6, laments the way interracial relationships in the gay community have come more not less difficult since Stonewall; the idea of 'categories of pleasure' I have adapted from Jackie Goldsby, 'What It Means to be Colored Me', *Out/Look*, no 9, Summer 1990, p5, in which she also asks about her relationship with a white woman, 'where, in the context of lesbian political discourse on race, can we acknowledge that our knowlingly crossing boundaries of race and class *is* a part of our desire for each other?' Thanks to Bill Nichols and Alex Doty for pointing out this article to me.

loving black women, we're always talking about a double transgression. What is striking about interracial homosexual desire (the case with the white male photographer's desire for the black male body) is that from the point of view of official culture, this is a double-crossing that cannot be ideologically rehabilitated – it is incorrect on two counts. But Mapplethorpe's transgressive desire is really a triple transgression – a class infraction as well as a gender and race infraction of social rules – although this has only been noted by critics sceptical of the power differential in his work.

While interracial homosexual desire may be culturally incorrect on two counts (at least), and therefore ideologically troublesome in the culture at large, it is strangely invisible in the gay and lesbian community where it should theoretically thrive, given the culture of acceptance. By invisible, I mean that 'race' as a 'category of pleasure' cannot, as yet, be articulated, except perhaps in local chapters of the radical group 'Black and White Men Together'.[31] So the question has to do with the way an interracial taboo is operative in both the subculture and the host culture.

31. Juliet Mitchell, *Psychoanalysis and Feminism*, Vintage, New York 1975.

In the mainstream discourse on Mapplethorpe, attention has been fixed primarily on the way the photographer has found sexuality where it is not supposed to be (in children, between men). 'Race' as a category of pleasure is implied in *Black Book*, is indeed its overarching premise, but the stir over Mapplethorpe's black nudes has been more over the incorrectness of his aesthetic usage – the high art form in relation to the low life black model – than over his implicit staging of sexuality between races. Clearly the offence of homosexuality is a greater crime in the eyes of official culture, also indicated by the contemporary dictum against homosexual marriages; interracial sexual infringement being only a secondary 'crime gainst nature'. But much more work needs to be done on the way the two crimes may be seen to cancel each other out: the way men and women already 'lost' to homosexuality, who transgress deeper by engaging in interracial sexuality, are eventually 'written off' as a whole by the normative culture.

To discuss these troubles to dominant culture in terms of the nature/culture dialectic is only one way of addressing taboo crossings, and only the beginning. We might also ask which loss is more devastating to white male society. Is it the white woman lost to the lesbian or the white woman lost to the black man? Since the former taboo coupling is unimaginable (in the white male cultural mind) because the body wasn't designed for it, it either tends to be invisible or may be easily dismissed as freak aberration. But the latter taboo coupling, because it is fully imaginable with reference to the 'normal' heterosexual drive is not so easily dismissed as freakish. It may become more threatening as it is increasingly acknowledged that women too have sexual desires, and that involvement with men of a different race is a matter of choice. If natural bodies are designed for this coupling, however taboo, only culture (at once resilient and unbending but fragile and changing), stands in its way.

V WHAT PSYCHOANALYSIS CAN AND CAN'T TELL US ABOUT FANTASIES OF RACE AND SEX

I'd like to return here to the question of objectification versus fetishization. What do Mercer and others mean when they speak of this photography as white fetishization? Are the implications of using Freudian terminology the same for African American studies as for women's studies, where Juliet Mitchell's original argument, that psychoanalysis can be turned to feminist advantage, seems to have won acceptance?[32] Recently, black critics have hotly debated the relevance of Continental theory to African and African American literature. Although these debates have primarily had to do with the compatibility between poststructuralism and black writing, the question is equally applicable to the relation between psychoanalysis and images of black male sexuality. In the course of these discussions, black critics have considered what it means for them to engage inhospitable philosophical traditions in the service of reading black texts.

The most persuasive argument on behalf of using Continental theory in relation to African and African American texts is that the integration of the two produces unpredictable offspring. What is it that happens when theory meets text? To paraphrase Derrida, once a text has been 'translated', in any way, it never comes back.[33] Black criticism especially, says Henry Louis Gates, never leaves the text where it found it. But the transformation is reciprocal: the theory transforms the text and the text transforms the theory. What is produced is a 'construct neither exactly "like" its antecedents nor entirely new'.[34]

I would argue that Freudian theory will never be quite the same again after Kobena Mercer's use of it, as in his analysis of *Man in a Polyester Suit* where he sees a significant play on the myth of the big black phallus, a play produced by giving white male culture a literalization of its own conception (the black male as nothing more than his cock). Mercer also finds the logic of disavowal in Mapplethorpe's work. But instead of the boy discovering the absence of the penis in the girl child, which occasions the production of the phallus as powerful fetish against the castration the boy fears, the white photographer's logic brings the penis back to different ends. As Mercer puts it, Mapplethorpe's logic goes something like this: '*I know* it's not true that all black men have big penises, *but* in my photograph they do.'[35] The photographer's disclaimer has the same structure as 'I know that she is not castrated, but nevertheless she is.'

In connecting the myth of the big black penis with the castration complex as he does, Mercer discovers something new about castration anxiety – that it is about making comparisons: mine is bigger than yours; mine is there, yours isn't. It is about not having any or not having enough, and again the white male is the measure. It is also about having the power to disclaim social and economic realities, and having the position to put other, more advantageous and flattering versions of reality in their place. This is easier to see in the second move of Freud's fetishist than in the first. First, the fetishist stands

32. Jacques Derrida, *The Ear of the Other*, Schocken Books, New York 1982, as quoted in Diana Fuss, *Essentially Speaking*, Routledge, New York, 1989, p83; I am indebted to Fuss for this way of reading black texts.

33. Henry Louis Gates (ed.), *Black Literature and Literary Theory*, Methuen, New York 1984, p4.

34. Mercer, 'Skin Head Sex Thing', *op. cit.*

35. Homi Bhabha, 'What Does the Black Man Want?', *New Formations*, no 1, Spring 1987, pp123-4; for a companion defence of the use of psychoanalysis in colonial studies see Stephan Feuchtwang, 'Fanonian Spaces', *New Formations*, no 1, Spring 1987, p127.

aghast at what is not like himself in the Other. But it is in the second, companion move that he bestows a new status on an unlikely object, a value disproportionate to its original worth. The fetish is then a kind of trophy and magical protection in one. It guards against castration as it gleefully triumphs over it. Could it be that this analysis offers us some insight into the mindset of the conquering imperialist in his first encounter with the Other? He says to himself (in the inner voice of imperialism): 'I don't understand what I see before me because I can't recognize myself in it, but, whatever it is, I will turn it to my advantage.'

In answer to the charge that Continental theory is an interloper in black cultural criticism, I should also say that there is really no turning back, especially as we increasingly acknowledge the importance of Frantz Fanon. Because, via Fanon, the philosophical foundation of studies in colonialism, already laid, depend upon the notion that colonizer and colonized alike require the Other in order to constitute the self; and this is basic Lacan. Note the utility for studies of race and representation in Homi Bhabha's quotation of Lacan:

> In the case of display, ... the play of combat in the form of intimidation, the being gives of himself, or receives from the other, something that is like a mask, a double, an envelope, a thrown-off skin, thrown off in order to cover the frame of a shield.[36]

Now that I have shown that it may be possible to discuss the relationship between colonizer and colonized in psychoanalytic terms, let me ask about the political implications of working this critical vein. In 'Critical Fanonism', (in one of his most outwardly political moments), Henry Louis Gates responds to the current uses of Lacan in African American studies. Fanon's 'self-divisions' (Martinique, Paris, Algeria and Tunisia), Gates says, represent the 'agon between psychology and politics, ontogeny and sociogeny, Marx and Freud'. And he concludes: 'In the context of colonial binarism, we've seldom admitted fully how disruptive the psychoanalytic model can be.' Why? It is disruptive because it has stood for 'a productive relation between oppressed and oppressor'. This is political objection number one. I also find in Gates a second political objection when he says that where the 'Freudian mechanisms of repression are set in relation to those of colonial repression ... it's still unclear whether we are to speak of convergence or mere parallelism.'[37] It is the danger of confusing the social, the historical, and the psychoanalytic that constitutes the political problem, something Kobena Mercer and Isaac Julien have pointed out in their observation that Freud's example of disavowal in his classic essay on fetishism in Chinese foot-binding. They call for a more culturally specific understanding of such a practice not available through Freud.[38]

The use of Freudian teminology, then, always leaves us with a job of political clarification to do. Or, as Linda Williams has noted in her astute comparison between Marxist and Freudian notions of the fetish, the dilemma is that the 'social fact must be factored in ... to the Freudian fetish.'[39] If there is a better

36. Henry Louis Gates, 'Critical Fanonism', *Critical Inquiry*, Vol 17, no 3, Spring 1991, p469, p470, pp466-7.

37. Kobena Mercer and Isaac Julien, 'De Margin and De Centre', *Screen*, Vol 29, no 4, Autumn 1988, p9.

38. Linda Williams, *Hard Core: Power, Pleasure, and the 'Frenzy of the Visible'*, University of California Press, Berkeley and Los Angeles 1989, p204.

39. Richard Dyer, 'Don't Look Now – The Male Pin-up', *Screen*, Vol 23, nos 3-4, September-October 1982, p66.

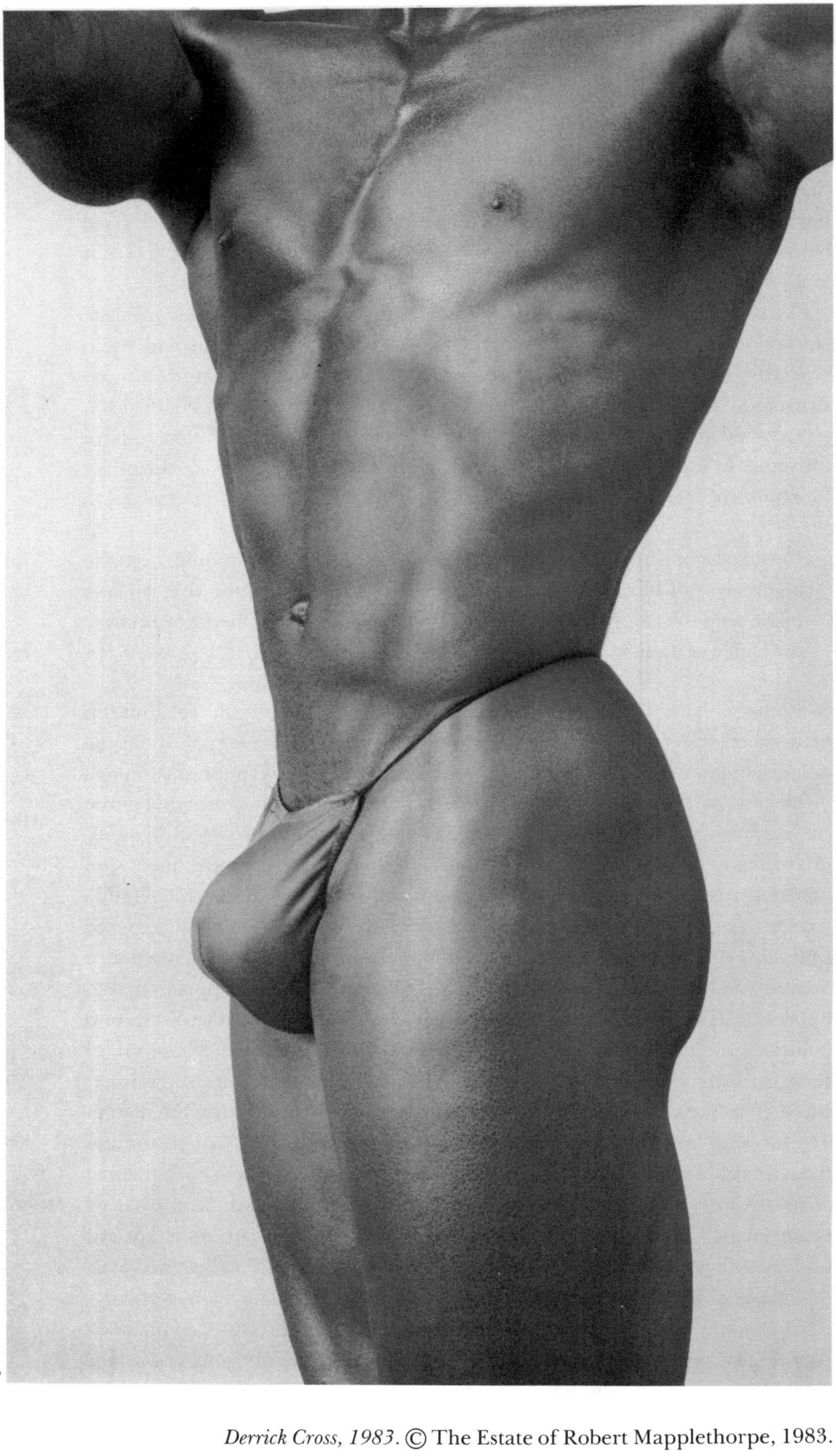

Derrick Cross, 1983. © The Estate of Robert Mapplethorpe, 1983.

political objection to psychoanalytic theory than the absence of politics from this theory, I have yet to find that objection.

Insisting on a political orientation also means listening to the many feminists who voice grave doubts that the scenario of castration and fetish-production can tell us anything about women's desired objects since women have been left out of this theory from the beginning. As Richard Dyer once remarked, why should women be implicated since they have nothing at all to fear from castration?[40] Mapplethorpe may have staged these photographs in ways that echo classic fetish construction, and certainly this would explain the deep ambivalence Mercer attributes to them. But their construction as fetishes doesn't go very far towards helping us to explain the attraction they have for women. And here I want to talk about middle-class straight white women in particular.

VI WHITE WOMEN/BLACK SEX

I say middle-class because it is as high art that the Mapplethorpe photographs have been introduced into the broader culture. Indeed, for the current generation of young art history students, the *Black Book* nude studies may be the equivalent of the textbook images of Michaelangelo's *David* which stirred an earlier generation of college students. (Several graduate student women asked me if they could borrow the book to study the photographs of the uncircumcized penis since they had never seen any.) In this way, for some straight women, the nude studies take on the task of what Richard Dyer suggests is the higher function of pornography – the 'education of desire'.[41] 'Art' becomes the alibi for satisfying curiosity and seeking sexual knowledge through looking.

It is a new generation of women better educated in desire who responded so enthusiastically to the image of football star Roger Craig in a Macy's ad for Calvin Klein briefs appearing in a San Francisco newspaper last summer.[42] And this generation has been further 'taught' by the choreography of African American dancer Bill T. Jones, particularly through his provocative nude solo work. In contemporary culture, one image leads to another in the training of subversive desire, and it is impossible not to notice that Calvin Klein's Roger Craig is nothing more than a Mapplethorpe photograph flipped.

But there is something else important going on in the white approach, an approach too tentative and timid to be called appropriation. Yingling (I think quite usefully) situates Mapplethorpe's nudes within developments in the gay male culture in New York, in which the eroticization of a simulated male/female role difference has been replaced by the eroticization of racial difference.[43] But this is not the only instance of one difference standing in for the other. Many women in United States culture have historically been taught to understand sexuality entirely in terms of racial difference. Lillian Smith once described the sexual education of Southern children as based on an analogy with segregation. A white woman is taught to think of her body as

40. Richard Dyer, 'Gay Male Porn – Coming to Terms', *Jump Cut*, no 30, 1985, p27.

41. Noel K. Wilson, 'Tailback Shows Off Tight End', *The Daily Iowan*, 22 June 1990.

42. Yingling, *op. cit.*, p10.

43. Lillian Smith, *Killers of the Dream* (1949) W.W. Norton, New York and London 1961, p87.

racially divided into those parts which are dark and untouchable and those that are not. As she describes this lesson:

> Now, parts of your body are segregated areas which you must stay away from and keep others away from. These areas you touch only when necessary. In other words, you cannot associate freely with them any more than you can associate freely with colored children.[44]

Growing up, Southern children were made to feel as guilty about crossing the colour line as they did about crossing the sex line to touch the dangerous parts of their own bodies.[45] The implications are not the same for female as they are for male children. It is by now a truism that male culture has shifted the burden of representing sexuality to the Other – to blacks and to women. This enables men to distance themselves from their own sexual excesses and misdeeds, which are performed then by the dark parts of the male body acting independently of the rest of it.[46] Consider, however, the implication for women for whom the same distancing might exaggerate fear of (and disgust with) their own sexuality, a sexuality belonging not to themselves but to some Other, belonging elsehere yet located in their own bodies.

But there is something more at stake than the alienation from one's body which feminism has already diagnosed for us. Could it be that for the Southern woman of a particular generation, learning about her own sexuality must always be tied to knowledge of the dark Other in a particular way? Given this fact of the education of Southern women, one would surmise that sexual liberation must be inextricably linked with racial desegregation. Lillian Smith gives us a new scenario with which to understand the relation between race and sexuality. In this scenario, the white body differs from the black body in one key respect: whereas the black body is integrated, the white body itself is segregated.

'Race,' says Henry Louis Gates, 'has become a trope of ultimate, irreducible difference between cultures, linguistic groups, or adherents of specific belief systems which – more often than not – also have fundamentally opposed economic interests.' Is it by means of this trope, then, that one comes to understand gender difference, as another ultimate and irreducible distinction? Gates, however, reminds us that 'the biological criteria used to determine "difference" in sex simply do not hold when applied to "race".' And yet the imperfectness of the comparison is what should interest us, for, as Gates goes on, it is because of the arbitrariness of race that it works as the 'ultimate trope of difference'.[47] This arbitrariness explains why 'race' has worked so well to mystify sexuality for Southern children.

Mercer was right when he first wrote that the Mapplethorpe photographs 'project[ed] certain sexual and racial fantasies about the black male body'.[48] There are fantasies of that body as available and submissive (note the number of models with closed eyes); there are fantasies of encounters with uniformed soldiers, primitives, boy children, athletes, and Greek statues come-to-life.

44. *Ibid.*, p84.

45. See, for instance, Tom Ryan, 'Roots of Masculinity', and Richard Dyer, 'Images of Men in the Media', in Andy Metcalf and Martin Humphries (eds), *The Sexuality of Men*, Pluto Press, London and Sydney 1985.

46. Henry Louis Gates, 'Writing "Race" and the Difference it Makes', in Henry Louis Gates (ed), *'Race', Writing, and Difference*, University of Chicago Press, Chicago and London 1986, p5.

47. Mercer, 'Imagining', *op. cit.*, p62; but see also Judith Butler, 'The Force of Fantasy: Feminism, Mapplethorpe, and Discursive Excess', *Differences*, Vol 2, no 2, 1990, p106, for more on how such representations are equally 'producer and produced' by fantasy.

These are classic gay male fantasies which supposedly have nothing to do with women. But for women (some of whom are literate in these codes and some of whom are not), what fantasies are 'on offer', if any? I suppose that there may be fantasies of defiance as well as fantasies of discovery worked out over these 'borrowed' and shared love objects. Such fantasies may be possible because Mapplethorpe's nudes offer none of the imagery of the black male 'threat' to pristine womanhood. And thus, I don't see that Mapplethorpe's images have anything to do with miscegenation, with black seed spilled in white wombs. But I do think that they have already had to do with arousal, awakening, and yearning, even for women who would not know what to do with these bodies if they had them.

Thanks go to Susan Jeffords, Susan Willis, Ed Hill, and Kobena Mercer for making important contributions to this essay.

SUBJECTIVITY, IDEOLOGY AND DIFFERENCE
RECOVERING OTHERNESS

Couze Venn

I

Laura Mulvey, reflecting on the changed circumstances of the 1980s following the optimism of feminist struggles of earlier years writes: 'It cannot be easy to move from oppression and its mythologies to resistance in history: a detour through a no-man's land or threshold area of counter-myth and symbolization is necessary.[1] That same sense of the drawing to an end of a particular period of activity and analyses applies to the issues around racism and the struggles to break free from old dominations rooted in colonialism and its legacy.

This paper is an intervention in a particularly insecure moment for politics and for theory, framed between, on the one hand, the 'postmodern' and poststructuralist rejection of totality and grand narratives and, on the other, the diversification of political direction which the recognition of difference and the postcolonial reality of divergent national states have entailed. The question of what is to be done has become acutely regionalized, even individualized, caught in the struggles around race, gender, class and the urgency of living satisfying lives in the spaces we manage to secure for ourselves. Current strategies for action and resistance can appear as disorganized as capitalism has apparently become, if we are to believe observers like Scott Lash and John Urry and Claus Offe.[2] Furthermore, the post-cold war period reconstituted the issue of the 'end of history' trumpeted by apologists of the 'American way of life' like Daniel Bell. This has serious implications both for the legitimation of alternative models and modes of development for 'Third World' countries, and for the project of rethinking the postmodern world.

The problem can be posed against the backdrop of the massive effort expended in the colonization of nature and consciousness on a global scale which for Ernest Mandel characterizes 'late-capitalism'. Specifically, it focuses on the cultural resources for resisting domination which exist or could be produced, and on the bases upon which alternative futures can be imagined and planned. The insecurity I noted earlier has to do with the fact that until recently a broad Marxism could inform and guide this counter-hegemonic move, either through the critique of capitalism or in supporting the ethical commitment to the idea of modernity as the project of universal human emancipation and enlightenment.

We now have to rethink the question of agency and of the making of history, and do so without losing sight of the reality and meaningfulness of human lives, something which the privileging of totality had disastrously forgotten. It is a question which engages with the concepts of ideology and of subjectivity, but which now requires their urgent reconceptualisation.

1. Laura Mulvey, 'Changes: Thoughts on Myth, Narrative and Historical Experience', in *History Workshop*, no 23, p3.

2. Scott Lash and John Urry, *The End of Organized Capitalism*, Polity Press, Oxford 1987, and Claus Offe, *Disorganized Capitalism*, Polity Press, Oxford 1985, present a view of capitalism which moves away from analyses which see it as a system.

A great deal of important analytical and cultural work has been produced in the period of decolonization which brings us to this new threshold, marked by the crisis of socialism and the ascendancy of the New Right. If old certainties and signposts have become suspect for the task of critique and for overcoming postmodernist political pessimism, the agenda for change tied to subjectivity remains fruitful – i.e., the reformulation of the problem of ideology in relation to the formation of subjects and the functioning of apparatuses of power in the subjective process. My reassessment of this problematic will pass through Althusser to the extent that the issues of the efficacious strategies, sites and forms of struggle implicated in Mulvey's remarks have a starting point in his work, particularly in the borrowings from Lacanian psychoanalytic theory and in the way in which semiotic and discourse theory and the theme of otherness have thus become central for understanding change.

I think that the issues now hinge on the production of 'counter-discourse',[3] of counter-memories and narratives that 'change the rules',[4] production which feeds into the struggle to decolonize the mind. In order to clarify and contextualize what is at stake in the shift of focus I am proposing, I shall begin by briefly considering the main elements of what has developed into two broad approaches to the study of racism and racial difference, which imply quite different strategies for change.

A broadly Marxist approach examines racism mainly within the framework of the critique of capitalism. Racism is seen as an aspect or an effect of class struggle,[5] or the product of colonialist and imperialist ideology supporting the exploitation of the 'Third World'.[6] Racism here is regarded as an ideology in the old sense, serving the interest of the ruling class or functioning for the maintenance and reproduction of capitalism. Studies informed by Althusser and Gramsci refer the crisis in 'race relations' to the thesis of a crisis in hegemony in social democracy. A response to the crisis is the eruption of moral panics which invest non-white groups with the mark of danger and seek to reconstitute the community and nation by founding its cohesive unity on the construction of collective opposition to the alien Other. Racism is thus thought to play a key role in securing or re-establishing hegemony.[7]

It is also argued that racism takes on specific reconstituted forms according to varying ideological functioning. It thus operates as other ideologies do, constituting new 'historical' and 'ideological' subjects for 'ideological discourses'.[8] Stuart Hall has argued that non-white subjects, by the same token, live their relation to their real conditions of existence 'in and through the imaginary representations of a racist interpellation', that is to say, as 'inferiors'.[9] He concludes with the important reminder that ideologies are also open to contestation and provide elementary forms for the 'cultures of resistance' (such as through the 'symbolic inversions' of 'black power').[10]

Today, in the light of a multiplicity of politics around 'difference', there is a recognition of a plurality of interests, suggesting the *possibility* of new forms of alliances in what would be the continuing struggle to overcome or transform capitalism.[11] Alongside this development there has emerged an important

3. R. Terdiman, 'Deconstructing Memory: On Representing the Past and Theorizing culture in France Since the Revolution', *Diacritics*, 1985, pp13-36.

4. Hayden White, 'The Narrativization of Real Events', *Critical Inquiry*, 1981, pp793-8.

5. A. Sivanandan, *A Different Hunger*, Pluto Press, London 1983.

6. E. Williams, *Capitalism and Slavery*, André Deutsch, London 1964.

7. Stuart Hall *et al.*, *Policing the Crisis*, Macmillan, London 1978.

8. Stuart Hall, 'Race, Articulation and Societies Structured in Dominance', in *Sociological Theories: Race and Colonialization*, Unesco, New York 1980, p342.

9. *Ibid.*

10. *Ibid.*

11. Established differently in Paul Gilroy *et al.*, *The Empire Strikes Back*, Hutchinson, Birmingham 1982, and Ernesto Laclau and Chantal Mouffe, *Hegemony and Socialist Strategy: Towards a Radical Democratic Politics*, Verso, London 1985.

body of texts which is concerned with how racial difference has been discursively constructed and with the analysis of the effects of the discursive for subjectivity and identity. Clearly, its central contribution is towards the understanding of the cultural mechanisms which have gradually become a condition of the exercise of colonial and post-colonial power. This work examines the forms and the texts in which the history of these relations has become sedimented as part of the 'cultural capital' of the 'West'. Equally, the expressions of dissent, the voice of the racially oppressed, are dissected to reveal their cultural significance. This approach, as distinct from the Marxist one, utilizes an apparatus of concepts and theories drawn from poststructuralist writings generally.

These analyses of colonial discourse and the construction of otherness gesture towards a cultural politics, but indicate no specific strategy, and by themselves can only establish imprecise links between the production of texts in the broad sense that Fredric Jameson has defined it[12] and political action of the kind that would transform social relations (and not merely at the individual level).

The danger is real enough of the solidity of racism melting into the thin air, of a philosophy of pure textuality, a danger Edward Said points to and attempts to correct when he argues that:

> Even if we accept (as in the main I do) the arguments put forward by Hayden White – that there is no way to get past texts in order to apprehend 'real' history directly – it is still possible to say that such a claim need not eliminate interest in the events and circumstances entailed by and expressed in the texts themselves ... texts are worldly ... they are a part of the social world, human life ... the realities of power and authority ... are the realities that make texts possible ... these realities are what should be taken account of by criticism and the critical consciousness.[13]

A crucial question is implied here about the relation of history to text – that is, the relation of the 'realities' of material practices to the discourses inscribed in or 'representing' them. The materialist focus on practice, though correct, especially in its correction of the privileging of ideas/texts, nevertheless misses out the effects of the discursive. On the other hand, the privileging of texts in the understanding of history misses out the fact of a specific gap between texts and historical 'reality' which arises from the effects of power and domination in the production of texts. That is to say, it does not take account of the fact that the less powerful and the oppressed do not write their texts and their history except as part of a politics of resistance, namely, as part of what the oppressor strives to silence and suppress and what the discourse of domination demeans or marginalizes.[14]

If there is 'nothing past texts', then it is vital that the means for their subversion and the production of counter-discourse be found. The problems

12. Fredric Jameson, *The Political Unconscious*, Methuen, London 1983.

13. Edward Said, *The World, the Text and the Critic*, Faber and Faber, London 1984, pp4, 5

14. See, for example, the work of the Subaltern Studies Group, in R. Guha and G. Spivak (eds), *Selected Subaltern Studies*, Oxford University Press, New York and Oxford 1988, who argue that narratives and representations of historical events are themselves instruments in the making of history; they belong to the adversarial space in the struggles of power and resistance, domination and liberation. Dominant history is the 'prose of counter-insurgency'.

involved in this task are but the other face of issues around 'counter-ideological' practices, which deal with how subjectivity can be transformed. If this is the point at which we have arrived in the development of political and analytical work about 'race', then a post-Althusserian approach suggests that we draw upon both sets of discourses in reposing the old questions. This requires an understanding of the problems in each broad position as well as the means to move to some new conceptual coherence. In my discussion I shall note the former and suggest elements which can help towards the latter.

It is now well established that the main area of difficulty with the Marxist critique of racial, class and gender oppression has concerned the functioning of ideology in accounting for subjectivity and agency. Outside of 'vulgar Marxism', the critique of capitalism from the 1920s has increasingly taken the form of the critique of ideology (for example, in the work of the Frankfurt School). The development of the problem through Gramsci and Althusser has co-opted psychoanalytic theory; and in the context of the slogan asserting that 'the personal is political', theoretical work has come to prioritize the issue of subjectivity – 'The politics of ideological struggle thus becomes exclusively a problem of and around "subjectivity" in the Lacanian sense.'[15]

It is certain that psychoanalysis has proved to be a very useful tool in a variety of struggles which intrinsically problematized gender, sexuality and identity. But it is recognizably a double-edged weapon since it remains contaminated by phallocentrism and is ever open to appropriation by 'ego psychyology', as Lacan has demonstrated.

However, I think one should take seriously Paul Ricoeur's argument that psychoanalysis is allied to the understanding of the project of hermeneutics as demystification and the reduction of illusion. It thus participates, together with the movement that 'let speak what once was said', in the task of modernity to 'bring into the open the crisis of language that today makes us oscillate between demystification and restoration of meaning.'[16] Such a task requires that 'we listen to symbols.'[17] My interest in this view is the connection it makes with the suggestions made by Mulvey and by Hall concerning culturally disruptive forms of resistance, and with Jameson's discussion of a 'utopian hermeneutic'[18] which could serve the aim of the critique of oppressive ideologies and the 'affirmation of collective solidarity'.[19]

One other important departure in the post-Althusserian period which moved away from the old problematic of ideology altogether follows Foucault who avoids the concept not only because it tends to appear in opposition to something like the truth, but because it refers to the notion of an epistemic subject and is made to depend for its effectivity on some other instance like the economic.[20] In the place of class struggle and of contradiction he points to the play of power and resistance, although for him resistance seems to be both a condition and an effect of the exercise of power. Although these new conceptual tools have resulted in much fruitful work, serious problems remain when we want to address the issues of gender and racial difference.[21]

If we turn to the approach informed by literary and cultural criticism and

15. Stuart Hall, 'Recent Developments in the Theories of Language and Ideology: A Critical Note', in Hall *et al., op.cit.*

16. Paul Ricoeur, *Freud and Philosophy*, Yale University Press, New Haven and London 1970, p27.

17. *Ibid.*

18. Frederic Jameson, *op.cit.*

19. *Ibid.*, p291.

20. Michel Foucault, 'Truth and Power', in M. Morris and P. Patton, *Foucault: Power, Truth, Strategy*, Feral Publications, Sydney 1979.

21. See the discussion in Mandy Merck, 'Difference and its Discontents', *Screen*, Vol 28, no 1, 1987, pp2-9, and Jacqueline Rose's essays in *Sexuality in the Field of Vision*, Verso, London 1986.

poststructuralism, another set of problems emerge centered mainly on the relation of history to text and of discourse to subjectivity. Barthes[22] claims that historical discourse, because it is woven according to a narrative structure, is a form of ideological elaboration. This claim is based on the argument that the narrative form of representation, because it must assume a centered constitutive consciousness, leads the subject to mistake a specific constituted meaning of 'reality'. The question of the place of narrative in historiography contains many other considerations, apart from the location and epistemic status of the subject of historical understanding, as Hayden White has demonstrated.[23] One pertinent aspect is that existing narratives of the past are always class, gender and race and culture specific – historical memory being itself a specific construct, often subject to conscious manipulations.[24]

Terdiman[25] argues that, from the nineteenth century, history became the discipline of Western social formation, the 'distillate', (as White[26] has put it) of the past circulating and participating in the regulation of the present. Terdiman also points out that history, in taking on the function of preserving the past also 'occluded the individual dispossession of the past'.[27] A stark example of this is given by Tompkins.[28] She examines the question of how one decides 'what really happened' in the face of the challenge to the study of history arising from the claim that point of view is determined by the speaker's frame of reference. It follows from this claim that there can be no independent means of verifying the 'true' facts of history – nothing 'outside the texts'. Applying this reasoning to Indian history in America, she finds that the question of truth is not just an academic and epistemological one, but a moral one as well, since we know that the result of the encounter between Europeans and Indians has been virtual genocide. Yet many standard history texts relating the colonization of America have little to say about the Indians; they are absent because, as Tompkins demonstrates through a deconstructive analysis of primary sources, they 'did not matter' to the authors.

Texts, then, are suspect. The privileging of texts in understanding history at the same time privileges both the producers of texts and what is recognized by a discursive community as valid and legitimate. The writing of women's history and colonial history from the point of view of the oppressed shows that the production of counter-ideological and subversive texts is possible. The problem is not just the writing of an other history but understanding the process of change and variation in textuality and in history. Any theory which regards the bounds of historical reality to be those established by texts must be able to account for such a process. It must, therefore, recognize the effects of conflict and domination, that is, the effects of power in the textual process and thus relate the latter to historically specific material practices tied to the exercise of power.

Furthermore, the cultural conditions that make a particular discourse possible and intelligible are a consideration which adds weight to the suspicion we should attach to Western discourse about the Other. Speaking about apartheid, Derrida makes the point that 'the history of apartheid (its

22. Roland Barthes *et al.*, *Poetique du Recit*, Editions du Seuil, Paris 1977.

23. Hayden White, 'The Question of Narrative in Contemporary Historical Theory', in *History and Theory*, Vol 23, no 1, 1984, pp1-33.

24. Eric Hobsbawm and T. Ranger (eds), *The Invention of Tradition*, Cambridge University Press, Cambridge 1983.

25. R. Terdiman, *op.cit.*

26. Hayden White, *op.cit.*

27. R. Terdiman, *op.cit.*, p19.

28. S. Tompkins, '"Indians": Textualism, Morality and the Problem of History', in *Critical Inquiry*, Vol 13, 1986, pp101-19.

"discourse" and its "reality", the totality of its text) would have been impossible, unthinkable without the European concept and the European history of the state, without the European discourse on race – its scientific pseudo-concept and its religious roots, its modernity and its archaisms – without Judaeo-Christian ideology and so forth.'[29]

So, the whole of the 'West' writes the history of the Other, strives to bind the Other to that history through the effects of discourse on subjectivity, and thus to lock the Other in its masterly gaze. The means and conditions whereby the Other may slip away to an other place, the subterfuges and camouflage of this contest are the central issues to the wider project which informs this study.

It is in this context that I will examine the deep-seated discursive alliance of logocentrism, phallocentrism, and ethnocentrism at the core of Western thought. The implication is that in order to rethink the issues around subjectivity and otherness, and the consequences for political and ideological struggle, one would need not only to be wary of Western analyses of racial difference, but also to understand what may or may not be appropriated. For this reason I make a critical detour via Althusser and Lacan, hoping in the process to arrive at the point where the elements of a new problematic of subjective change and forms of resistance can be specified.

29 Jacques Derrida, 'But Beyond ... Open Letter to A. McClintock and R. Nixon', in *Critical Inquiry*, Vol 13, no 1, 1986, p165.

30. Louis Althusser, 'Ideology and Ideological State Apparatuses', in L. Althusser, *Lenin and Philosophy and Other Essays*, NLB, London 1977.

II INTERPELLATION, AGENCY, RESISTANCE

When one considers the question of the subjectivity of the Other within the problematic established by Althusser, enormous problems immediately surface.[30] For instance, can we blandly declare that 'black' people inscribed in the same ideological state apparatuses as 'white' subjects end up 'freely accepting' their place in the scheme of things? Clearly, even if some 'black' people seem to accept 'their place' with docility, one can hardly fail to notice that the effects of the apparatuses of interpellation for the Other are inconsistent, uncertain, different. There are good grounds for wondering what is really going on here – over and above the problems already picked out in the debates about Althusser's theory of ideology.

The case of 'black' subjectivity in relation to religion, one of the key apparatuses, will further highlight the problem. The canonical view derived from Althusser would be that the rituals and beliefs, the positioning of subjects in relation to God/the Subject in Christian religious practices, produce willing Christian subjects who accept their subjection, indeed do not perceive it as subjection. Yet Christian religion has played an important part in resistance from the time of slavery in the West Indies and America, and it has done so because its principles of equality in the eyes of God, its valuing of suffering and poverty for salvation, and its assurances to the meek and the down-trodden of the rewards to come, could not only provide spiritual comfort but also be turned into a rhetoric of resistance. Gospel music, for example, is an admirable case of the appropriation of an aspect of a dominant practice – European Church music – by a subordinate group in order to preserve group coherence, express its solidarity, and to keep alive aspects of the group's threatened culture, whilst appearing to conform and to accept the oppressor's culture and authority. Gospel music utilizes the rhythms and cadence of black music, the collective making of music, the repetition and 'cut',[31] the specific use of human voice and so on to refashion the hand-me-down of white culture – a lovely example of the multi-accentuality and mobility of the text in relation to politics.

31. J.A. Snead, 'Repetition as a Figure of Black Culture', in L. Gates Jr (ed), *Black Literature and Literary Theory*, Methuen, New York and London 1984.

32. Homi Bhabha, 'Signs Taken for Wonders: Questions of Ambivalence and Authority Under a Tree Outside Delhi, 1817', in F. Barker *et al.* (eds), *Europe and its Others*, University of Essex, Colchester 1985.

Now, Althusser does say that every ideological apparatus is also the site and stake of struggle. But he mainly means class struggle and one fought out more in terms of a grand strategy of power – wars of manoeuvre or position – than at the level of how individuals 'live' their existence, what sense they make of it, and what part of it they are able to subtract from the power of oppressors.

Religion indeed plays its part in the play of power and resistance in the formation and capture of subjects, including in the colonial situation, as Homi Bhabha had discussed.[32] Althusser's theory, though, can only make sense of the Other's resistance by reducing it to an aspect of class struggle in capitalism, thus denying its specificity and difference, and sliding the 'black' or the (ex)colonial subject under the universal subject, a subject who receives its '*lettres de creance*' only within Western thought. The trouble is that, in the problematic of interpellation, imaginary misrecognition works as an impasse for the subject who cannot transcend it except through class struggle and its theory, namely, historical materialism.

I want briefly to examine how this comes about. In Althusser, the category of imaginary – a shuttle concept – works to effect a suture between two discursive figures in his thought: that of ideology in 'ideology etc' (see note 29) and that of knowledge in his earlier work, hence its central importance. The imaginary produces forms of recognition, that is to say, forms of the mode in which social relations are 'lived'. The function of ideology is to ensure the recognition effect for subjects. Given that recognition is coupled with misrecognition along the axis of the imaginary relation to the real, ideology – precisely through recognition in the imaginary – produces knowledge which 'represents' the 'lived' relations of the subject to the real and not the 'real' relations. Ideology is caught in this specular maze where it constantly misrecognizes the 'real' in the imaginary recognition which it creates. It effects a closure in the space of knowledge, a closure which only a science can open up by breaking with the epistemological space of ideology/pre-science.

Within Althusser's problematic, then, ideology continues to have a double function: it is both the term which explains subjectivity and the measure of an epistemological judgment about the relationship of knowledge to the real. For Althusser, as much as for Foucault and Western thought generally, a relationship of knowledge to being remains the central philosophical and political question. The ontological theme is constantly found at work in all theorizations of the subject of modernity.

The effect of the particular concept of representation in his theory is to anchor even more firmly ideology in the terrain of epistemology, namely, by fixing the basic form of the relationship of knowledge to truth to the criterion of the adequacy or inadequacy of a knowledge to an independent real. The consequence is that although Lacan's problematic of subjectivity is put to work in reformulating subjects' ideological formation, an opportunity is missed concerning the place of history in the process of constitution. I refer to the fact that, for Lacan, psychoanalysis takes as its domain 'concrete discourse insofar as this is the field of the transindividual reality of the subject ... [whilst] its operations are those of history, to the extent that history constitutes the emergence of truth in the real.'[33] This historicity of the event makes possible the subjective reproduction of the past in the present. In a basic way it is history which provides the stage where the subject appears. In addition, in relation to the outside, the signification of events is mobile. History and the process of signification for the subject are very much the core of Lacanian psychoanalytic theory, for the essential dimensions of psychoanalytic experience are 'in addition to the historical theory of the symbol: intersubjective logic and temporality of the subject'.[34]

The second missed opportunity revolves around the concept of the imaginary. In Lacan, it is very much one axis of a triple complex of relationships, involving besides, the symbolic and the real. The mechanism of the imaginary combines several equally crucial processes. First, a relationship to the Other as described in the 'schema L'.[35]

Following Heidegger, Lacan argues that intersubjectivity has more to do with the symbolic relationship. Equally, the question of who I am arises from within the symbolic order, the order of culture. The imaginary and the symbolic co-exist, but, in order to be positioned in discourse in the place of the 'I', the infant must accede to the symbolic order. Lacan's inference from the schema L is that:

> It is thus that if man is drawn to think about the symbolic order, it is because from the beginning he is caught in it in his being. The illusion that he has formed it by his consciousness results from the fact that it was by way of a specific lack arising in his imaginary relation to his mirror image/other [*semblable*] that he was able to enter into this order as a subject'.[36]

If we follow Lacan's meaning of recognition in the understanding of the mirror stage as an identification, recognition is not that of a previously constituted subject, but is itself the transformation produced in the subject when it assumes an image [*imago*]'.[37] It marks the moment of emergence of the 'I' in a primary form prior to identification with the Other (objectification) and the positioning of the subject in language. This means that it is with the subject's entry into the order of culture, that is to say, into an intersubjectively constituted domain of signification, that the 'I' is properly established.

It is clear, as Wilden has argued,[38] that the symbolic, the imaginary and the real co-exist and intersect in the subject. The real is not the same as external reality, but what is real for the subject: 'they are the functions linking the

33. Jacques Lacan, *Ecrits I*, Editions du Seuil, Paris 1966, p135.

34. *Ibid.*, pp169, 170.

35. 'Schema L', *Ibid.*, p66.

S (Subject) a (other)

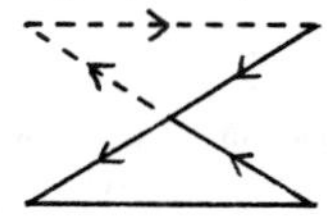

á (ego) O Other

S–O is the symbolic axis
a–a' is the imaginary axis

36. *Ibid.*, p66.

37. *Ibid.*, p90.

38. A. Wilden, *Speech and Language in Psychoanalysis* John Hopkins University Press, Baltimore and London, 1981.

subject to others and to the world.'[39] This plurality of the subject is what is given in the formula: 'the unconscious is the discourse of the Other.'[40] In a very fundamental sense, it is through discourse that subjectivity is established.

For Lacan, what is at stake in psychoanalysis is that grain of reality which desire[41] keeps alive in the face of symbolic conflicts and imaginary fixations, and which it manifests in intersubjective experience. This is a formulation which tends to interiorize resistance, or else to couple resistance with the return of the repressed. For the imaginary relationship, because of its denial of the unconscious elements that structure it, has the effect for the subject of securing an identity between subject and consciousness, so that the subject acts as if it were the constitutive subject: it is as if it is the subject as self-centred individual who resists. It is impossible, then, to recover the repressed, but the repressed does return. For the 'black' person, for instance, it can, according to Fanon[42] manifest itself in paranoia or self-hate, or in violent impulse toward the (white) love/hate object of identification, a response tied to the narcissism and aggressivity in the mirror stage.

In Althusser's schema of interpellation, curiously, the symbolic is played down – curiously because he himself emphasized its centrality in Lacan.[43] Since culture is effectively absent, as is history, he cannot account for the cracks and fissures in subjective identity and unity which allow and enable resistance and dis-identification. In fact, struggle is radically exteriorized with respect to the subject. The subject can only recapture its history by placing itself on the side of the class whose destiny is to make history. Subjects, as bearers of history, can only be in the stream of history if they position themselves (or are positioned) from the point of view of revolutionary struggle; the only possible knowledge is that produced by revolutionary theory, historical materialism.

Lacan, as we have seen, grants history a central place, but in his problematic it is radically interiorized because caught in the relation of symbolic to the imaginary and essentially divided off from consciousness by the lack which splits off recognition from cognition, and whereby, presumably, cognition desires to know and possess completely its objects: to capture Mythos within the gaze of the Logos, closing the gap which the will to power of logocentric cognition itself opened up. As I have noted, resistance is also interiorized, owing more to that part of desire uncaptured within the symbolic order than to historically located political conflict and goals.[44] One crucial aspect one could explore here would be about how this kind of gaze territorializes, repeats a master-slave thematic.[45]

III THE DISCOURSE OF THE OTHER

What do the more recent studies within the other approach I outlined earlier contribute? Bhabha, for example, concerns the construction of the Other in colonial discourse.[46] He emphasizes the basic ambivalence at the heart of colonial discourse which both fixes and assigns its place to the (non-western) Other, yet strives to capture an otherness it conceptualizes as wild, chimeric,

39. Lacan, *op.cit.*, p161.

40. *Ibid.*, p24.

41. Note the distinction between desire, need and demand in Lacan, and the binding of the notion of lack with that of desire.

42. Frantz Fanon, *Black Skin, White Masks*, Paladin, London 1970.

43. 'Freud and Lacan', in Althusser, *op.cit.*

44. The problems of founding all resistance on the force of desire involves the kind of objection discussed by P. Dews in 'Power and Subjectivity in Foucault', in *New Left Review*, no 144, 1984, pp72-95.

45. I have explored this more fully in Couze Venn, 'History Lessons: Formation of Subjects, (Post) colonialism, and an Other Project', in Bill Schwarz (ed.), *The Expansion of England*, Routledge, London forthcoming.

46. Homi Bhabha, 'The Other Question ...', *Screen*, Vol 24, no 6, 1983, pp18-36.

excessive and unknowable. Such an ambivalence allows colonial discourse to claim for itself always already to know its object, precisely in its recalcitrant inscrutability – no doubt a misrecognition, masking a fracture in the mechanism of power/knowledge.

His argument is that the construction of the colonial subject in discourse and the exercise of colonial power through discourse requires an articulation of forms of racial and sexual difference. Such an articulation he points out 'becomes crucial if it is held that the body is always simultaneously inscribed in both the economy of pleasure and desire and the economy of discourse, domination and power.'[47]

He examines the way in which a discursive apparatus hinged on the recognition and disavowal of racial, cultural and historical differences produces knowledges of colonizer and colonized which authorize practices of surveillance and enable the setting into place of a system of incitement to act and speak centered on forms of pleasure and unpleasure. The system of representation is homologous to Realism in its ambition to capture the Other/colonized in a timeless and transparent discursive space where it appears as a fixed reality. This 'regime of truth' supports a 'governmentality' which makes possible the rational 'administration of subject peoples'.

This Foucauldian *analytique*, extending beyond Edward Said's approach to the problem of Orientalism,[48] moves towards a problematization of the stability of the discursive economy which has apparently succeeded in containing the Other within the boundaries of Western rationalism and logocentrism. For, as Said's remarks about the Orient indicate, the site and space of otherness is also the site of dreams, fantasies, obsessions, myths – a site where transgression (for the Western subject) is possible.

Bhabha's work radically challenges the coherence and closure attributed to colonial discourse. This releases the full implication of the instability of its discursive field, enabling him to examine the problem of the 'repressed' in the other scene of the stereotype, namely, that framed by the tropes of savagery, anarchy, lust which are the signs of both identification and alienation – desire and fear for colonizer and colonized. He explores this play of the recognition and disavowal of cultural and racial difference through Freud's notion of fetishism, arguing that the stereotype/fetish refers to the closure which disavowal effects in the 'circulation of the chain of absence and presence in the realm of the Symbolic'.[49] The fetish in his schema is made to do the work of suture, closing the space of the representation of difference; this points to the way the colonized is captured for and within colonial discourse.

It seems, then, that the stereotype, a central point of subjectification in colonial discourse, is not so much a false representation of reality as a 'fixated', 'fetishized' form of representation, denying the play of difference in its simplifying repetition of a phantasized originality. The consequence is that colonial discourse does not have a space for the recognition of difference in the symbolic, a possibility that would free the signifier skin/culture from ideologies of racial and cultural domination. The effect is a disavowal of difference (in the

47. *Op.cit.*, p19.

48. Edward Said, *Orientalism*, Routledge and Kegan Paul, London 1978.

49 Homi Bhabha, *op.cit.*, p27.

imaginary misrecognition of an authentic, ordinary [and white] subject, as Althusser might put it) and in the kind of symptoms described by Fanon in *Black Skin, White Masks*. Yet the stereotype has a 'knowledge value' because of its positivity in the constitution of subjectivities. Disavowal, however, introduces a lack which undermines the colonizer's logocentric discourse and prevents closure: the repressed returns.

A key argument is that this 'knowledge' nevertheless admirably serves the administrative practices of a 'governmentality in which the "ideological" space functions in more openly collaborative ways with political and economic exigencies'.[50] This is because, according to strategies of normalization and discipline, the apparatuses of power functioning in the Church, the barracks, the school, the law courts etc. appear as the visible – though fetishized – objects of the colonizer's superiority rather than as the instruments of subjugation and domination. Thus the relationship is masked, misrecognized.

It follows that the process of subjectification indicated in my remarks produces subjection as an overdetermined effect working at once at the psychic and the discursive levels. But the subject so produced is fundamentally split – 'A grotesque mimicry or doubling', or an amputated, mummified subject tortured in its soul, as Fanon earlier described it.

Indeed, one could note that for Fanon,[51] because of the co-articulation of colonial discourse (in which the stereotype of blackness circulates) with the black subject's experience of his/her body and with a distorted and alienated history of his/her race, the split is a triple one: axed between body, race and ancestors, anchored there by what he has called the 'epidermal schema'.

Of course, this split subject, living its multiple contradictions in a phantasmagoric imaginary where aggression, guilt, desire are 'projected' and 'introjected',[52] moving across metaphoric and metonymic fields where await the condensed or displaced marks and substitutes of already unstable, obscured signifiers of skin, race and identity, this subject profoundly destabilizes the whole discursive field in which it is caught.

Spivak[53] has explored the impossibility of the dominated, the 'subaltern' speaking (as autonomous subject) because of the epistemic violence of the discourse of the Master in his imperialist project. The colonized is reduced to silence in the text of the imperialist discourse, forced to collude in the colonizer's will to power. Women are doubly oppressed in colonial ideology, since patriarchal imperialist ideology adds to the native patriarchal oppression. The effect of imperialism has been to domesticate the Other in his/her own eyes, to make the 'native' see her/himself as 'Other'. Resistance, at the level of theory, is an affirmative deconstruction of the texts of the colonizer to tease out the exclusions, the constructions, the lies at the heart of these texts.

When posing the question of subjectivity, psychoanalysis seems the obvious place to look; Fanon, before Althusser, Bhabha and Spivak had followed that path. The problem from the point of view of theorizing 'black' subjectivity or otherness is that if psychoanalytic theory is itself a culturally and historically specific product and part of Western intellectual discourse, and if it is the

50. *Ibid.*, p35.

51. Fanon, *op.cit.*

52. A. Mama, 'Race and Subjectivity: A Study of Black Women', unpublished PhD Thesis, University of London, 1987.

53. She explores this theme in several places, notably in Gayatri Spivak, 'The Rani of Sirmur', in F. Barker *et al.* (eds), *op.cit.*, and Gayatri Spivak, 'Imperialism and Sexual Difference', in *Oxford Literary Review*, no 8, 1986, pp226-40.

whole of Western thought that participates, directly or indirectly, in the subjugation of the Other, then we need to question seriously the universalism of its concepts.

IV SUBJECTIVITY AND BEING IN LACAN

I propose to do this questioning because I want to establish first, the culturally specific character of the premises of psychoanalysis through an examination of the place of sexuality and the ego in it and second, the different basis which such a critique indicates for a theorization of the Other as subject. I shall approach this through Lacan's discussion of speech and language in psychoanalysis for reasons which I hope will become clear as I proceed.

These theoretical meditations are crossed by Lacan's break with the 'orthodox' school, the 'Discours de Rome' (1953) marking a key moment. They are therefore the place where psychoanalytic theory is interrogated about its epistemological foundation and its status as knowledge. Lacan makes it clear that the terms of his reassessment of Freud's work recognizes the central importance of anthropology, philosophy and linguistics for the reconstruction of psychoanalytic theory, for these knowledges mean that 'it is impossible not to make a general theory of the symbol, the axis of a new classification of the sciences, in which the human sciences would once more occupy their central place as sciences of subjectivity'.[54] Psychoanalysis is in this way located on the terrain of the human sciences, marking a displacement from the interests of a medicalized therapy or from a theory of instincts founded in biology.

54. Lacan, *op.cit.*, p165.

The centrality of history and of the symbolic domain in Lacan's theorization of the subject, which I discussed earlier, already points to the principles founding this reformulated science of subjectivity. This reconstruction makes much better sense when we pay attention to the different problematic of the subject at work in Lacan's theory.

The allusions and references in his examination of speech and language support the view that the central issue in his problematic was the subject as it has figured in philosophy from Descartes – the subject belonging to the 'ego's era'. His discussion of ego, the self (*moi*) recognizes its modernity in the sense that it is only from the seventeenth century that there appears this notion of the coherent, unitary and rational subject, this being whose measure is consciousness confronting the chaos of the outside world. The metonymies of such a subject are the '*belle ame*' of Hegel, the 'interior man' of Husserl, the notion of '*moi*' in Heidegger, the Sartrian 'being-for-itself', to mention the terms explicitly referred to in Lacan's text.

It is clear from Lacan's arguments that he had thought through the metaphysics of lack which gnaws at the core of theories of the *cogito*. Perhaps in Western culture this lack refers back to an original imperfection of being. Christianity, like most religions, harbours such a view: if God exists, then human subjects must be less than perfect, being forever less than God, something that Feuerback, besides Nietzsche, well understood in their different ways. Since Descartes, the subject has been granted a degree of autonomy and will, but a sense of limit remained. We know the trajectory which charts the will to recover for the subject the possibility of a plenitude, from Kant's transcendental subject to Hegel's absolute subject – the monad or else the goal of the phenomenology of mind – and the more phenomenologically founded theorizations of Husserl and Heidegger and their development in Sartre and Lacan. The difference is that Lacanian psychoanalysis is an attempt to restate this problem in empirical, psychic *and* linguistic terms. Yet it retains an apparatus of concepts that recirculate the same deep-seated uncertainty about the epistemic and ontological status of the human subject, for example, in the notions of lack (of course), ideal ego, death drive, empty speech/full speech, imaginary relation, splitting and so on.

The question which underpins his project is the form of existence of the '*moi*', the 'I', the Cartesian subject of consciousness, whether as effect or myth, or as a 'misrecognition' sustained in language. The distance from any 'ego psychology' is emphasized when he explains that:

> It seems to me that the 'I think', to which it is intended that presence be reduced continues to imply ... all the powers of the reflection by which subject and consciousness are confounded – namely, the mirage which psychoanalytic experience places at the basis of the misrecognition of the subject and which I myself have tried to focus on in the '*stade du miroir*' by concentrating it there.[55]

Indeed it is clear that the thesis that the unconscious is the discourse of the Other not only proposes the multiplicity of the subject but undermines the foundation of theories of a unitary ego and *cogito*. For elsewhere he claims both that the 'unconscious is that part of concrete discourse insofar as it is transindividual'[56] and that the unconscious participates in conscious thought. Yet although the 'unconscious is marked by a blank or occupied by a lie ... its truth can be found again':[57] in monuments such as the body, in semantic evolution, in traditions, in the traces preserved in distortions, in archival documents.

How this is possible is explained when we examine the conceptual apparatus a little closer. The remarks that I have cited above about the mirror stage demonstrate that Lacan's ego is the effect of the interiorization of the Other through identification in the mirror stage.[58] It implies an alienated self. For Lacan, following Sartre and Husserl, the ego is also transcendent and not interior to consciousness. To understand how this works we need to focus on the place of desire and the process of recognition in his theory, concepts of which Althusser, Fanon, and Bhabha (as well as others) have made much use.

The notion of desire in Lacan must be seen as a development of the notion as it appears in Hegel and is elaborated by Heidegger.[59] It connects with the ontological basis of the concept of lack of being discussed above.[60] The Hegelian thematic of desire for recognition, elaborated in the master-slave

55. Lacan, 'Maurice Merleau-Ponty', *Les Temps Modernes*, nos184-85, 1961, pp245-54.

56. Lacan, *op.cit.*, 1966, p136.

57. *Ibid.*

58. The mirror stage is first proposed in 1936, informed by a reading of Husserl and the seminars of A. Kojeve on Hegel. Later formulations (1946-51) take account of Sartre's existentialism.

59. It is thus quite different from Freud's view.

60. The notes of Laplanche and Pontalis, *The Language of Psychoanalysis*, The Hogarth Press, London 1980, indicate this when they write: 'Desire appears in the rift which separates need and demand: it cannot be reduced to need, by definition, it is not a relation to a real object independent of the subject but a relation to phantasy; nor can it be reduced to demand, in that it seeks to impose itself without taking the language or the unconscious of the other into account and insists upon absolute recognition from him.' [p483].

schema, is given its psychic reality in Lacan in the notion of lack of object which fuels desire. It is this lack of object which drives the infant to occupy the position designated by 'I'. How this is accomplished is explained by the Schema L, an aspect of which I discussed earlier. We recall that Lacan argues that the illusion of a constitutive consciousness arises from the subject's imaginary relation to his Other and that it was by way of the lack in that specular relation that the subject could enter the symbolic order. Furthermore, the mechanism of recognition/misrecognition implies that consciousness is transcendental and the transcendental ego is relativized:

> In the capture it suffers because of its imaginary nature, it masks its duplicity, namely that the consciousness in which it finds the guarantee of an unquestionable existence ... is not at all immanent in it, but in fact transcendental since it relies for support on the unitary hyphen of the ideal ego. Thus the transcendental ego itself becomes relativized, implicated as it is in the misrecognition in which the identifications of the ego are inaugurated.[61]

One could say that the subject is itself the being which appears in the gap between presence and absence; in other words it is the locus, the point of intersection in discourse which assigns to it the place occupied by 'I'.[62] Importantly, this appearance on the scene of the symbolic is negotiated via the Oedipal scenario, whereby the rule of culture is superimposed on that of nature in the name of the Father, symbolized in the Phallus, the Signifier of the Law and of cultural order. The phallus functions as the lost object at the origins; it is the transcendental referent in psychoanalysis putting a stop, as '*point de capiton*' to the indefinite sliding of signification. Thus is resolved existential unbeing, at the cost of entering culture as subject, but a subject condemned to 'live a lie'.

61. Lacan, *Ecrits, II*, Editions du Seuil, Paris 1971, p169.

62. Note Lacan's closeness once again both to Heidegger here for whom the subject is the being 'determined by the potentiality for discourse' (Martin Heidegger, *Being and Time*, SCM Press, London 1962, p47), and to A. Kojeve: 'It is the conscious Desire of a being which constitutes that being as an ego (*Moi*) and reveals it to be such by driving it to utter: "I".' (A. Kojeve, *Introduction á la Lecture de Hegel*, Gallimard, Paris 1979, p11.)

V THE PLACE OF THE OTHER

What is interesting about this discourse is not only that it results from a question posed initially in the form of the possibility of the Cartesian subject and that it allies the logocentrism of that project to phallocentrism: my contention is that the conceptualization of non-Western people as radically other – unknowable, alien, dangerous, as negation – is also very much part of the whole problematic of being, inaugurated with and inscribed in the concept of modernity.

Whilst the alliance of logocentrism and phallocentrism is relatively well established, the extension of this discursive knot to include ethnocentrism/ Eurocentrism, signalled in Derrida, is less readily accepted in spite of the demonstrations by Spivak and Bhabha. The way I understand it is in relation to the twin(ned) birth from around the seventeenth century of, first, the modern 'ratio' which not only privileges a specific notion of Reason but interweaves that notion with that of individualism; and second, the establishment of Western capitalism and colonialism, and its alignment with the progressive, accumulative and totalizing project of modernity, which I have explored elswehere.[63]

With the Cartesian subject, along with 'his' doubts, appears the figure Foucault described as the universal intellectual, this figure who takes on the responsibility for knowledge and who is charged with finding and telling the truth. The displacement in foundation is from a guarantee of order and truth to be sought in the scriptures and in God's creation and will, to one which is interiorized in the subject, or rather in the rational apparatus of the Cartesian *cogito*.

A parallel displacement mirrors this shift which is admirably captured in the displacement from the purity of soul of the knower to the purity of reason of the philosopher/scientist.[64] Foucault[65] has explored the forms of exclusion which accomplish this transformation in the Western episteme, in particular the exclusion of unreason.[66]

I would argue that the underlying principle was the exclusion of anything which could endanger the purity of reason and of the knower, and thus introduce uncertainty and undermine the logocentric discursive order. Conceptually, of course, reason and unreason, the Subject and the Other, are constructed within the same discourse according to a process of *différance*: 'Subjectivity – as much as objectivity – is an effect of *différance*, an effect inscribed in a system of *différance*.'[67] The conceptualization of difference as a polarity has been extensively explored within feminist theory by, for example, Gallop[68] who points to the anxiety produced by difference and the taming and binding of anxiety which the prism of polar opposites makes possible. Fanon throughout his work has similarly explored what this conceptualization of the Other as negative means experientially, how it feels in the bone.

Sibony[69] exploring the solidarity which exists between the rational and the racial (integrated in the term 'ratial') suggests the layers of anxiety and distress, the disavowed desire of the difference one perceives in the Other, which feed racism: 'Racism does not indicate intolerance to what is different but the fear or the panic-stricken horror in the face of the sameness which this difference hides, and because that hidden sameness stampedes one into the absolute difference of the void in the real.'[70] The other, at all costs, must be imprisoned in its otherness, made invisible or objectified.

Another crucial historical event was also taking place during that period when the modern, Western form of subjectivity was emerging which provided rational power with the opportunity to exercise absolute mastery over its fearful object of desire – the Other. That event was the process of colonization and slavery. Tompkins[71] demonstrated the reality of that mastery in the brutal eradication of whole cultures and peoples, their reduction to the status of beasts, outside humanity.

It is worth noting the alliance of the discourse about the Other and that of political economy and of the state in the emergent period of capitalism. Locke's

63. See Couze Venn, *op.cit.*

64. Lacan, in an interesting remark, makes a connection between the purity of soul demanded of the alchemist and the question of the unacknowledged desire of the scientist. See Lacan, *The Four Fundamental Concepts of Psychoanalysis*, Penguin, Harmondsworth 1979.

65. See in particular, his *Les Mots et les Choses*, Gallimard, Paris 1966, and *Histoire de la Folie a l'Age Classique*, Gallimard, Paris 1972.

66. One should also bear in mind Derrida's examination in *L'Ecriture et la Difference*, Editions du Seuil, Paris 1967, which is partly critical of Foucault's analysis of the *Cogito*.

67. Derrida, *Positions*, Editions de Minuit, Paris 1972, p48.

68. J. Gallop, *Feminism and Psychoanalysis*, Macmillan Press, London 1982.

69. D. Sibony, *La Haine du Desir*, Christian Bourgois, Paris 1984.

70. *Ibid.* p49.

71. J. Tompkins, *op.cit.*

'Second Treatise of Government' is a key example of how the dispossession of indigenous non-Western nations of their land and autonomy – on the grounds that they were savages who could not make good use of it or govern themselves 'rationally' – became a central condition for legitimizing private property and its individual accumulation. Lebovics[72] has argued that without the land 'freed' for the West by colonialism in the New world, Locke's contention that there was ample land to satisfy the needs of private accumulation without endangering the proviso that there must be 'enough, and as good' land left would have been clearly unconvincing. Without that provision the whole doctrine of consent also falls down. It is clear that representations of otherness are not mere textual constructs: they have been anchored in the solid grounds of slavery, colonialism and capitalist practices.

The thesis I am proposing is that it is in that historical conjuncture that the colonized is conceptualized as radically Other, not only barred from entry into the cultural order of the 'West' but installed as the sign of what threatens it – the myth of the savage, the heathen – and the measure of its difference. So representational discourse does not theorize racial difference precisely because it cannot do so without recognizing the Other as subject and thus, by the same token, relativising the Cartesian *cogito*. Such a recognition would fundamentally undermine the absolute character of the subject of any logocentric discourse.

In addition, once the particular concept of otherness – and its exclusion – had become established in colonial discourse and given material reality in the existence of Western empires and the specific form of racism inscribed in colonial experience, it became impossible to untie the knots by which the Other had become immobilized in oppressive relations. Indeed the only avenue open to the colonized to accede to the status of 'Western' subject was to attempt to become (or be formed as) white through acculturation, the theme Fanon and Bhabha have differently explored, describing its fractures and ambivalences.

The second thesis I am going to propose is that in rethinking subjectivity and racial difference, we should regard the privileging of the sexual scheme in psychoanalysis to be tied to the Western metaphysical discourse I have noted above, in addition perhaps to what Plaza [73] has referred to as 'male desire' and power. My analysis indicates that the reason for the search for a mechanism which functions to put a stop to the state of unbeing – at the same time as it arrests the indefinite sliding of the signifier – has to do with the whole problematic of being in Western philosophical discourse. The fact that a mythical narrative (the Oedipal scenario) and mythical figures (Narcissus, Eros) are inserted to generate the organizing principles which fix the subject in culture is itself significant, not least for the way in which Mythos and Logos are made to refer to each other in a metaphysical imaginary. But then the psychoanalytic project is itself an amazing play of mirrors.

What this means for the understanding of otherness and racial subjective difference is that we need to counter the force of this discourse-of-being, which is interwoven with a discourse about sexuality, as Brennan has interestingly

72. L. Lebovics, 'The Uses of America in Locke's Second Treatise of Government', in *Journal of the History of Ideas*, Vol XLVII, no 4, 1986, pp567-81.

73. Feminist critiques of 'phallomorphic power', (e.g., in M. Plaza, ' "Phallomorphic Power" and the Psychology of "Woman" ', in *Ideology and Consciousness*, no 4, pp4-36), and of phallocentrism (as established in M. Montrelay, *L'Ombre et le Nom*, Editions de Minuit, Paris 1977, and L. Irigaray, *Ce Sexe qui n'en est pas un*, Editions de Minuit, Paris 1977, provide similar kinds of observation, although we should be careful not to confuse sexual and racial difference, even if the examination of sexual difference in psychoanalysis has provided some lessons for theorizing racial difference.

explored.[74] (This is in part the reason Fanon introduced the epidermal schema.) It is interesting also that skin has cut across the divide between men and women in recent gender politics. Additionally, what I am saying is that the necessity for a signifier like the phallus, which assigns to other signifiers their place and fixes the subject as a centre, only arises if we assume the existence of a will for a unique order in a culture. Only a dominant and universalizing order, and the totalizing discourse allied to it, would seek such a project or assume its existence in the discourse of its self-understanding, its self-consciousness.

Clearly there can exist subordinate, at times competing, orders inscribed in different discursive formations and circulating in non-normalized/normative social practices in a culture, carried by a number of narratives such as those about women, immigrants, black/colonized people, etc. There can be different pivotal signifiers – Fanon's example of skin – locked into different symbolic matrices. The concept of multiple subjectivity is implicated in this point of view.

One must assume that the norms of the dominant order continue to have effects within subordinate ones and thus on subjectification; this, after all, is the measure of its domination. Another related issue is whether the coherence of the subject is the effect of these different matrices pulling in the same direction by means of some ruling or unifying discourse, in a manner similar, but not identical, to Althusser's suggestion that ideologies were united beneath what he called the 'ruling ideology'.

If the question is no longer that of accounting for a subject (or subject effect) as constitutive, then we should attempt to do without the mirror stage and the Oedipal scenario, or at least limit its application to the modern western form of sociality. This means that we can begin to rethink the problem posed in terms of recognition/misrecognition – a problem arising from the assumption of a constitutive or Cartesian subject or the desire to deconstruct that assumption. Perhaps the couple, identification/disidentification,[75] gestures in the right direction, opening towards a domain of history, intersubjectivity and the symbolic/significatory as well as psychic domain already present in Lacan (though located in a different problematic). In that context the whole issue of how the infant enters the cultural order, how it becomes a subject or a particular subjectivity, can be conceptualized with a (reworked) psychoanalytic framework as well as knowledge drawn from existing practices about the effects of power and of signifying practices in examining concrete data.[76] The problems which now emerge refer more directly to the impact of history and of cultural practices on subjectivity.[77]

Faye,[78] in his examination of how narratives function in fascist ideology, notes that the suppression of Mythos by Logos inaugurated by Greek philosophy begins an era when judgment between true and false becomes the norm for understanding human experience and history. The questioning of the possibility of an objective truth in history does not abolish the issue of truth and falsehood since there is 'on the one side the narration which refuses to decide between true and false and on the other side the narration for which

74. T. Brennan, 'History After Lacan', in *Economy and Society*, Vol 19, no 23, 1990, pp278-313.

75. See the arguments of M. Pecheux, in *Les Verites de la Palice*, Maspero, Paris 1775, and C. Venn, 'Beyond the Science-Ideology Relation', unpublished PhD thesis, University of Essex, 1982.

76. There is a beginning of this approach established in J. Henriques *et al.*, *Changing the Subject*, Methuen, London 1984.

77. The problems for historians implicated in the recognition of a place for a theory of subjectivity in the interpretation of history are sketched in T.C. Ashplant 'Fantasy, Narrative, Event: Psychoanalysis and History', in *History Workshop*, no 23, pp165-72.

78. J-P. Faye, *Theorie du Recit*, Herman, Paris 1972.

such a refusal erases all difference between science and ideology'.[79] He points out that every account of history, true or false, can have a positivity in the sense of 'changing the face of history itself. Thus any theory of knowledge presupposes a theory of narration.'[80] For him this means that as we move away from a notion of science founded in Logos, the question of an objective truth becomes 'how is historical narration possible?'.[81]

So it could be argued that from the point of view of political action it is not a question of a science, like historical materialism, exercising power over our rational calculations, but of the existence of a narration which is on the side of the truth. With regard to subjective investment the effects for identification which specific narratives of events have are manifest, as in for example the history of women's and 'black' people's resistance. The problem becomes one of understanding the mechanisms of the survival, effectivity, circulation and transformation of such narratives in people's daily lives.

If we consider history, sedimented in social, material and signifying practices, to have pervasive effects in the process of subjectification, then when focusing on non-Western subjects, we would need to examine the mode of circulation of non-dominant discourses, the tropes around which they have become organized and the specificity of the practices in which they appear. The kind of 'affirmative deconstruction' and 'restorative genealogy' this suggests would need to take account of the extent to which some of the knowledges informing such work already carry disabling elements central to the discourse of the oppressor, as Spivak has noted in her discussion of the historical work of the Subaltern Studies Group;[82] the effect of the dominant culture in the everyday lives and subjectivities of the Other; the effect of dislocation; the forms – songs, sayings, emblems, rituals, etc. – in which a history of resistance has left its traces; the instability of all these discourses for subjectivity.

We should think also about the elaboration of what Fanon had initially called the 'epidermal schema'. Pursuing that example one could say that the black subject can always imagine occupying the position designated by the metaphor 'white' but is constantly thwarted because of the 'epidermal schema'.[83] The fixity of skin as signifier, in any case, constantly threatens closure for subjectivity. One could ground this work theoretically within the kind of analyses which has been done about the body – the development of its capacities; the incitement of its pleasures; its location as site and target for strategies of normalization and discipline; in addition, its place in processes of subjectivity and cultural identity (how it is shaped, dressed, presented; the forms and sites of its display, its 'representations' and constructions in texts such as films, music, dance, etc.); and its urges and goals as 'desiring machines'. I am not suggesting that the politics of pleasure authorizes us to dispense with the theorization of political goals and social change, for serious conceptual shortcomings still exist which the lingerie of desire cannot cover up.

79. *Ibid.*, p30.

80. *Ibid.*

81. *Ibid.*, p29.

82. Spivak, *In Other Worlds*, Routledge, London and New York 1988.

83. Bhabha's analyses in 'Signs Taken for Wonders', *op. cit.*, and in 'Of Mimicry and Man', in *October*, no28, 1984, pp125-33, admirably develop this theme with respect to the colonized in India, but with implications which generalize the processes at the theoretical level of explanation.

VI BELONGING, BECOMING, CHANGING

Concerning subjective change, it is important to recognize that an oppressed group's history, often localized, for example, in a mining community, in a ghetto, in shanty towns, can be aligned with a wider historical discourse such as that of the working class, or of colonized or black people's resistance. Its signification as a memory is thereby transformed – the 'we' of the community becoming subordinated to a greater subject by sliding under its signifier (e.g., race, class, women). Localized struggles can thus become affiliated to a wider one. The danger is that struggles and solidarity are not necessarily in opposition to systems of domination, as the appeal of fundamentalisms well illustrates. There is clearly an abiding need for theories and narratives which co-ordinate struggles on the side of a liberatory project.

The experience of 'splitting' as an effect of the culture of modernity can also provide conditions for the forging of a resistant subjectivity where transgression is possible within the fissures in dominant discourse that exist because the dominant culture is not all of one piece and unitary, but fractured and fraught, the terrain of contestations. These fissures are the place of fantasy, carnival, the repressed history of the oppressed and of the flow of desires that cannot be captured or which have been denied expression. There is, therefore, the possibility of occupying unclaimed positions in discourse, of escaping fixity, of renewing the play of '*différance*'. This is possible in part because of the multiple positionality of subjects[84] and because skin, in the present culture, irremediably and constantly returns the non-white Other to the margins, to the position of the outsider, to the condition of unbelonging. But significant change can be produced not individually, but through the *collective* recovery and reactivation of the repressed or forgotten history in forms of counter-discourse where the erased links of the metonymic chains of intertextuality can be recovered.

My argument is that these texts – for women, the Other, the colonial – have sometimes to be constructed in the margins of established history, attempting a kind of textual archaeology of memory as in a number of black and 'Third World' writings and other cultural forms, where historically based narratives circulate.[85] In any case, as White has put it, 'this affiliation of narrative historiography with literature and myth should provide no reason for embarrassment, however, because the systems of meaning-production shared by all three are distillates of the historical experience of a people, a group, a culture.'[86] It is worth repeating the point that knowledge of the 'facts' about, for example, the exploitation of 'Third world' countries, do not necessarily or automatically occasion subjective or political change. Truth in itself does not dispel ideology. Truth must be allied to a narrativization, a plot which reconstitutes the historical and subjective dimension of lived experience, by locating events in a 'configuration' of events, as part of a story line which evokes the presence of the past in the present. Events need to acquire a symbolic charge before they can enter life as a signifying memory. Indeed, when most

84. See J. Henriques *et al., op.cit.*

85. For some examples, see L. Hutcheon, 'Beginning to Theorise Postmodernism, in *Textual Practice*, Vol 1, no 1, 1987, pp10-31.

86. White, *op.cit.*, pp793-8.

effective they can pass into everyday language, as with for example the 'Dunkirk Spirit' in Britain, or Soweto as a symbol of apartheid.

I am going to try and relate this to something in Althusser which is worth retaining – a place for a narration which globalizes struggle (for him, class struggle and the theory of revolution) and thus assigns a place to regional struggles in a wider scheme of things. This would not be globalization in the name of a universal class or subject whose becoming is the goal of History, for such a discourse already belongs to a particular tradition in Western philosophy, its 'metanarrative'[87] subsuming gender and racial difference under a 'metasubject' who is the narrator of history, its consciousness and conscience. I understand such a globalization – once frowned upon by Foucault because of its totalizing and totalitarian temptations – to refer not to a reading of historical materialism which accepts its claims to be an objective truth, to a discourse which appeals to our rationality, but to one which can be aligned with immemorial themes.

87. J-F. Lyotard, *The Postmodern Condition: A Report on Knowledge*, MUP, Manchester 1984.

88. Jameson, *op.cit.*

I suggest this for several reasons. Postwar capitalism has now become thoroughly globalized, dominated by multinationals whose economic strategies have little place for national interests. The workings of finance capital further secures and solidifies this situation. In that sense the struggle to overcome oppression and exploitation in different places and sites have a common adversary and share some important goals. Fredric Jameson's argument for retaining the 'utopian dimension' of a 'positive hermeneutic'[88] – without the privilege he accords to class struggle and without the older humanist inferences – has some purchase for the ideological struggle which is part of that global effort for change.

This leads me to my second reason – namely, the extent to which a postmodernist mass culture has captured the space of imagination and identification on a world scale. In the context of the already established cultural imperialism of the West, this is a development which requires that we take seriously the question of the mechanisms and processes whereby the ex-colonized is constituted and seduced for practices of consumption and modes of being which still look to the West but with a different gaze. One cannot undo the work of 'ideology' or challenge the dominant law without this struggle both at the level of the symbolic and the psychic, and the related level of the production of material life. These are the considerations which inform my suggestion for forms of narrative and forms of text which can keep open the closures operated by dominant ideologies.

I am not suggesting that this should replace theoretical work. Rather, I would like to think it possible to search for different theoretical and narrative discourses and forms, subversive to the opposition of reason to emotion which characterises logocentrism, whereby the One would bear the imprint of the Other in its very construction, in dialogical fashion. Furthermore, the importance of such texts for struggle and for dis-identification is that their existence makes possible the displacement, onto a terrain of history, of a countermemory – events and action which could be politically diluted by being reduced to purely subjective goals and investments. In this way they contribute to the interiorization of a history of struggle and have effects for subjectivity: for the two processes are interwoven, the one conditioning the other.

In his analysis of totalitarian languages, Faye concluded that what is important is that 'the narration (*récit*) which accounts for the manner in which oppression has been made acceptable begins liberation.'[89] The liberatory project of Enlightenment has for a long time informed the narratives, including Marxism, which have inspired struggles against oppressions of various kinds. Foucault, reflecting on that project, thought that it should be replaced by a critical ontology on the grounds that the former seeks to reveal an essential self temporarily distorted by prevailing conditions, while the latter entailed an historical and collaborative project.[90]

In 'The Uses of Pleasure' he makes clear the view that critical ontology suggests an ethos, an art of oneself whereby we take ourselves to be the object of a project of becoming which is aesthetic and critical. This is especially so for the modern subject whose specific characteristic is the sense of belonging 'to the questioning of that to which we belong'.[91]

This aesthetic dimension to the project of transforming oneself opens up an interesting connection with the notion of the sublime in the sense that the subject reaches for an ideal imagined self which transcends yet completes it; it would be an experience of the truth, goodness, and beauty which the time of dire wishes for oneself. The narcissism inscribed in this process is reminiscent of Kant's argument about the sublime and Lyotard's[92] development of the connection between 'the sublime' and ethical and aesthetic judgement. This suggests that a moralization is involved in the process of becoming, tied (presumably) to values inscribed in narratives of subjective identity existing in a culture. The implications for theorizing ideology are worth pursuing, especially for the connection between the biographical dimension and the wider socio-cultural processes. The ideal self, after all, is not something fashioned out of its own imaginings, it is shaped by models, described and circulating in narratives of being, already located as subject position in 'imagined communities'.

New foundations are needed, absent in Foucault, which counter the possibility of an aesthetics of self serving the interests of individualism. The work of Levinas provides some of the conceptual elements for this task, particularly the redefinition of human beings which prioritizes the principles of responsibility for the Other, founded in the idea that our condition is not that indicated in the concept of being-for-itself but, on the contrary, that of being-for-the-other. One can juxtapose the complex thinking of Levinas with Benhabib's[93] reinterpretation of Habermas' communicative ethics because of the fruitful affiliations which her 'communicative utopia' suggests. She argues that the rejection of the philosophy of the subject in the context of struggles in late capitalism can enable emancipation as well as 'the formation of communities of need and solidarity'[94] based on the principles of friendship, love and solidarity.

Of course, principles alone cannot eliminate the reality of widespread oppressive power relations and the ideological work of the texts of oppression.

89. Faye, *op.cit.*, p136.

90. Foucault, 'What is Enlightenment', in P. Rabinow (ed.), *Foucault Reader* Pantheon Books, New York 1984.

91. See the discussion by R. Coles, 'Foucault's Dialogical Artistic Ethos', in *Theory, Culture and Society*, no 8, 1991, pp99-120.

92. Lyotard, *Le Differend*, Editions de Minuit, Paris 1983.

93. S. Benhabib, *Critique, Norm, Utopia*, Columbia University Press, New York 1986.

94. *Ibid.*, p353.

The problem for analysis is not the existence of these texts, for they cannot be wished away. The problem concerns the development and diffusion of insurgent ways of reading them – in other words, the development of the means for their appropriation in counter-hegemonic moves.

An important part of this project is the development of the kind of theory whose function is 'to contest, to overturn a reality, social relations, the relations of human beings to things and to others which are glaringly unbearable'.[95]

95. Lyotard, *Derive à Partir de Marx et Freud*, Union Generale d'Editions, Paris 1973, p210.

INTERRACIAL DIALOGUE IN RAP MUSIC

CALL-AND-RESPONSE IN A MULTICULTURAL STYLE

Gregory Stephens

I'd like to say 'nuff respect' to R.J. of KAZI and Root One in AusTex and Jay Trachtenberg of KUT-Austin – two 'white guys in love with black beauty' (in Ziggy Marley's words) who provided invaluable assistance. This paper was drawn in part from *Droppin' Science: Rap Music's Postmodern Critique*, my Master's thesis at California State University, Hayward.

I INTRODUCTION

Popular culture can be seen as a form of interracial communication – often acting as a mobile crossroads for the symbolic interaction of various socio-cultural groups. Rap music is a particularly volatile site for this kind of 'electronically mediated' interracial dialogue. The oppositional critique of 'conscious rap' – an artform rooted in the discourse of 'black liberation' – is being adapted by an increasingly multi-ethnic subculture in order to develop 'imagined communities' that transcend racial and national boundaries. I have previously made a content analysis of the discourse of black 'conscious' rappers, framing their reconstruction of African American liberation theory as a parallel form of postmodern critical theory. Here I will focus more on the way in which recent Latino and 'white' rappers have inserted themselves into this discourse. My broader aim is to examine the implications that multi-ethnic use of the African-derived call-and-response process has for the development of more inclusive and responsive forms of democracy.[1]

Rap music vividly illustrates 'the discursive nature of the boundaries through which we define ourselves', as Dick Hebdige has remarked.[2] Hiphop, the subculture from which rap emanates, was originally located mainly in African American urban communities. Now that rap has gained 'mainstream' mass media acceptance and influence, an unresolved racial tension has emerged within the artform. Some participants are using this vehicle to forward an exclusive, often 'anti-white' concept of 'black consciousness', even as many others use the same artform inclusively in an effort to eradicate race-consciousness.

I interpret rap as a 'double-voiced' discourse which arises from the 'collision between parallel discursive universes'. Multiracial participants are using this 'dialogic discourse' in a call-and-response process that is spawning a *mutually created language*, and thus redefining the boundaries of racial identity. I present evidence for this analysis in three ways:[3] 1) 'conscious rap' artists apply an Afrocentric code to source documents like the Bible in order to decode 'his-story'; 2) as a collage artform, rap incorporates cultural sources transcending race; 3) non-black artists have inserted themselves into the discursive formation of this emergent, oppositional mythology, decoding in their own way concepts like 'blackness'.

What do we make of a phenomenon in which black nationalist rap groups like Public Enemy attract largely non-black audiences? Former Public Enemy 'Minister of Information' Professor Griff has said: 'we had a mission ... to raise

1. On 'electronically mediated' dialogue, see Mark Poster, *Mode of Information*, University Chicago Press, Chicago: 1990; Benedict Anderson, *Imagined Communities*, Verso, London (1983) 1991; Gregory Stephens, 'Rap Music's Double-Voiced Discourse: A Crossroads for Interracial Communication', *Journal of Communication Inquiry*, vol 15 no 2, Summer 1991. This piece examines four broad themes of 'conscious' rap – self-critique, social critique, cultural critique, and racial critique.

2. Dick Hebdige, 'Subjects In Space', *New Formations*, no 11, Summer 1990, pvi. Not all boundaries in the imagined communities of African-rooted musics like rap are discursive, of course. We might think of it as a *symbolic order of rhythm*.

3. Henry Louis Gates, Jr, *The Signifying Monkey: A Theory of Afro-American Literary Criticism*, OUP, New

the consciousness of our people, and we didn't. We didn't attract black people; we had all-white audiences. Black people didn't want to hear what we had to say.'[4]

Griff is of course exaggerating for effect. Furthermore, by (predictably) thinking in black and white, he is ignoring rap's other audiences – Latino, Asian, etc. But anyone who has seen Public Enemy on tour with the rock group Anthrax during the summer of 1991 knows that he is not far off the mark.

Rap is 'black America's TV station', Public Enemy's Chuck D claims. Many performers on that station consider the music their property. They are singing 'It's a family affair', and often defining that family on the darker side of the colour line. Yet they can look out at their audience and see a sea of non-black faces, or turn on the radio and hear their Other chanting back at them in 'their' own language.[5] In a postmodern irony, an artform that often attempts to define racial boundaries is simultaneously transgressing them. Thus, rap music represents a challenge to traditional definitions of racial representation.

By applying both Euro- *and* Afrocentric definitions of signifying and signification to rap's intertextual, double-voiced discourse, I attempt to demonstrate how rap's 'two-toned' symbols convey different meanings to different members of its multicultural audience. Engaging these 'parallel discursive universes' in a dialogue is an effort to bridge Western and non-Western conceptions of language, 'permitting a context in which analyst and subject can talk together as equals'.[6] This electronic call-and-response process may, in turn, give us a preview of how multicultural societies arrive at a 'crossroads to a new transnational culture', as Homi Bhabha has written[7] – a culture that both honors differences and defines shared goals.

II TEXT AND CONTEXT

Dialogue between persons of European and African descent must incorporate both of their respective worldviews. I use the terms Afrocentric and Eurocentric to signify these worldwide, strictly as ideal types. By 'Eurocentric' I don't signify the often pejorative contemporary usage of the word. Eurocentric is simply shorthand for European-rooted, just as Afrocentric is shorthand for African-rooted. Likewise, 'Afrocentric' does not denote here an exceptionalist stance – as some black nationalists would have it. Rather, I use the term in a sense similar to Cornel West's 'Afro-American humanist tradition'.[8] Finally, it must be stressed that in the realm of popular culture, there are no *pure* forms of African- or European-derived speech patterns. Both cultures have been engaged in centuries of cross-fertilization.

Eurocentric Theories of Dialogic Discourse

The European conceptions of signification which I have applied to rap music all have an interactive focus: namely postructuralism and dialogism. For Murphy, 'researchers are communicatively competent when they comprehend the *linguistic pragmatics* of their subjects.' Hence, 'every research instrument that is

York, p. xxiv; Mikhail Bakhtin, *The Dialogic Imagination* (ed. Michael Holquist), University of Texas Press, Austin 1981. The idea of processual analysis' has been explicated by Renato Rosaldo, *Culture and Truths*, Beacon, Boston 1989.

4. *Daily Texan*, 23 June 1990.

5. Mark Derby, 'Public Enemy: Confrontation', *Keyboard*, September 1990. Shinehead's 'It's A Family Affair' quotes Sly Stone in his call for unity, and then chants off a lengthy list of African American entertainers to make explicit his definition of family.

6. C. Jan Swearingen, 'Dialogue and Dialectic: The Logic of Conversation and the Interpretation of Logic', in Tulio Maranhao (ed.), *The Interpretation of Dialogue*, University of Chicago Press, Chicago 1990, pp47-71. Dialogic textual analysis should be a 'union between minds rather than understanding of texts'. (p68).

7. Homi Bhabha (ed.), *Nation and Narration*, Routledge, 1990, p4.

8. Cornel West, *Prophesy Deliverance!*, Westminster Press, Philadelphia 1982.

adopted must be viewed as a means to engage subjects in dialogue.' Habermas believes that 'the dominant paradigm is no longer the observation, but the dialogue.'[9]

Bakhtin distinguished 'dialogic' from 'monologic' discourse. Dialogic discourses are 'a bridge thrown between myself and another ... a territory shared by both addresser and addressee.'[10] Kristeva renames this concept as the 'dialogical word'.[11] Dialogical words bridge the Self with its Other. This concept is especially fruitful for the 'common discourse' of intercultural communication. The insistence on signifying *process* rather than signifying *systems* opens to an understanding of *processual meaning* – a prerequisite for interracial dialogue.

The dialogical word and intertextuality serve as a bridge between Eurocentric and Afrocentric theory. Intertextuality is 'the interpenetration of two or more signifying practices', in Kristeva's view.[12] Since the Afrocentric signifying practice is rooted in oral, *vernacular* traditions, in order to achieve 'dialogic discourse' we will have to expand our understanding of texts in order to incorporate 'electronically mediated'/oral sources. In other words, we will have to address ourselves to the canonization of non-written texts.[13] A preliminary map of this process is provided by the Afrocentric theories of discourse outlined by Gates and Asante.

An Afrocentric Theory of Discourse

'A euro-linear view seeks to predict and control. An afro-circular view seeks to interpret and understand,' writes Asante. To illustrate: Popper described theories as 'nets to catch what we call "the world": to rationalize, to explain, to master it. We endeavor to make the mesh ever finer.' But what do we get with this catch? An object removed from its natural environment, and suitable for framing. As Murphy notes, 'technical methods operate like a fishing net, immobilizing whatever is caught.'[14] A postmodern Afrocentrism would, instead of weaving theoretical nets, ask whether or not we ought to be learning to swim.

As ideal-types, Eurocentric discourse is speaker-oriented and unidirectional; Afrocentric discourse is audience-oriented and interactive. 'A speaker governs the use of language under tutelage of the audience,' writes Asante of the Afrocentric call-and-response paradigm. Recently, Callendar and Cameron have studied the call-and-response process in black Pentacostal churches, and observe that 'spontaneity' and 'turn-taking' appear to be norms in black culture. Foucault noted that because European science has considered its texts as fixed, it looks back to origins. By contrast, Afrocentric culture sees texts not as fixed, but emerging from interplay between speaker and audience, created through call-and-response. While Europeans built cathedrals as monuments to their spirit, 'Africans built their monuments in their bodies, with rhythm.'[15] The difference, metaphorically, is between truth in stone and truth in motion.

Gates writes that black texts – and Afrocentric theory – cannot be 'only black', since 'all texts signify upon other texts.' Rather, its role is 'to define itself with – and against – other theoretical activities'.[16]

9. John Murphy, *Postmodern Social Analysis and Criticism*, Greenwood Press, Westport, CT 1989, pp46, 52. Jürgen Habermas, *Theory and Practice*, Beacon, Boston 1973, p13.

10. Mikhail Bakhtin, *Problems of Dostoevsky's Poetics*, Manchester University Press, Manchester 1984. V.N. Volosinov, *Marxism and the Philosophy of Language*, Seminar Press, New York & London 1973, p86.

11. Julia Kristeva, 'Word, Dialogue, and Novel', in Toril Moi (ed.) *The Kristeva Reader*, Basil Blackwell, Oxford, 1986.

12. John Lechte, *Julia Kristeva*, Routledge, London 1990, p104.

13. Abiola Irele, 'The African Imagination', *Research in African Literatures*, Vol 21, no 1, 1990, pp49–67.

14. Molefi Asante, *The Afrocentric Idea*, Temple University Press, Philadelphia 1987, p18. Karl Popper, *The Logic of Scientific Discovery*, Science Editions, New York 1968, p59. Murphy, *op.cit.*, p44.

15. Asante, *op.cit.*, p13. Christine Callendar and Deborah Cameron, 'Responsive Listening as Part of Religious Rhetoric: The Case of Black Pentacostal Preaching,' in Graham McGregory and R.S. White, *Reception and Response: Hearer Creativity and the Analysis of Spoken and Written Texts*, Routledge,

Simulating a Dialogue of Euro- and Afrocentric Theory

Both postmodern Euro- and Afrocentric theory stress inter-subjectivity. On this common ground important parallels can be drawn. Both define themselves as *oppositional*. Gates' concept of 'parallel discursive universes' is similar to the concept of 'parallel cultures' in the arts world.[17] Central to both versions of critical theory is the idea of signifying, signifying practice, or the mode of signification.[18] Signifying is for Gates a *processual* paradigm: 'in the black tradition [figures of signification] denote *ways of meaning*' (as opposed to meaning). Deconstructive critics have similarly argued that interpretation should focus on '*how texts mean* – rather than ... what they mean'.[19]

Eco suggests we are entering a communication era in which control is shifting from sender to receiver. Whoever 'succeeds in making a given audience discuss the message it is receiving could reverse the meaning of that message', he writes, recalling the Afrocentric idea of speakers being under tutelage of their audience. Eco and Asante are essentially talking about call-and-response, a process now being played out in rap's multiracial arena.[20]

III RAP MUSIC: A POSTMODERN/WEST AFRICAN BRIDGE

Robert Hilburn of the *Los Angeles Times* observed that 'the controversial ... street sound of rap [had] grabbed the creative momentum' from rock music.[21] This power has both a commercial and a creative side. M.C. Hammer and white rapper Vanilla Ice sold 16 million copies of their 1990 releases as of February 1991 after a combined 35 weeks atop the American pop charts. 'Conscious rappers' like Boogie Down Productions and Public Enemy are also consistent million-sellers. In order to understand the impact this music's discourse is having on contemporary culture, it may be helpful to conceive of rap music as a West African-postmodern bridge.

Now the notion of drawing parallels between African and European art is currently under attack in some quarters. At issue here is how to deal with *difference*. Some argue that a search for commonality merely serves as a pretext to whitewash significant cultural differences, and the postcolonial legacy of power imbalances still often tied to these differences. Stuart Hall rightly criticizes the way in which postmodernism 'can become a kind of lament for one's own departure from the centre of the world'. In (over)compensation for this sort of insular soft-headedness, the differences of race, class and gender are often recited as a sort of holy trinity. Those who argue that these differences are not absolute, but of relative importance, risk being dismissed as hopelessly naïve, or even accused of being racist, sexist, etc.[22]

My view is rooted in personal experience. I am of Irish descent and married to a woman of African descent. I worked in the 1980s as a songwriter for a black-led, multiracial dance band in Austin, Texas. I conceive of myself as an inhabitant of a 'racial frontier'; as a consumer and a co-creater of an interracial culture, and as a speaker of what is essentially a mutually created language. From this vantage, I think many on the 'Left' overcompensate for historical

London 1990, p175; Michel Foucault, *Archaeology of Knowledge*, Pantheon, New York 1972; Michael Ventura, *Shadow Dancing in the USA*, Jeremy Tarcher, Los Angeles 1985.

16. Gates, *op.cit.*, ppxxiii-xiv.

17. Michael Brenson, 'Artview', *New York Times*, 23 September 1990. The concept of 'parallel cultures' is attributed to Thomas Ybarra Frausto, Assistant Director of Arts & Humanities, Rockefeller Foundation.

18. The Afrocentric usage of 'signifying' is outlined by Gates, *op. cit.* For 'signifying practice', see Kristeva, *op.cit* 1986, and Dick Hebdige, *Subculture: The Meaning of Style*, Methuen, London 1979. On 'mode of signification', see Scott Lash, *The Sociology of Postmodernism*, Routledge, London 1990.

19. Gates, *op.cit.*, pp11, 24. K.M. Newton, *Interpreting the Text: A Critical Introduction to the Theory & Practice of Literary Interpretation*, Harvester Wheatsheaf, London 1990, p95; Robert Dunn, 'Postmodernism: Populism, Mass Culture, and Avant-Garde' in *Theory, Culture & Society*, vol 8, no 1, February 1991.

20. Umberto Eco, *Travels in Hyperreality*, Harcourt Brace Jovanovich, San Diego 1986, pp142-3.

*under*recognition of difference by now *over*emphasizing said difference. Unfortunately, the issue is too often framed as an either/or equation.

There is a stream of diasporic African thought that claims all popular music to be 'black', and is quite emphatic in its rejection of claims by whites to any significant contribution to this culture. Greg Tate tells the story about jazz drummer Max Roach calling the writer Frank Owen a 'racist white cocksucker' and throwing him out of his house. Owen's offence was to assert that hiphop isn't a 'pure' black art form, since it samples liberally from 'white' rock groups. Tate retorts, 'Their tired-ass riffs were heisted from black folks in the first place.'[23]

Tate is a talented critic whom I admire. But he seems to be indulging in racial romanticism, trying to recover some pure cultural source. Now, respect where respect is due is one thing. Certainly popular music owes more to Africa than any other source, and of course many 'white' artists have made fortunes imitating 'black' styles. But to imagine that this music is anything other than a hybrid creation is delusional. Should we call Stravinsky black because he was influenced by jazz, or Miles Davis white because he was influenced by Stravinsky? What do we make of the widespread admiration of country'n-'western by African musicians? Or the fact that most Algerian Rai music is now made in Paris? Once music enters the marketplace, it is all but impossible to claim any kind of racial ownership.

By defining rap as a West African/postmodern bridge, I am taking a both/and position. Difference and commonality don't have to be mutually exclusive. Surely we are sufficiently complex that we can both retain a strong ethnic identity, and participate in the give-and-take of a common culture. There is another stream of black critical thought that recognizes this open-ended potential of 'racial identity'. Stuart Hall insists that ' "Black" is essentially a politically and culturally *constructed* category,' while Cornel West emphasizes 'the profoundly hybrid character of what we mean by "race", "ethnicity", and "nationality".'[24]

I have detailed elsewhere rap's characteristics as both a West African and a postmodern artform, and only summarize this argument here. In 1966, Robert Farris Thompson described West African dance and music as 'danced faiths' which provided 'a means of comprehending a pervasive strand of contemporary culture'. Parents didn't 'get' their children's rock'n'roll, he wrote, 'because of their ignorance of black artistic traditions, which even blue-eyed youngsters seem to have absorbed.'[25] Thompson's comments still apply today. Some of the West African traits he mentioned, quite visible in rap, are a percussive performance style, multiple meter, call-and-response, and songs and dances of social allusion/derision.

While manifesting African roots, rap is also clearly postmodern. Rap's tales of urban life's ruptures and its ambiguous relation to 'mainstream' American culture reflect an indeterminacy. Its decanonization is evident in both style and substance – by defying musical rules, by describing 'his-story' as a genocidal ideology, etc. Rap is a hybrid form, putting samples of cultural icons

21. Robert Hilburn, 'Rap: The Power and the Controversy', *Los Angeles Times*, 4 February 1990.

22. Stuart Hall, 'The Emergence of Cultural Studies and the Crisis of the Humanities', *October*, no 53, Summer 1990, p22. Typical of the timely but somewhat reactionary critique of drawing parallels between European and non-European art is Marianna Torgovnick's *Gone Primitive*, University of Chicago Press, Chicago and London 1990. See also Hal Foster, 'The "Primitive" Unconscious of Modern Art, or White Skin Black Masks', in *Recodings: Art, Spectacle, Cultural Politics*, Bay Press, Seattle, WA 1985, and Susan Hiller (ed.), *The Myth of Primitivism*, Routledge, London 1991.

23. Greg Tate, 'Diary of a Bug', *Village Voice* 22 November 1988.

24. Hall and West both quoted in Cornel West, 'The New Cultural Politics of Difference', *October*, no 53, Summer 1990, pp104-5.

25. Robert Farris Thompson, 'An Aesthetic of the Cool: West African Dance', *African Forum*, Fall 1966, pp85-102. A similar typology is presented by Thompson in his book *Flash of the Spirit*, New York Randon House, 1983, pxiii. My outline of rap's West African/ postmodern parallels is in 'Rap Music's Double-Voiced Discourse: A Crossroads for Interracial Communication', *op.cit.*

of the past into a contemporary format, integrating elements of rock and reggae. Rap is a do-it-yourself performative art that is constantly being 'revised, answered, acted out'.[26] Finally, rap is an *immanent* forum for 'language animals' that reinvent themselves through the manipulation of symbols.

IV DROPPIN' SCIENCE: AN AFROCENTRIC CRITIQUE

Asante sees 'resistance to oppression, liberation from stereotypes, and action in anticipation to reaction' as the three central themes of Afrocentric discourse. This oppositional stance, like European critical theory, is concerned with the reordering of underlying symbols and rule systems. Writes Asante, 'Since the ruling power tries to impose silence by presenting an *undebatable word*, the receiver must present the *most debatable symbol*.'[27] Since my focus is on rap's debatable symbols, I have concentrated on what Boogie Down Productions' KRS-One calls 'conscious rap', or 'black consciousness rap', as X-Clan sees it.

In hiphop subculture, a rapper telling 'what's *really* goin' on' is said to be 'droppin' science'. Three connotations of this term frame my critique of rap's discourse on race: 1) 'droppin' science' implies, to use Weber's terminology, the 'prophetic imagination'.[28] In hiphop, 'science' is not received from an 'expert' but is created by the individual rapper under the guidance of black culture heroes like Malcolm X. A T-shirt popular among black youth illustrates the belief in a 'separate knowledge' and this tradition's prophetic continuity – 'Marcus, Malcolm, Martin, Marley, Mandela, *and Me*'; 2) it is dropped in a 'ghetto code' (Gil Scott-Heron) that gives its audience a practical knowledge unavailable to the out-group; 3) traditional scientific knowledge is being *dropped* in favor of an 'Afrocentric' perspective – defined here as 'African American Liberation Theory'. In X-Clan's words, 'I'm quite illogical but never been a savage/Been scientific but I never have to map it.'

In an early-1980s rap, 'Black History/The World', Gil Scott-Heron disowns what he sees as the whitewashing of history in words that have been echoed repeatedly:

> If interpreting was left up to me
> I'd swear every time that version ain't mine
> That's why it's called His-Story.

This reference to his-story as a fiction created for the benefit of white males is repeated often in rap. In his album 'By All Means Necessary', KRS-One comments, 'So when you're there in class learning his-story/Learn a little of your story, the real story.' Public Enemy say much the same thing: 'History shouldn't be a mystery/Our story's real history, not his-story.' As do the Jungle Brothers: 'Lookin' for the True Black Days of Glory/But your readin' history – That's HIS-STORY!'

This dis-identification with 'mainstream' culture reveals itself in wordplay. Television becomes 'tell-lie-vision'; a library is a 'lie-bury' – the place where lies

26. Ihab Hassan, *The Postmodern Turn: Essays in Postmodern Theory and Culture*, Ohio State University Press, Ohio 1987, pp169-72.

27. Asante, *op.cit.*, pp169, 31. My emphasis added.

28. Max Weber, *Sociology of Religion*, Beacon, Boston (1922) 1963.

are buried. 'Land of the free and the home of the brave' is rendered 'land of the thief and the home of the slave'. A PhD is a 'psychological human disorder'. KRS-One challenges conventional wisdom on why blacks fail:

I fail in your class cause I ain't with your reasoning
It seems to me that in a school that's Ebony
African history should be pumped up strongly.

And he does just that, reinterpreting Judaeo-Christian culture's central text from an Afrocentric view:

Moses had to be of the black race
Because he spent forty years in Pharaoh's place
He passed as the Pharaoh's grandson
So he had to look just like them

KRS-One has started a collective of 'edutainers' called 'Humanity Educated Against Lies'. Their album 'Civilization vs. Technology' focuses on the rewriting of his-story. KRS-One, as the organizer, is at pains to provide an inclusive theoretical overview: 'Black and white ain't the real fight/That's the only thing the media hypes ... Before you're a color you're human.'

But some rappers under his umbrella are not quite so charitable. Kushite urges his people to 'erase the old' and to 'declare independence from the white bondage'. Since he believes blacks are the 'original peoples', he urges them to 'snatch back authority' and become 'straight up imperialists'.

Some black nationalist-inspired rappers, such as Brand Nubians, express not only cultural pride but superiority:

We come to make people aware that black means first
400 years we've been made to feel cursed
But now, it's our time to rule ...
To be exact, dominant means black
But some have a hard time trying to swallow that.

Much of rap's ideology comes from a mythologized memory of the black power movement. X-Clan uses code words which signify white inferiority. 'Vultures' or 'culture vulture' refers to the belief that whites have no culture except that which they have stolen from non-Europeans. 'Cave-boy' is a generic reference to white males which signifies a diseased consciousness developed in the absence of the sun. 'Devils' reflects the influence of Nation of Islam teachings formulated by Elijah Muhammed and popularized by the early Malcolm X.[29] X-Clan uses the 'crossroads' as a central metaphor for what they conceive of as a meeting place for 'the blackwatch' who enact revenge on 'cave boy oppressors'. They place this crossroads in a mythical Egypt and put a 'blacks-only' sign at the frontier – decrying 'the legendary thief who tried to make Greece sinkin' Paris into Egypt'.

29. Charles Ahearn, 'The Five Percent Solution', *Spin*, February 1991.

Ice Cube, a 'gangster' rapper who has tried recently to incorporate political commentary, has taken to an extreme tendency in black nationalist thought to fight racism with racism. In 'Horny Lil' Devil', he threatens to kill white males who desire black women. 'Black Korea' advocates arson of Asian shopkeepers in black ghettos. Rejecting any hope of coalition-building, Ice Cube dismisses successful blacks as 'tryin' to be white or a Jew/but who are they to be equal to?'

Positively Black takes opposition to its (il)logical end: 'Think like your enemy thinks/Do all you can do to make your enemy sink'. Over a sample of Marley's 'Could You Be Loved', their song 'Enemies Got Me On the Run' repeats Public Enemy's claim of 'the worldwide conspiracy to destroy the black race'.

KRS-One, 'conscious rap's' most eloquent spokesman, on the one hand subscribes to the drugs-as-genocide-of-blacks theory; on the other hand, he has denounced the concept of group blame. In 'The Racist', KRS-One lists four types of racism against blacks, followed by this biting indictment of black racism:

The last but not least racial prejudice
Is the black man speaking out of ignorance
Whitey this and chingchow that is not how the intelligent man acts
You can't blame the whole white race for slavery 'cause this ain't the case
A large sum of white people died with blacks
Trying hard to fight racial attacks

Queen Latifah expresses frustration at continuing racial hatred and calls for a change:

Why is it so hard to be sisters and brothers
I hate when they hate me, I hate when I hate them
There wouldn't be problems if we didn't create them
The time is now to mend and be friends.

Mixed race British rapper Rebel MC offers his own existence as proof that an interracial culture can emerge – 'Black and white we can unite … I'm living proof.'

A new genre of rap is emerging, groups like Definition of Sound and P.M. Dawn, which some have labelled 'New Age Rap'. It takes a somewhat utopian view of race relations. Definition of Sound devote much of their album 'Life and Love' to emphasizing the changing character of race relations and the dangers of being frozen in poses of victimization. They advise their peers, 'Life is not an angle it's a 360 spin/To think one way is not to think positively.' Urging blacks not to 'fall down in sorrow for your self-pity', DOS offers this King-like vision:

I'm able to see about a day where the sun of peace shines
Upon where black, white, yellow and red – they're all intertwined …
In this lifetime anything can be done

Forget about the color and unite as one ...
It could be solved ... anything can evolve.

Rap music is explicitly oppositional, but it is also housed in a structure designed to bypass the limitations of an oppositional stance. Rhythm is the vehicle of this transcendence; rhythm is 'the basis of African American transcendence'. Transcendence is achieved through a dialectical tension – the freedom to 'do one's own thing' within the structure of a moveable unity, keeping it 'on the one'.[30] Rebel MC can signify this entire worldview and cultural tradition by repeating the simple refrain, 'Riddim a full of culture y'all'. This philosophy of transcendence does not respect colour lines – hence Clinton's quasi-millenial vision of 'One Nation Under a Groove', recently reconstituted in Janet Jackson's appeals to a 'Rhythm Nation' which is 'pushing toward a world rid of color lines'.

30. Gregory Stephens, 'Fashion Dread Rasta: On the One in Jamaica with Bob Marley's Children', *Whole Earth Review*, Summer 1988.

31. Kevin Mattson, 'The Dialectic of Powerlessness: Black Identity and Affirmative Action', *Telos*, no84, Summer 1990, pp177-84; Mark Costello and David Foster Wallace, *Signifying Rappers: Rap and Race in the Urban Present*, Ecco, New York 1990, p87.

DJ Shazzy chants that anyone who can 'Keep It Flowin' ' will experience her music's healing and equalizing power:

And if your rhythm's sick this song will make it better
Hear the bass kick strong with every letter ...
At any age, race, rank or color
You could move as smooth as any other.

To Euro-Americans or other cultures which have traditionally separated mind and body, this is a call with redemptive appeal. This is quite visible in the film 'Commitments', when an Irish band dubs themselves 'The Saviours of Soul' and speaks explicitly of using soul to bring a healing process to their people.

Ska Danks (of H.E.A.L.) insists on the universality of the African culture: 'Black or white, Indian, Tai or Chi/Half a half, one a one ... Every body African'. This line, echoing Black Uhuru's lyric that 'The Whole World Is Africa' holds out the promise that African culture, and African music in particular, has the potential to unite all people, to write the bassline for a new multiracial song.

The more antagonist rap would seem a forbidding environment for non-blacks. But many of them seem to feel that the bark of their black peers is worse than their bite. Furthermore, as we have seen, they can choose whether to identify with the exclusive lyrics of black consciousness rappers, or the inclusive message of conscious rap.

More fundamentally, 'Rap is postmodern (pastiche) art par excellence,' as Mattson notes. Thus we encounter the irony of a self-consciously "closed" music's obsessive use of samples that must by nature be open.'[31] There are surprising reflections in this hall of mirrors. Chuck D was inspired by Afrika Bambaataa's 'Zulu Nation', but Bambaataa says he got the idea not from South Africa but from the British movie 'Zulu' starring Michael Caine. Schooly D's 'Signifying Rappers' is built on a sample from rock legend Led Zeppelin, who in turn drew from the blues. De La Soul samples Liberace, and uses David

Bowie as a career model. As Costello and Wallace put it, 'When you sleep with a source you sleep with everyone your source has slept with.'[32]

By putting past cultural voices in a contemporary context, rap allows the audience to signify anew upon these sources. Thus Malcolm X is reconstituted as the 'white man is the devil' orator, or as the post-Mecca peacemaker, depending on one's orientation. Just as black rappers have used an Afrocentric code to find themselves in historical landscapes previously presumed to be the province of whites, so non-blacks are using rap's double-voiced symbols as entry points to a cultural landscape that often presents itself as only black. And non-blacks, having discovered in rap's symbols a common ground, are proceeding to make their own contributions to this discourse. Having learned the 'linguistic pragmatics' of the predominantly African American speakers in this multicultural form, they are proceeding to engage them in dialogue. Thus, in the call-and-response tradition, the Rhythm Nation raps back.

V CALL-AND-RESPONSE: THE RHYTHM NATION RAPS BACK

The Caucasian Persuasion

The cave dweller drops lyrics a capella (3rd Bass)

At least since the 1950s, 'hip' white youth have identified strongly with black music. From early blues-based rockers, to the Talking Heads, the cutting edge of rock music has always been defined on the borderline with black, Latino or 'world' music. In 1992 this is no different, except that the cutting edge 'rock' musicians just happen to be black.

The process by which white youth have borrowed from black culture has been well documented.[33] There is a less-documented but equally important reverse process: from jazz's assimilation of Euro-American music to rap's 'plundering' of cultural sources such as old TV themes and 'breaks' taken from rock records.[34] A call and response – a dialectic – has been going on between these parallel cultures long enough that we can discern the beginnings of a mutually created language. Now we are seeing the emergence of white rap acts who explicitly signify identification with black (or transracial) culture.

For instance, 3rd Bass slams colour stereotypes:

Black cats bring bad luck
Bad guys wear black
Musta been a white guy started all that.

On the song 'No Master Plan, No Master Race', 3rd Bass develops this philosophy more fully, professing that 'Original man's a black man/said by a Caucasian'.

The all-white rap group 'Young Black Teenagers' strongly identifies with African American liberation. In 'Proud to be Black', they stake out their claim on this 'contested cultural arena' with an insistence that 'Blackness is a state of mind':

32. *Ibid.* ('Zulu' reference is in Costello and Wallace.) On De la Soul's influences, see *Rolling Stone*, no 602, 18 April 1991.

33. Hebdige, *op.cit.* See also Roger Hewitt, *White Talk Black Talk: Inter-racial Friendship and Communication Amongst Adolescents*, CUP, London 1986; Simon Jones, *Black Culture, White Youth*, MacMillan, London 1988; Paul Willis, *Common Culture: Symbolic work at play in the Everyday Cultures of the Young*, Westview Press, Boulder 1990.

34. The story of hip-hop's birth and borrowings has been told often. One of the better accounts is Greg Tate, 'Hip Hop Nation', *Village Voice*, 19 January 1988.

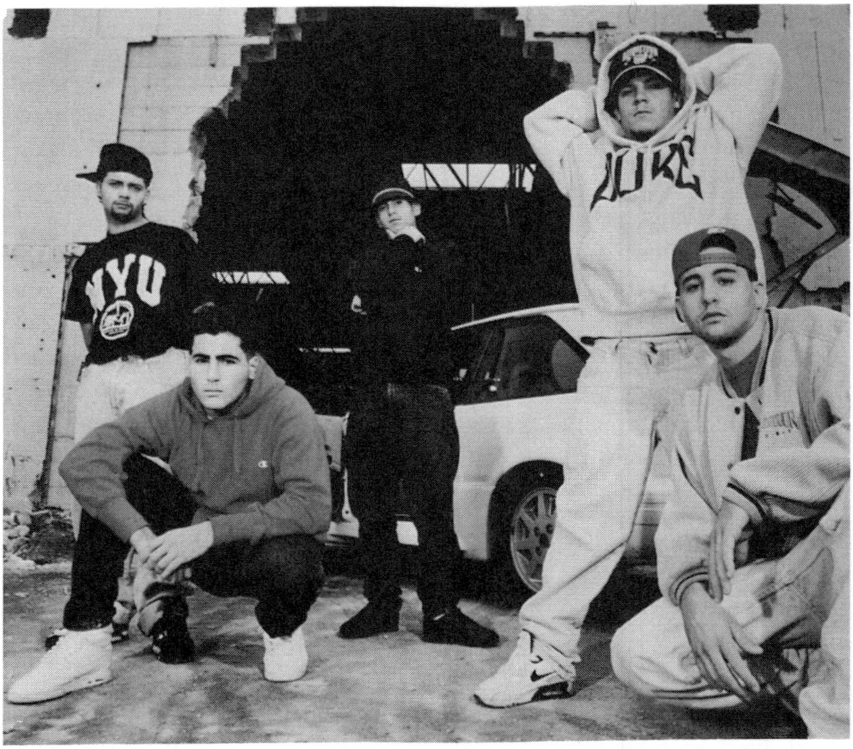

Young Black Teenagers

So to whom it may concern here's a fact
That the minute you hear a rap you think black ...
The truth is sharp and proven that
It ain't where you're from it's where you're at ...
New styles, new rules, new facts
That's why we're proud to be black.

Though YBT begin 'Proud to be Black' with the admission that they are 'born of the Caucasian persuasion', some black DJ's have protested that this is just another instance of 'culture vultures'. The group defends itself by pointing out that they grew up in black neighborhoods and were considered 'black' by their peers. Soul Records co-owner Bill Stephney (who records YBT and was one of the originators of 'the Public Enemy concept') defends the group by saying that they 'will make African people in this country question what the term "black" really means.'[35]

35. Leah Garchik, 'Personals', *San Francisco Chronicle*, 9 January 1991.

At the same time, white rappers tend still to be very self-conscious about their presence on this contested turf. You can see this in the way the thin-skinned Vanilla Ice invents ghetto credibility, retracts part of it, and then tells his critics to 'kiss my white ass'.

The New Jersey-based 'Caucasian' Tony D (who produces Poor Righteous Teachers) is blunt in telling his black peers to ease off the white-bashing:

Damn, I said I know who I am
So you don't have to remind me every time you shake my hand
Point blank, understand, don't you think I notice
There's a mirror in my room ... I have 20-20 vision

3rd Bass are more subtle. They invert stereotypes of 'whites' being forwarded by some Afrocentric razz artists, remarking slyly that 'the cave dweller drops lyrics a capella'. But this insecurity manifests itself most of all in the in-fighting that has developed among white rappers. It seems to be almost an inverse manifestation of the conventional wisdom that used to operate about there only being room for one black artist in any field at any given time. Now that white rappers are under fire by their black peers, they often seek to establish their credibility not only by professing their allegiance to the fight against racism, but by attacking the alleged sincerity of other white artists. 3rd Bass spend much of their second album distancing themselves from Vanilla Ice, and even includes a scene in the video 'Pop Goes the Weasle' in which a Vanilla Ice lookalike is clubbed by the 3rd Bass Posse.

Tony D seeks to delegitimate 3rd Bass at every opportunity. He tells MC Serch 'you forgot you were a bleach boy', compares him to Vanilla Ice, and tells the group they are just 'another replacement for the Beastie Boys'. In rap argot, they're 'frontin' ':

In the shoe polish you take your bath
You got to learn history before you conquer math
You rub it on your body thinkin' you'll get knowledge ...
The teacher might of taught you but you learned wrong
It shows in the writing of your songs.

Tony D seeks to legitimate himself, in comparison, by reasserting his awareness of difference:

Black is black and white is white
There's no changin' or rearrangin' this subject ...
I'm fillin' my mind up to capacity
With knowledge of self – I know whom I am
I'm not down with the kiss ass program.

At the same time, he describes hiphop as 'the music that we created' and feels qualified to lecture black radio:

Seems to me that the radio should play the truth
To enlighten today's black youth
Cause your education is not teachin' them
It only weakens them as the rebel to violence.

In the end, Tony D comes back to a stance of recognizing but transcending difference that is very like that of 3rd Bass:

> When I look at a human you can say I'm color blind
> Cause I see them with my eyes but I judge them with my mind.

The Latino Connection

> Being the fine line between the black and the white man. (Latin Alliance)

Latino rappers probably better illustrate rap's ability to cross colour lines, since they are less obsessed with defending their legitimacy. Their multicultural heritage gives them solid ground from which to provide their own unique critique of his-story. For instance, the group Aztlan Nation reframes the illegal alien issue: 'I didn't cross the border, the border crossed me.'

Cuban American rappers like Mellow Man Ace and Mexican American rappers like Kid Frost have staked their claims to hiphop's contested turf with a richly articulated discourse on Latino contributions to rap in particular and American/New World culture in general. 'What we tried to do is break stereotypes that rap is a black art form,' says Kid Frost – the 'Hispanic Causing Panic'. 'Rap is not a black art form, rap is an *urban* art form,' he explains his philosophy, 'It's not where you're from, it's where you're at' – echoing the YBT.[36]

36. Kid Frost interview on KALX-Berkeley, 24 June 1990.

Frost has produced a stable of rap artists – the 'Latin Alliance' – hailing from Nicaragua, France, Spain and Puerto Rico. On their collective album, the concept of a community or a nation which transcends racial/national barriers is quite explicit. On 'Valla En Pas (Go In Peace)', the Hip Hop Astronaut describes his identity as 'being the fine line between the black and the white man'. The song 'Latinos Unidos' describes the Latino connection to African slavery:

> Puerto Ricans survived 400 years of slavery
> Based on pride, persistence and bravery ...
> That only made us much stronger
> Now we're multiracial and we're slaves no longer.

Pride in a multiracial and multicultural identity is a persistent theme of Latino rappers. ALT, a rapper on the Latin Alliance compilation, asks, 'What is the true definition of American/Does it belong to any one race or culture?' The answer, from a Latino perspective, is clear: an American lives on a crossroads, a convergence of cultures. ALT comes from 'Two mountain streams flowing together/It's Hispanic and French blood, create a lyrical flood.' The Lyrical Latin (from the Latin Alliance) looks to his Nicaraguan heritage; others even look back to Germany, since Germans have had, of course, a major impact on some Latino nations – particularly in Argentina and Brazil.

Like their Afrocentric peers, Latino rappers sometimes entertain messianic

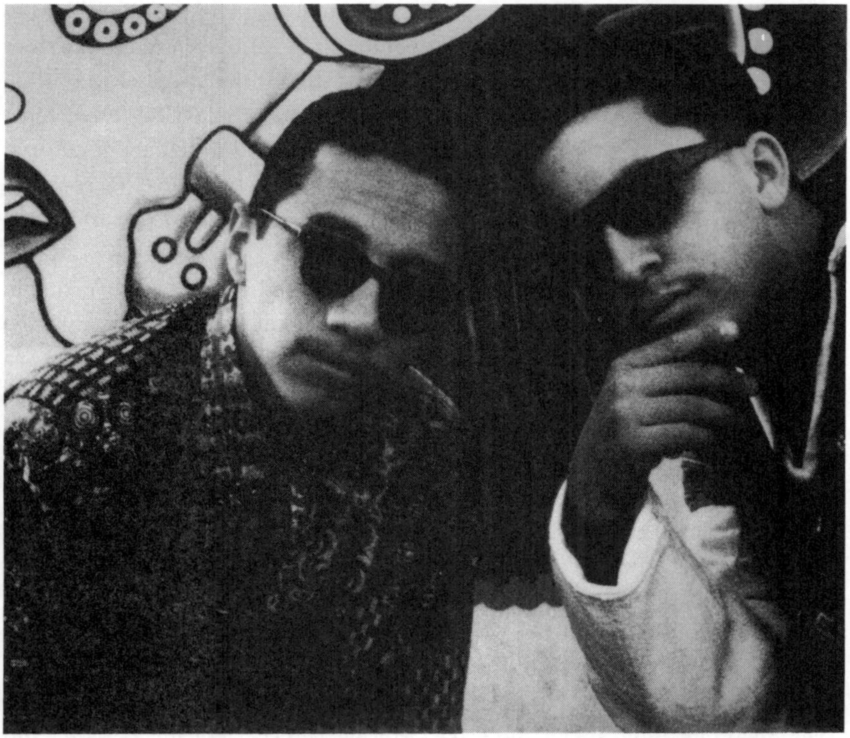

A Lighter Shade of Brown

or imperial dreams. 'If for once all Chicanos got together/No longer the minority but the majority', dreams Kid Frost. The Hip Hop Astronaut imagines, 'maybe one day we'll have the upper hand'. And like Afrocentric rappers, Latinos are intensely critical of Eurocentric education. 'What they teach in school is the dumbest/And don't talk no shit about Christopher Columbus', say Frost and ALT on 'Runnin'. They see a quite different history behind the history of the United States flag:

Red for the bloodshed
White for the white man
Blue for the women of the red man, right man?

But like KRS-One and many black 'conscious' rappers, the Latinos are primarily concerned with uplift, and not with 'dissing' any other group. In the words of the Hip Hop Astronaut:

To the Latin community, it's time to get the immunity
Free from any type of racial negativity …
Don't be misled, we're not trying to put any ethnic group down
We're just trying to bring ours up.

This uplift is accomplished, in part, by recontextualizing Latino cultural heroes and musical fragments. For instance, a Lighter Shade of Brown retells the story of 'Pancho Villa' from a Chicano perspective – that of the 'original vato' who, acting as a sort of Mexican Robin Hood, 'had the whole USA after him'. Another cut reworks the Latin Rascals classic 'Groovin' ' to tell about cultural values in the contemporary Chicano community. 'Spill the Wine' borrows the old Eric Burdon/War song and refashions it as a sort of Latino variant of Bob Marley's 'Three O'Clock Roadblock'.

The ethnicity of Latinos is marked by an unabashed pride in its diversity, in its multiracial, bilingual adaptability. A particular point of pride is the ability to engage in what the Speech Communication field calls 'code switching'. In 'Ya Estuvo', Kid Frost announces to a sceptical black rapper that 'I'm going to bust this one in a bilingual mode', and then proceeds to run each verse down in both Spanish and English. A Lighter Shade of Brown advises 'suckers dissin'' to 'Pay attention to an invention that caught your attention/We call it Spanglish/A Bit of Spanish combined with English.'

The group is 'always comin' funky to any old tempo' because they've got 'Paquito Soul' – a little bit of soul, or Latin Soul, by inference. It is when we look at what constitutes 'Paquito Soul' – at the structural foundations of Latino rap – that we understand just how inclusive this variety of hiphop is. For instance, the song 'Latinos Unidos' is based on samples from Dr John's 'Funky Nassau', Average White Band's 'Cut the Cake', Herbie Hancock's 'Palm Grease', and 'Subway to Venus' by the white punk/funk band, the Red Hot Chili Peppers.

This celebration of hybridity in Latino culture can be seen in Latino rappers' widespread use of War samples. We could almost say that War is to Latino rap what James Brown is to black rap. The significance is in War's musical history as a multicultural crossroads: they are a primarily 'black' band who first made a name for themselves backing an Englishman, Eric Burdon; then developed a uniquely Latin sound in songs like 'Low Rider' that used the harmonica of Denmark's Lee Oskar as its signature.

The implications of this cultural and ethnic gumbo for race relations are clear: 'the true definition of an "American" – quote, unquote,' as ALT put it, cannot 'belong to any one race or culture'. Rayski Rockwell (Latin Alliance) advises, 'So don't be enemies, know that I'm saying?/Negative lifestyles bring bad memories'.

In a broader sense, artforms primarily pioneered by American blacks (like hiphop) do not belong to Americans, any more than they can be owned by blacks. As Simon Frith has pointed out recently, American artforms are essentially cultural myths which have some geographic roots but few geographic limitations. 'America itself, as a pop cultural myth, no longer bears much relationship to the USA as a real place *even in the myth*,' writes Frith, since 'its very cultural forms are now everywhere available.'[37] African American liberation theory and the 'black beats' which carry it have gone international. It can no more be called only black than Christianity can be called 'only Jewish', or

37. Simon Frith, 'Anglo-America and its Discontents', *Cultural Studies*, Vol 5, no 3, October 1991, p268.

democracy can be defined as only the concern of the white male landowners who wrote the United States constitution.

Eco's assertion that a group which discusses the message, or 'challenges the sender' as Asante says, is able to 'reverse the meaning of that message', seems to be precisely the point of 'droppin' science', in its multicultural application. We have seen how conscious rappers apply an Afrocentric code to recover their place in historical landscapes from which they had been written out. With a knowledge of double-voiced discourse, non-blacks can in turn decode concepts such as 'blackness', 'soul', and 'America'. In the process, they are discovering in rap's double-voiced symbols and musical architecture a world in which cross-fertilization between 'blacks' and 'non-blacks' is a historical and ongoing process.

No matter how far back we go in cultural history, we find a crossroads – a site of intercultural dialogue. Martin Bernal and others have represented the evidence, for instance, that Mediterranean culture was a hybrid byproduct of the cross-fertilization of African, European, and Semitic peoples. So to look for 'pure' origins in Greece, Egypt, or the Middle East – or in contemporary cultures – is to perpetuate 'symbol imperialism' against which both Euro- and Afrocentric critical theory have aligned themselves.[38]

VI THE ROLE OF THE CALL-AND-RESPONSE PARADIGM IN MUTLI-ETHNIC SOCIETIES

The case of non-black participation in rap demonstrates that, although the social landscape between race and culture is still contested turf, a type of linguistic pragmatics is emerging on this cultural frontier which transcends racial boundaries. Groups like Young Black Teenagers are helping to inspire a long-overdue debate on the cultural meaning of 'blackness'. While blackness has been vigorously defended in racial terms in the United States, the term has been given a more inclusive meaning in other locales. For instance, Asians in South Africa often designate themselves as black because they identify with the anti-apartheid movement rather than the white minority regime.

Dub poet Linton Kwesi Johnson was a nationalist in 1980 but today rejects the idea of colour-coded identity. 'Blacks have a stake in the future of Europe because we're Europeans, too,' he says. 'A couple of black guys took great offence because they couldn't come to terms with that fact. For them, European is a racial category; for me it is a geographical one.'[39]

In a critique of Young Black Teenagers, Joe Wood poses the challenge this way: 'We blackfolk need to redefine our changing blackness ... Can right-thinking whites be a part of our "we"? He concludes that YBT, as culturally black, represent 'Phase II' of America's 'racial reconstruction project', which consists of 'redefining the fictions of blackness and whiteness.'[40]

This process can begin by naming our common discourse. This is not an assimilationist stance, but a recognition that in addition to our unique Afro- and Eurocentric roots, we also share a common culture. This is the culture Janet Jackson names when she speaks of a 'Rhythm Nation'. We can also see

38. Martin Bernal, *Black Athena: The Afroasiatic Roots of Classical Civilization*, Rutgers University Press, New Brunswick, NJ 1987.

39. Jason Fine, 'Poet Evokes the Pulse of the Streets', *Daily Californian*, 2 March 1990.

40. Joe Wood, 'Who Says a White Band Can't Play Rap?', *Village Voice Rock & Roll Quarterly*, 19 March 1991.

potential transracial cultural communities in what Linton Kwesi Johnson calls 'Bass Culture', in Bob Marley's ideal of 'One Love', or in what Junior Reid, Definition of Sound and others call 'One Blood'.

After Everett Hughes, I see this turf as a *racial frontier*. Hughes wrote: 'The true unit of race and ethnic relations is not the single ethnic group, but the situation, embracing all of the diverse groups who live in the community or region.' For Jack Forbes, 'the very essence of a frontier is the interaction of two or more peoples.' Thus, 'frontier studies must properly focus their attention upon inter-ethnic behaviour.'[41]

The sociology of race relations has often been, as Blumer once remarked, 'fixated on a prejudice-discrimination axis'.[42] However, as critical sociology and communication studies move towards interactive paradigms, there has been an increasing recognition of the need to define shared values.

In this light, it is important to understand that call-and-response, the Afrocentric dialogue paradigm, is a communication process ideally suited to multicultural settings. Chernoff speaks of 'the reciprocity inherent in rhythmic call-and-response'. Abrahams notes that stories or discourses in a call-and-response context 'are called upon not just to deliver a specific message but to initiate talk about that message.' Thus, the 'antiphonal structure' of such interactive communication puts 'the individual in continual dialogue with his community, allowing him at one and the same time to preserve his voice as a distinct entity and to blend it with those of his fellows'.[43]

The utility of call-and-response for intercultural problem-solving is that it allows speakers to 'turn to their advantage dissenting as well as assenting voices in the audience'.[44] This is clearly evident in the way in which, for instance, Public Enemy samples irate callers to their own radio shows. 'Call-and-response is a distinctively African and African American form of discourse,' writes Callahan, but 'it is also especially well suited to the vernacular culture of an experimental democratic society.' Black speakers imagine national identity as 'a collaborative improvisatory national tradition of call-and-response'. Such an adaptive 'ideal speech situation' requires a society that 'remains emergent and experimental, open and responsive to new voices, new stories'. Rap music is call-and-response in a multicultural style; a form of reciprocity that features a 'continuous alternation of feedback' between speaker and audience.[45] It may be, in practice, the closest thing multiracial (would-be) democracies like England and the United States have to a popular, inclusive 'ideal speech situation', despite the attempts of some to define it as an exclusive family debate.[46]

If 'symbol imperialism, rather than institutional racism, is the major social problem facing multicultural societies,' as Asante suggests,[47] then rap's multicultural audience must challenge its speakers as to whether its 'most debatable symbols' are being used inclusively. And if speakers within 'black' forums are to be 'under tutelage of their audience', as that audience becomes more and more multicultural, they will have to adopt appropriate speech patterns. To pretend to be 'only black' in this context is to be untrue to Afrocentric concepts of communication.

41. Everett and Helen Hughes, *Where Peoples Meet: Racial and Ethnic Frontiers*, Free Press, Glencoe, IL 1952, p 19; Jack Forbes, 'Frontiers in American History and the Role of the Frontier Historian', *Ethnohistory*, volXV, Spring 1968.

42. Quoted in Michael Banton, *Racial Theories*, CUP, London 1987, p110.

43. John Chernoff, *African Rhythm and African Sensibility*, University Chicago Press, Chicago 1979, p167; Roger Abrahams, *African Folktales*, Pantheon, New York 1983, pp1-15; Lawrence Levine, *Black Culture & Black Consciousness*, OUP, New York 1977, pp33, 221.

44. John F. Callahan, *In the African-American Grain: The Pursuit of Voice in Twentieth-Century Black Fiction*, University of Illinois Press, Chicago 1988, p15.

45. *Ibid.*, pp16, 19; Thomas Luckmann, 'Social Communication, Dialogue and Conversation', in Ivana Markova and Klaus Foppa (eds), *The Dynamics of Dialogue*, Harvester Wheatsheaf, 1990, p47.

46. The concept of an 'ideal speech situation' is spelled out by Jürgen Habermas in *Legitimation Crisis*, Beacon Press, Boston 1975.

47. Asante, *op.cit.*, p56.

'Black' music acts like a 'wave' at sporting events: once the wave starts rolling, you can't ask certain people not to stand up. When the call-and-response starts cooking, you can't pick and choose who's going to answer. It seems to me that instead of trying to draw colour lines around our music, we ought to be proud that black grooves are writing the basslines to a new multicultural song.

In hiphop, white rappers like Third Base and Tony D, biracial rappers like Rebel MC and Neneh Cherry, Latino Rappers like Kid Frost, and black rappers like KRS-One, all use black music and liberation theory as a base. But they use this tradition inclusively. The outcrop can no longer be defined along colour lines. With this mutually created language, participants can engage in 'negotiation strategies' through which they can 'transcend the trappings of their respective cultures'.[48] This dialogic discourse provides a model of our movement towards the cultural crossroads where we can truly come to know 'what diversity means'.

48. Stella Ting-Toomey, 'Identity and Interpersonal Bonding' in Molefi Asante and William Gudykunst (eds), *Handbook of International and Intercultural Communication*, Sage Publications, Newbury Park, CA 1989, pp369-70.

Recordings

Boogie Down Productions, 'By Any Means Necessary', 1988; 'Ghetto Music: The Blueprint of Hip Hop', 1989; 'Edutainment', 1990, Zomba/RCA.
Brand Nubians, 'Brand Nubian', 1989, Elektra/Asylum.
Neneh Cherry, 'Raw Like Sushi', 1989, A&M.
Definition of Sound, 'Love and Life: A journey with the Chameleons', 1991, Circa Records.
H.E.A.L., 'Civilization vs. Technology', 1991, Elektra.
Ice Cube, 'Death Certificate', 1991, Priority.
Janet Jackson, 'Rhythm Nation', 1989, A&M.
Linton Kwesi Johnson, 'Bass Culture', 1980, Mango/Island.
Jungle Brothers, 'Done By the Forces of Nature', 1989, Warner Brothers.
Kid Frost, 'Hispanic Causing Panic', 1991, Virgin.
Latin Alliance, 'Latin Alliance', 1991, Virgin.
Lighter Shade of Brown, 'Brown and Proud', 1991, Pump/Quality Records.
Poor Righteous Teachers, 'Holy Intellect', 1990, Profile.
Positively Black, 'Positively Black', 1989, Select.
Public Enemy, 'Fear of a Black Planet', 1990, Columbia.
Queen Latifah, 'Nature of a Sista', 1991, Tommy Boy.
Rebel MC, 'Rebel Music', 1990, Desire/Polygram.
Gil Scott-Heron, 'Moving Target', 1982, Arista.
Shazzy, 'Attitude: A Hiphop Rapsody', 1990, Elektra.
Shinehead, 'Unity', 1988, African Love/Warner Brothers; 'The Real Rock', 1990, African Love/Elektra.
3rd Bass, 'The Cactus Album', 1989; 'Derelicts of Dialect', 1991, Def Jam/Columbia.
Tony D (Harvee Wallbanger), 'Droppin' Funky Verses', 1991, 4th & B'Way/Island.
X-Clan, 'To the East, Blackwards', 1989/90, 4th & B'Way/Island.
Young Black Teenagers, 'Proud to be Black', 1991, Soul Records.

To Do or Not to Do Without the Word

Ecstasy and Discourse in the Cinema

Jean-Jacques Lecercle

I INTRODUCTION

In a letter to Adorno, written in 1938, Walter Benjamin deplores the advent of talking movies:

> It is increasingly clear to me that we must interpret the launching of the talking movie as a deliberate attempt by the film industry to put an end to the revolutionary primacy of silent movies, which to a greater extent provoke uncontrollable and politically dangerous reactions.[1]

Half a century later, this statement has the flavour of paradox. No one would seriously dream of going back to silent movies as a way forward for the art as a whole. If, which is doubtful, there is still a place for silent film, it is at best in marginal, and experimental, circles. Language having conquered the cinema for good, Benjamin's opinion must be treated as an oddity, one of those things one might well repent having said.

Yet I would like to treat it as the sympton, not of a deciduous conjuncture, but of a perennial unease, the unease caused by the invasion of nonverbal arts by logocentrism. We could give a mythical account of such contagion by describing a semi-paradisiac state before the fall into language, when a firm distinction was maintained between the nonverbal practice of visual and oral arts, and the verbal practice of criticism of these arts (for it would seem that we can never entirely do without language). And we could describe an equally mythical state of dereliction after the fall, when language has contaminated nonverbal arts (there are letters or words in paintings, and films talk), whereas criticism has gone one step further and been invaded by the science of language, linguistics or semiotics. What is problematic, of course, is not so much the first movement. One could easily show that there have always already been words in paintings (in a sense, Western painting has emerged from the illuminations of capital letters in mediaeval manuscripts), and titles and captions in silent films. This is not necessarily (not at all) a sign of logocentrism: in a famous analysis, Lyotard interprets this,[2] in the case of paintings, as the emergence of the figural (what he calls the 'bad form', bad because not immediately recognizable in the sense of not mimetic – the figural, as opposed to the discursive, is the very reverse of logocentrism). If logocentrism there is, it is to be found in the second movement, the extension of the field of linguistics on to other projects, for instance the 'text' of the film, which will be envisaged

1. Walter Benjamin, letter to T.W. Adorno, 9 December 1938 (my translation), *Briefe*, Surckhamp, Frankfurt, 1966.

2. Jean Francois Lyotard, *Discours, figures*, Klincksieck, Paris 1978, pp135-7.

from the vantage point of a narrative substance, paradigmatically analysed and syntagmatically synthesized.

It is, however, increasingly clear that this form of logocentrism is undergoing a crisis, that a turning point has been reached, which is reflected in the *Zeitgeist*. Linguistics can no longer today because of its internal state of confusion claim to be the imperialistic model it was in the 1960s and 1970s. There are many signs of this: the involution of Chomskian linguistics, the development of alternative fields in the study of language, like critical or feminist linguistics, the return to non-formalist and non-positivist philosophies of language, like Bakhtin's or – this will be my point – Walter Benjamin's. In this context a semiotics of film is no longer the urgent enterprise it used to be. Perhaps the time has come to think again of the cinema outside, or without, linguistic models.

II BENJAMIN'S INTUITIONS

If we go back to the letter to Adorno, Benjamin seems to be saying three things. First, the question of language in the cinema is a political question. The invasion of movies by language is a political intervention, deliberately engineered by a social agent, the film industry, for its own political purposes – to calm down the revolutionary impulses of the masses, to provide a new form of opium for them. One might have thought that the reason for the introduction of this technological innovation would be mainly economic – to capture wider audiences. But it is not. Or rather, since Benjamin harps on the same theme in his celebrated essay on the work of art in an era of mass (mechanical) reproduction, the reasons for the change are inextricably political *and* economic. The new technology is a response to the economic crisis – talking movies, according to Benjamin, have enabled the film industry to attract capital from electrical firms. But there is also a global political response to the crisis – fascism – so that there is a link, even if only indirect, between talking movies and fascism. Benjamin's argument here is contorted: one of the immediate effects of the birth of talkies is that it has restricted the audiences of films, for linguistic reasons, to national audiences (this is before the practice of dubbing has been adopted). At the same moment, the Nazis are insisting on a return to national cultural values. (With hindsight, and coming from a country whose television has been invaded by American soap operas, this argument clearly does not work.) The whole story seems to have an anti-Freudian moral: putting the story into words does not bring awareness but only the worst of illusions (the new opium of the people – modern commonplaces would ascribe this role to TV images, rather than words). Or is it a Freudian moral after all? Keeping things silent preserves the potential violence of desires and symptoms. The silence of silent movies is a locus for the deployment of instinctual drives.

Second, Benjamin suggests that such drives are revolutionary, and silent movies politically progressive. There is nothing obvious in this. We could attempt to explain the statement on historical grounds: this is the quasi-Marxist

Benjamin, the admirer of Brecht and Piscator, and of the use they made of films in their theatre productions. The letter was written when the apex of the tradition of revolutionary films was still the silent movies of Eisenstein (*Battleship Potemkin* rather than *Alexander Newsky*). Perhaps we could even attempt a less contingent justification, and try to analyse talking images, as opposed to silent ones, as a source of illusion, as always already enlisted on the side of the dominant ideology – the passage to talking movies involving a political and ethical dereliction. I doubt, however, that we could construct a convincing argument along those lines, even if the difference between silent and articulated language can be accounted for in no trivial terms within Benjamin's philosophy of language.

Third, and this is the most general, but also the most interesting point: reactions to silent movies are uncontrollable; the silent image fosters violence (which turns out to be revolutionary violence). This is where the shift I have hinted at occurs. Such power is usually ascribed to words – propaganda, pamphlet or slogan, it is discourse which is usually thought to provoke action, raise class consciousness and rouse revolutionary anger. Here, it is the image – and I am not certain that we must interpret Benjamin's praise of silent movies along the lines of Brechtian distanciation – which is seen in terms of Spinozist *conatus*, as force and desire, as the truly performative medium, because it has the immediacy of presentation rather than the distance of representation.

We could derive two consequences from Benjamin's argument. The first is that the struggle within the cinema is a struggle to recapture the idea of the genre, in Benjamin's sense (the *Trauerspiel* as genre, according to him, is an aesthetic quasi-Platonist idea). And this essence of the cinema is pre- and anti-linguistic. The languageless picture is not only the medium of the art, but its essence – films are photographs that move, not pictures that talk. The second consequence is that the political struggle within the cinema concerns the question of the image in a new fashion. Revolutionaries, of the type Benjamin sympathizes with, belong to a culture of discourse – of the slogan, the leaflet, the pamphlet, the resolution, the report to the Central Committee, or even the eight volume treatise. This discourse is heavily sedimented, too dependent on a tradition of discourse really to break new ground. (We may remember here Deleuze and Guattari's version of what linguists know as the 'performative hypothesis': the origin of every utterance, even the most innocuously constative, is a slogan.) The only way to escape from these originary slogans, to cut loose from the unwelcome determinations of origins and open up to the demands of the future is to pass on, before and beyond language, to the immediate revolutionary force of the image.

These consequences are rather trivial. I am not even sure that I can rightly ascribe them to Benjamin. And they have little to do with the actual history of the cinema. However, it seems to me that they suggest a theory of the relation between image and language, which is neither facile nor trivial, and which will cast some light on the question of logocentrism. In order to show this, I must accept two detours, one brief, one long.

The short detour will take us through Walter Benjamin's philosophy of language. To tell you everything at once, what I am looking for is a concept of two levels of language, one which I shall call articulate language (present in talking films, and in all films *qua* narratives) and another which I propose to call general or higher language, one of the characteristics of which is that it is silent (and silently present in nonverbal arts – logocentrism being thus defined as the invasion of articulate language into the realm of general language). Such a concept we find, albeit in a more complex form, in Walter Benjamin's idea of a hierarchy of languages, from the silent language of God to the inarticulate language of things. In between lies the articulate language of man, which, because of its position in the Great Chain of Language, is endowed with contradictory characteristics. On the one hand it has inherited from God and His higher language the power of naming, thus being able to intercede between creation and creator by translating the mute language of anonymous beings into a higher language where they receive proper names (the giving of proper names is the point where man is closest to God).

On the other hand, as a result of the linguistic version of the fall, the language of man has declined into the formulation of judgments (the judgment is the word that formulates a sentence, in both senses of the term). This is where language, as an instrument of judgment and communication, is farthest from God. Translation, therefore, is the name of the human language game, and it has two, contradictory, effects: by naming it intercedes, by communicating it betrays. There is a displaced version of this contradiction in the *Trauerspiel* book, where Benjamin contrasts script and sound, voice and writing.[3] The spoken word, like natural sound, is material, part of the original expression of creation (onomatopoeia is the last trace of this in articulate language). Script, however, is abstract, it is an emanation of pure intellect, the vehicle of *Bedeutung*, of significance. It is in relation with the spoken word and its 'unthinking exaltation' that the term 'ecstasy' appears. Instead of a two term contradiction, we now have a three term gradation: *silence* is the medium of the higher language of creation; *script* is the intermediary and contradictory language of abstraction (which betrays), but also of *Bedeutung* (which is closer to the divine order); *voice* or *sound* is the inarticulate language of material creation, inevitably excluded from the divine realm, yet free of the failings of judgment. The real problem of the talking movies is not that there is sound behind the screen – sound is the brute language of things which echoes in its distant and modest way the silence of the higher language. It is that the sounds are not voices but spoken scripts, attempts at communication and narrative, which no longer translate voices into the higher language of naming, but ineptly babble.

3. see J. Roberts, *Walter Benjamin*, Macmillan, London 1982, p145.

This theological account of the nature of language which lies beneath Benjamin's apparently left-Marxist attack on talking movies, still leaves the exact relationship between image and articulate language in the dark. At best, what I have suggested, without producing a convincing explanation, is that the way out of logocentrism in nonverbal arts is to concentrate not on verbal or articulate language, but on the language of the image; at worst, I am only redoubling the logocentric fallacy by trying to account for the image under a linguistic metaphor. I need to take a second, longer detour, the purpose of which will be to explore the nature of this *ecstasy* which Benjamin ascribes to sound, and which I am proposing to ascribe to images.

III DELAYING WORDS

I shall start with a pessimistic statement, pessimistic from the point of view of my attempt to move away from logocentrism: there is no escaping language. The image, whether it talks or not, whether it moves or not, is caught in language. For, if we follow Benjamin in his Great Chain, language is the medium of all relationship – between things, between men, between things and man, man and God, God and things. I had better stop here, for I am beginning to sound like Beckett's Watt. If I were even more pessimistic than I am, I could even maintain that articulate language, which is after all our main, if not our only, point of access to the Great Chain, is the model, and the locus, for the acting out of all relationships; it is the archetypal medium of translation/intercession. There is a passage in Walter Benjamin's *Berlin Childhood*,[4] where he remembers going butterfly-catching. The real subject of the passage is an account of the relationship (a silent, inarticulate one, in a language dimly perceived by the child as 'foreign') between butterfly and flower. But articulate language is not absent, as the memory of the scene is associated with a word, '*Brauhausberg*' (brewery hill), which triggers it. Proust's *madeleine* is not a sensation, or an image, but a word: there is no escaping the word. So we shall equally celebrate the cinema as language, and language in the cinema as the bearer of the translation process. I could even phrase this in the terms of Merleau-Ponty, by evoking the reversible relationship, or chiasmus, between film and audience. The film is seen by the audience and talks at them: there is a sense in which the audience is gazed upon by the film, not only in those innumerable *abyme* scenes where a film audience is represented on the screen, not only in those innumerable close-ups where a character's face is looking straight at us (in an obvious attempt at interpellation), but in *all* films insofar as the audience's reactions, their viewing, are both anticipated and guided by the film. This chiasmus, that interweaves film and audience, is a dialogue which makes language the very flesh, *la chair*, of the cinema.

4. Walter Benjamin, 'Butterfly-hunting', *Berliner Chronik*, Surckhamp, 1980.

The problem of logocentrism, however, does not lie in this pervasiveness – rather than invasion – of language in films, but rather, as I suggested at the beginning, in the invasion of film criticism by the metalanguage of semiotics. The problem is that, in this type of film analysis, language is a *terminus a quo* rather than *terminus ad quem*. *Terminus a quo* implies that language provides the model for the analysis of films. We do unto films what we do unto texts. A principle of homology allows the importation of concepts and methods. The consequences are that the relationship is one of precedence (language first, film afterwards) and hierarchy (language on top, film beneath). But if the impossibility of escaping language is recognized not as a call for a methodological starting point, but as a goal towards which our hermeneutics of film must strive, in other words, if language in the cinema is a *terminus ad quem*, the situation is reversed. The word, silent at first and vocal afterwards, is what emerges in the movement of the moving picture, and this emergence is what analysis tries to capture, never entirely captures. This tropic movement towards language, this yearning for the word is the essence of non linguistic, as of linguistic, arts. All art is metaphor in the sense of Nietzsche. We must recall that Nietzsche distinguishes between an original tropic movement, where sensation is metaphorized (translated, Benjamin would say) into perception, image and/or sound; and the result of this first trope is metaphorized a second time into articulate language. It is clear here that language as articulate is *not* the necessary goal of the movement, rather a secondary development (whether we interpret it in terms of progress or dereliction is immaterial). And it is also clear that Benjamin's analysis of the birth of talkies is both right and wrong. It is wrong because the passage to the talking movie is always possible, inscribed as it is, as a *terminus ad quem*, in the essence of the cinema; and it is right, because, far from providing the starting point of analysis (where the film is treated as narrative and discourse), it points out that the access to language is only a stage in what I shall soon call the dialectics of language and the image.

Finally, it is also clear that my developments were already foreseen by Benjamin. For this is where I need two different concepts of language. General language it is that cannot be escaped, because it is the medium of all relationship, the tropic movement of established contact, already present in the first Nietzschean metaphor, as sensation is translated into perception. The image Benjamin uses for this is creation (the higher language of God is the only truly creative one). Articulate language is the product of the impulse given by general language, a product neither necessary nor inevitable, although not unwelcome. It appears with Nietszche's second moment of metaphor, when perception is translated into words (words which are, therefore, constitutively metaphorical: Nietzsche's view of language is less Adamic than Benjamin's). If we go back to film, we shall recognise that general language is always present in silent movies; that there may be a lack of higher language in the *bavardage*, the babble of voices in talking films. What is wrong with Benjamin's description is perhaps his historicization of a structural relationship.

Because all this is rather abstract, because I still have to prove that my phrase 'the general language of silent movies' is not merely another logocentric metaphor, I shall relate an experience, or experiment, which I hope will be sufficiently *parlant* to be enlightening. I acquired, some months ago, an ingenious contraption called a video recorder. This ingenious machine has an ingenious function which allows me, when I am watching a film, to interrupt it by freezing the image (I believe this is the right metaphor; the French use the pedestrian phrase, 'stop-at-image'). You understand the title of this section: the effect of this ingenious function is that it delays the word by stopping the film. For there are two immediate consequences to my pressing the requisite button:

there is no longer any movement on the screen, and there is no sound. My talking movie no longer moves or talks, reduced as it is to what as an adolescent I used to watch with great interest while queueing at the cinema entrance: a still.

Let us make a thought experiment. Suppose we are watching *I Vitelloni*, Fellini's second film, and that I have frozen one image, towards the middle of the film. The scene now 'represents', as the phrase goes, a street at night, in the small Italian town where this autobiographical film is set. Everything is silent – the night is silent, the characters, lost in their egotistic worlds, are silent, on top of which, of course, the machine is now silent. There is silence everywhere, and yet there is language everywhere. First, what is this image we are now looking at, if not sedimented language, crying out for articulate description and recognition? You are, in fact, since I am referring to a precise moment in the film, waiting for me to describe it, in order to try and recognize it in your memory. You would recognize it if I described it (which I won't) because of the image's 'good form' (to speak like Lyotard), because of what he would call the massive presence in it of the discursive as opposed to the figural. There is such a thing as the 'Italianness' of Italian cities (and indeed in the middle of my image a shop sign reads 'Tabacchi'). The sediment in which this Italianness is made manifest is language: language is the very material of the image, crying out for articulate expression.

Even in terms of film technique, or of the analysis of photographs, the linguistic nature of the image has a name. Barthes calls it *studium*,[5] something similar to what is known in painting as composition. There is discursivity implicit in the very term 'study': the image is constructed as one builds up words into sentences, sentences into texts, and it is deciphered according to its syntax – the double articulation of language is the model for all syntax (meaningless elements regroup into meaningful higher units). The *studium* in the picture takes us dangerously close to articulate language.

5. Roland Barthes, *La Chambre claire*, Gallimard/Seuil, 1980, Paris pp47-9.

But in Barthes's analysis, the *studium* of a photograph is only a background, or a foil, for its *punctum*, the random and arbitrary point that breaks up the carefully composed structure and makes the image striking (or perhaps one should say 'piercing', as one talks of a 'piercing look'). And indeed, whether or not there is a recognizable *punctum* in it, the image is also something entirely different, something thoroughly nonlinguistic. It affects, or strikes, the audience *en bloc*, as a whole, and not merely as a composition. It is only analysis that produces composition – in the case of films, the artificial technique of freezing the movie, thus turning a dynamic into a static art. This overall effect of the picture can be referred to by other names. We will say of the image that it exerts visual force, like a successful performative aesthetic experience (perhaps we should call this 'invisionary force', on the model of 'illocutionary force'); that it produces an intuition in the audience, like a successful metaphor; that it has rhythm, like prosody. My points of comparison, you will object, are still linguistic, and we haven't left language. But performativity, metaphor and rhythm are precisely those parts of language that articulacy cannot reach: they lie beyond the dichotomies of articulacy, the true and the false, the literal and the figurative, syntagma and paradigm. They escape the analysis and synthesis of double articulation. In these regions, articulate language is always already, constitutively, delayed. Here, the image, on the way towards the higher form of language, general language, recovers its independence. We can give the force it exerts on the reader the name Benjamin used for sound as opposed to script: ecstasy. In theology this experience (this sense of fulfilment which the image gives beyond its sedimented and conventional Italianness, beyond the conventional nostalgia of the morning after the night before – we recognize the great Fellinian theme of '*les lendemains de fête*') is called epiphany, in love crystallization. We crystallize, for no obvious reason, on this image, which strikes us as memorable – I am, in fact, thinking of a specific shot in *I Vitelloni*.

Perhaps it is a little too easy to treat the frozen image on my video recorder as an embodiment of the language of silence, of non-articulate language. When I press the switch, the movie starts again; the music and the voices come back, a babble of articulate language, which is mere 'noise', in the technical sense of interference, to my ecstasy. The frozen film-image has a dual, a contradictory, nature: freezing the film means breaking the rhythm and betraying the art; but it also interrupts the babble and concentrates on the ecstasy. This is, Benjamin would argue, where silent movies show revolutionary aesthetic potential: they favour the ecstasy of the silent language of the image.

The status of the articulate commentary (including my own) now becomes clear. In classic Freudian terms, going from films to commentary involves a process of loss and gain – the loss of epiphanic force (as the capture of the subject by the order of signifiers involves the loss of her ineffable truth), and the gain of a dynamism which can mimic the dynamism of moving pictures (as the capture of the subject by language opens up the field of human relationships for him). Even if the babble hinders the ecstasy, there is a relationship of homology between moving pictures and talk: the rhythm of speech accompanies and fosters, as a form of background music, the rhythm of ecstasy. Freezing the image calls for a rhythm which is, at the same time, denied. (This is the difference between a film and a painting, where the rhythm is present in the programmed movement of the eyes of the spectator.) Speech unfreezes this rhythm: there lies the glory of talking movies, which not even Benjamin should deny.

My analysis, however, ends on some sort of aporia. The language of the image, the language of silence, what I have called general language, is ecstatic but static. Articulate language, on the other hand, is garrulous but dynamic, an active process of translation, language bursting into song.

In the usual paranoid fashion, I shall try to turn this aporia into a dialectic – the dialectic of language and the image, of general and articulate language. I am sorry to say it has five stages.

At stage 1, the image is still, or frozen. We have pressed the switch. This is a static moment of immediacy, the 'this' of the image: this is it, then. This immediate intuition is silent. We are in fact in the first stage of the Hegelian dialectic of sensation, the moment of *pure sensation*. There is no need of articulate language here: the image as pure presentation occupies the whole scene.

At stage 2, the image, still frozen, appears as a composition. We recognize the scene for what it is; it has a structure, which is the structure of discourse. Formally, it can be described in structural terms, as figure against background, for instance. Materially, it sediments older discourses (there is articulate language in sedimentation: what is sedimented is old phrases, sentences, catchwords). We have now reached the second stage of Hegel's dialectic of sensation: pure sensation is abstracted into language by naming. Articulate language now dominates the image. Using words implies that the image is not only cognized but recognized. In Hegel's terms, we have moved from sensation to *perception* (where we perceive forms which are such because informed by language). The words that the image utters are silent, but potentially (and, in the past of the image, materially) articulated.

At stage 3, the image, still frozen but recognized, is perceived as a whole. This is the moment of *intuition* or *impression* (I am leaving Hegel for good here). The image strikes, exerts its invisionary force, produces effects – the main effect on the audience is that of intuition in advance of understanding. This is no longer the 'this' of sensation but the 'that' of epiphany: so *that*'s it (after all). The image, as Spinozist *conatus*, now overshadows articulate language, goes far beyond it. The silent image is perceived in a flash (we are going from metaphors of hearing to metaphors of sight). No words are needed, and no discourse. Something occurs of the nature of what Lyotard calls the 'figural'. We could also remember here Walter Benjamin's description of the cine-camera as opening up for us the experience of the visual unconscious.[6]

6. Walter Benjamin, 'The Work of Art in the Age of Mechanical Reproduction', *Illuminations*, Fontana, London 1973.

At stage 4, the switch has been pressed, the image now moves. This move reintroduces articulate language in two ways. The first is obvious, as we have seen: the sound-track is back. The second is more important: the moving and talking image narrates. It is part of a syntagmatic chain. The talking movie talks in its images; so does, of course, the silent film. A story is being told; which can, or even has to be, retold in articulate language. In this moment of external understanding of the image as part of the narrative chain, articulate language, as the model for all semiosis, dominates the image. Words, not merely general language pervade: this is the explicit moment of what Lyotard calls the discursive.

At the fifth stage, our moving image is perceived as endowed with rhythm. The dynamic process of the moving image takes us from the mere crystallization or epiphany of static intuition (as in the illumination of suddenly realizing the force of a successful metaphor) to the climax of a rhythmic ecstasy – perhaps we should distinguish this from epiphany (the third stage) and reserve Benjamin's term for this, the fifth stage. Here the higher language of divine creation is, if not reached, which is impossible, at least approached. It is not so much that articulate language is here cancelled by the image, rather the rhythmic image takes us beyond articulacy and relegates it to the important yet subordinate place of a moment of transmission between the static image (Benjamin's language of objects) and its dynamic counterpart (Benjamin's creative language, striving towards divine language). Rhythmic intuition is both way beyond articulate language and into the higher language, which does not use words, and born by the rhythm of spoken language. At this stage, there is mutual contamination between image and articulate language. Articulate language contaminates the image by giving it rhythm; the image, if I may coin the verb, 'intuitions' articulate language. This is what metaphor is about.

I could give a Nietzschean account of this state of affairs. Articulate language is both bee and spider: it constructs (in perception) and imprisons (in narrative). It finds its freedom when liberated by the Saturnalia not of itself, but of the image, that takes it back to its origin in music and scream. This is my definition of the image – the Saturnalia of language, or the silent scream of the screen.

IV ECSTASY AND DISCOURSE

The problem, as I have tried to show, is not to oppose image and articulate language, but to understand their interweaving (*entrelacs*) and chiasmus, to use Merleau-Ponty's terms. The flesh of the higher language is the reversible relationship between image and articulate language.[7]

7. See M. Merleau-Ponty, *Le Visible et l'invisible*, Gallimard, Paris 1964.

To help us understand this better, I shall pretend to look at another picture, Franju's *Les Yeux Sans Visage*, and especially at one scene, where the ecstasy comes through horror – a black or, as Susan Sontag says, a negative epiphany. And truly the scene I am going to describe, in my own articulate words, is unbearable – a feeling necessarily betrayed by the description, which will nicely prove my point. The unbearable scene is not the climactic moment when the heroine lifts off her mask at last, thus revealing a face hardly human because of horrible burns. It is that other scene when the heroine's father, the evil surgeon played by Pierre Brasseur, operates on the kidnapped victim, and lifts off her face, which he wants to graft on to his daughter. We have a series of images (no need to freeze them here), which are:

a) silent (nobody says anything of course);

b) full of silent discourse (implicit discourses on the progress of science and the ethical questions it raises, on the state of the art of plastic surgery, on medical voyeurism as made famous a few years later by the celebrated medical programmes on French TV, on the myth of Frankenstein and its previous film versions of which this is an inverted transposition);

c) rhythmic – the horror is due not to the static sight of the helpless, drugged and bound victim, but to a series of movements: the lifting of the skin, little by little, inch by inch, from a face that is alive (we are witnessing what was always described in the cowboy films of my childhood as the ultimate horror – the lady is being scalped);

d) last, the scene exerts maximum invisionary force – the voyeuristic spectator is spellbound, nerves tingling with ambiguous horror.

In a few seconds (the shot lasts hardly more than that) we run through the whole dialectic of image and language. And articulate language is both strikingly absent from the scene, and yet implicitly present in two forms: first, as an inescapable moment of the experience itself, since our response to the horror of the scene, like Benjamin's butterfly-hunting memory, is triggered by words – words like 'scalpel' (French for 'surgical knife') and 'scalping', words that are, in the terms of another Benjamin, reservoirs of semantic potentialities which the image draws upon;[8] and second, as an inescapable instrument, after the event, nay during the event, of the formulation of our experience – not only the rather sedate words in which I have related the experience, but in the immediate exclamation of horror, 'Oh my God, he is scalping her!'.

8. A. Benjamin, *Translation and the Nature of Philosophy*, Routledge, London 1989, pp34-5, 126.

I have just used the word 'instrument'. That, for a philosopher of language, is a danger word. I could indeed attack my own analysis in two ways. I could show that we can have a similar experience through the sole medium of articulate language (Kurtz's 'the horror, the horror' immediately comes to mind), and even that articulate language is the better medium for this kind of ecstasy; I could also argue that at the bottom of this visual experience, there is always a word, or a text. Thus the whole scene is not only a commentary on the word 'scalp', but also on the word 'horror' itself – that face-lift is etymologically hair-raising. This could all be so except that, of course, the movement is entirely reversible: the origin of the word 'horror' is a visual metaphor, and linguistic horror works because it produces, if not strictly visual mental images, at least a perlocutionary effect which I might as well call pervisionary affect.

V CONCLUSION

It may seem that I sought to replace an obvious form of logocentrism (words have invaded visual arts) by an equally naïve, if more contorted, form of the same attitude: I have been trying to speak of words in terms of images (this referential illusion is, some would say, the highest point of logocentrism). In fact, what I have tried to do is to be faithful to the contradictory relationship between language and image, to their chiasmus, which in a fit of Hegelian delusion of grandeur I have called dialectic (should I have said dia-optic?). I have tried to be faithful to the paradox of their interweaving (the image is pervaded with general language; articulate language represses rhythmic language – performatives, metaphor, rhythm – which duly returns), of their mutual repulsion (the image threatens articulate language and is betrayed by it) and of their reciprocal dominance (language is visual, the image linguistic). My theme has been this version of the chiasmus, which accepts and denies Benjamin's assessment of the birth of talking movies: the talking picture is a seeing text.

CONFLICTING CHOREOGRAPHIES

DERRIDA AND DANCE

Sandra Kemp

> I am only asking you what is dance; each of you respectively appears to know; but to know it quite separately! The one tells me that it is what it is, and can be reduced to what our eyes see here; and the other holds very strongly that it REPRESENTS something, and is therefore not entirely in itself, but principally in us. As for me, my friends, my uncertainty is intact!
>
> Valery, 'Dance and the Soul'

This epigraph outlines the first concern of my paper: the relation between the interpretative and the expressive, or what might be called the 'translatability' problem in criticism. I would suggest that we come closest to the expressive in the first reading of a text, or in the experiences of watching a dance. An apt metaphor for this would be the distinction between programme notes and audience response: programme notes dwell on things that are usually imperceptible, unintelligible, or simply irrelevant to the audience. However, it is also the case, as Freud points out, that audiences can be resistant to the emotional effect of art, and derive pleasure from more intellectual comprehension. Speaking of himself, Freud says: 'Some rationalistic, or perhaps analytic, turn of mind in me rebels against being moved by a thing without knowing why I am affected and what it is that affects me.'[1]

Clearly then, 'translatability' is a matter of *how* we see, and of how we *respond* to what we see. It requires the realignment of subject and object, and especially the resolution of the contradictions between subject and object in their symbolic identification. As Baudelaire remarks:

> Faced with an object taken from nature and represented by sculpture – that is to say, a round, three dimensional object about which one can move freely, and like the natural object itself, enveloped in atmosphere – the peasant, the savage, or the primitive man feels no indecision; whereas a painting, because of its immense pretensions and its paradoxical and abstractive nature, will disquiet and upset him.[2]

It is significant that a number of post-Enlightenment philosophers turned to the expressive arts to resolve problems of knowledge, perception and cognition. This is particularly the case with music (and I would argue, by extension, with dance) because, as Hanslick points out, in these arts it is harder to distinguish between time and space, and between *affect* and thinking (i.e., you – the reader, the viewer – are supposedly more in control when turning the pages of a book, or looking at a painting, which you can do in your own time):

Earlier versions of this paper were given at Yale and at Cornell Universities in April 1991. I am grateful to Sally Banes, Lynn Enterline, Lynne Huffer, and Carla Kaplan for their comments.

1. Quoted in Pinchas Noy, 'The Psychodynamic Meaning of Music. A Critical Review of the Psychoanalytic and Related Literature', *Journal of Music Therapy*, Vol 3, no 4, 1966, p127.

2. *Salon of 1859*. Quoted in Naomi Schor, *Reading in Detail*, 1987, p131.

Without mental activity no aesthetic enjoyment is possible. But the kind of mental activity alluded to is quite peculiar ... because its products, instead of being fixed and presented to the mind at once in their completeness, develop gradually *and thus do not permit the listener to linger at any point or to interrupt his train of thought*..[3]

Not surprisingly then, for twentieth-century philosophers and theorists, the metaphor of *performance* creeps into, and becomes crucial in criticism of the arts, including supposedly 'unperformed' literature. In 'Funny Voices: Stories, Punctuation and Personal Identity', Jonathan Ree argues that:

> Many readers find it almost impossible to avoid approaching novels as schema for vocal performances, comparable to playscripts or vocal scores; we imagine the words spoken in specific voices, male or female, young or old, and with particular timings, pitches, dynamics or pronunciations. We gesticulate, chuckle, grunt and sigh. Some of us, in fact, can get quite hoarse after a couple of hours absorption in a good novel.[4]

This paper is framed by the question of why in the last couple of decades, so many contemporary literary theorists (for example, Derrida in *Choreographies*, and Annette Kolodny in *Dancing Through the Minefield*), use the metaphor of *dance* to represent their ideas, and in particular to signal the ways in which questions of theory are bound up with the material spread of language – its 'utterances', and its graphic distribution in space.

On this issue, the same question arises in all forms of criticism: how to put together the separate images that exist side by side in a painting, or in a literary text, or the simultaneous movements on stage of a dance. The art historian Barbara Cropper sees Caravaggio's paintings as collapsing the literary and the figural, the allegoric and the imitative, drawing our attention to the space between the symbolic and the real.[5] Touring Italy, Virginia Woolf was impressed by a fresco by Perugino: 'Each part has a dependence on the others; they compose one idea in his mind. That idea has nothing to do with what can be put into words.' By extension, Beiswanger in 'Doing and Viewing Dances: A Perspective for the Practice of Criticism' points out:

> This is to confuse art-making with message-bearing, as if participating in dance consisted of translating signs and symbols into images and feeling, conceptions and beliefs. If this were the heart of the matter, we would have reason to despair, for the 'there' of a dance would fade away and be lost (as it often is) in the 'meaning', the 'interpretation', the 'say' attributed to it. Everyone would have his own version of what the dance 'said', and there would be no way to get back to the dance's actuals, in which we all initially share.[6]

In this respect, the 'in-betweenness' of non-translatability is both non-

3. Quoted in Nicholas Cook (my emphasis), *Music, Imagination and Culture*, 1990, p42. See also Adam Smith, 'Of the Nature of That Imitiation Which Takes Place in What are Called the Imitative Arts', W.P.D. Wightman and J.C. Bryce (eds), *Essays on Philosophical Subjects*, 190, pp176-213.

4. *New Literary History*, Vol 21, 1990, p1046. Ree also notes: 'Charles Dickens wrote with public performance in mind. Sometimes he would act out his scenes before writing them down ... He had a mirror in his writing room, which he used in the same way that a composer uses a piano, to try how a passage will go in performance.' (p1045). See also Ursula Le Guin, 'Text, Silence, Performance', *Dancing at the Edge of the World: Thoughts on Words, Women, Places*, 1989, pp180; 184-5: 'People used to be aware that the written word was the visible sign of an audible sign. Apparently if the Romans saw somebody sitting reading silently to themself they nudged each other and sniggered ... A lot of the stuff we were taught to read silently – Jane! You are moving your lips! – reads better out loud. Reading aloud is of course the basic test of a kid's book.'

5. Quoted in Quentin Bell, *Virginia Woolf: A Biography*, vol 1, p138.

6. *Dance Perspectives: Three Essays in Dance*

metaphorical, and non-linear, precisely a question of the rearrangement of space. Juliet Dusinberre argues in 'The Literary and the Real' that:

> The suggestiveness of the metaphor itself imposes limits on perception ... It is not true that a rose by any other name would smell as sweet, or, as Bergson argues, that it smells different to every individual sniffer – because literature has given the rose a special place in perception. Nor is it that perception is the privilege of the well-educated because the symbolic rose has become so popularised that it usurps the real flower. Only a small child can smell a rose without romance.[7]

In 'Choreographies' Derrida's emphasis is on the non-linear, and on the discontinuous. It begins with a reference to Emma Goldmann – 'a maverick feminist from the nineteenth century who once said of the feminist movement: "If I can't dance, I don't want to be part of your revolution."' Derrida continues:

> Perhaps your maverick feminist was thinking of a completely other history: a history of paradoxical laws and non-dialectical discontinuities, a history of absolutely heterogeneous pockets, irreducible particularities, of unheard of and incalculable sexual differences: a history of women who have 'gone further' by stepping back with their lone dance.[8]

While literary theorists turn to the *performative* for their interpretative models, it's satisfying for my purposes, that the current turn towards narrative in dance, especially in postmodern dance, suggests that performance is examining the supplement of language. (I'm not saying that dance *needs* to be supplemented by language, but that so many theories are currently turning to the interdisciplinary to explain themselves suggests that the performative arts, like dance, contain multiple forms within themselves.)

As Sally Banes points out, the generation of choreographers that emerged in the 1980s had an insatiable appetite for narratives of all kinds: autobiography, biography, fiction, political document, interview, the use of sign language and other emblematic gesture systems. The pursuit of the story led Yvonne Rainer (whose *Trio A* was the *Finnegan's Wake* of dance) from dance *per se* into performance art, then film. The classic ballet had advanced plot through mute pantomime, but in postmodern dance the narration takes place on two simultaneous levels – verbal commentary and dancing. This has irritated and confused critics. Thus Cyril Beaumont comments on Frank Staff's version of *Peter and the Wolf* for the Ballet Rambert: 'The musical expression is so clear, and the verbal description is so vivid, the dancing seems superfluous.' The new model is, on the one hand, deliberately literal-minded. But the redundancy along multiple channels (a poetics of exhaustion), or the multi-layered 'text' punctured by allusions, subtexts, plural voices, heighten the irony. Both avant-garde and retrogressive, even its adult sophistication is yet another

Aesthetics, Vol 55, Autumn 1973, p11. Writing on the interviews with choreographers at the 1991 *Dance Umbrella Festival*, David Hughes notes: 'We have the impossible expectation of these sessions that the people who make their work with gesture should be able to articulate it at all levels through language ... And what tacitly underlies these sessions is the idea that the artists will tell us what the pieces are about. Understandably most are rather reluctant to do this.' *Dance Theatre Journal*, Vol 8, no 4, Spring 1991, pp17-18.

7. *Alice To the Lighthouse: Children's Books and Radical Experiments in Art*, 1987, p222.

8. *Diacritics*, vol 12, no 2, Summer 1982, pp67-8.

playful pose.[9]

Postmodern dance then foregrounds the issues I have been raising – of meaning and cognition, of appearance and reality, and of things as physical symbols and things as objects. Its reflexive relations with language are riskily creative. Sally Banes suggests that postmodern dance can have its cake and eat it in a way that the non-performing arts can never do, by combining 'the polymorphous pleasure of the body, with the adult pleasure of the analysis of the text'.[10]

II

> I mean that the ballerina IS NOT A GIRL DANCING ... and that SHE DOES NOT DANCE but rather, with miraculous lunges and abbreviations, writing with her body, she suggests things which the written word could EXPRESS only in several paragraphs of dialogue or descriptive prose. Her poem is written without the writer's tools.
>
> Mallarmé, 'Ballets'

The second epigraph primarily concerns 'writing with the body', or the bodily ground of critical response. It is generally accepted that only children and idiots move their lips when reading. Conversely that reading aloud is the basic test of a good children's book.[11] But in the performing arts, the intersections of speech, writing, text and body (the reflexive relations of dance and language), have led to new critical strategies. My concern here is with the ways in which we express 'affect' in criticism, or in the relation between abstraction and emotion. Again, the musicologists are to the point. Rose Rosengard Subotnik comments in 'Toward a Deconstruction of Structural Listening':

> As a music major, and later as a teacher, listening to scratched and otherwise dreadful monophonic recordings, I developed a strategy of listening which I have never entirely shaken, whereby I mentally 'correct' for inadequacies of sound or performance that distract from my structural concentration ... Is it possible that encouraging less dependence on the score when we listen, and on ways of perceiving that the score itself suggests, might help us to develop new and richer ways of speaking about music? And might not such an expanded language enhance even our conception of how structure operates, and what it signifies, in music?[12]

And in *Music, Imagination and Culture*, Nicholas Cook remarks:

> And in any case, music is full of things which even trained musicians find hard or impossible to hear in terms of their structural organisation; serial structures are merely the most obvious of these. What is more, people who can follow a piece in technical terms do not necessarily do so when they listen to it in the normal way, that is to say for pleasure ...

9. For postmodern dance see Sally Banes, ' "Happily Ever After"? The Postmodern Fairytale and the New Dance', unpublished article.

10. *Ibid.*

11. See note 4 above.

12. In Eugene Naramour and Ruth A. Solie (eds), *Explorations in Music: The Art and the Ideas*, pp120-1.

> And one might conclude from all this that the conventional theory of music, in which sonata forms, tonal structures, and thematic relationships play so large a part is no more than a theory of unheard of forms, imaginary structures and fictitious relationships.[13]

It is, of course, tempting to see readers, writers, dancers and audiences as mythical sites where the body, speechless and uncorrupted, plays. But this is to miss the *always already* inscribed hierarchies of power – what the literary critic Hortense Spillers calls 'the exquisite dance of textual priorities'.[14]

Again, this is where the expressive, or the performative, arts can provide an alternative to the repetitive tendency in literary theory to translate words into pure sign (Barthes calls this taking the 'event' out of language).[15] Adorno projects a time when 'the silent, imaginative reading of music could render actual playing superfluous.'[16] By contrast, it is difficult to dispense with the awareness of the body in dance, or at least, in modern dance.[17] It is, as I have said, the case that the body is already culturally conditioned or inscribed. But however well you may be acquainted with the history of, say, the dance piece (every technique involved in it, the choreographic design, at the *time* of watching), something else is at stake. This 'something else' exists in the moments of the dance *as they happen*. It doesn't exist before or after, and is not susceptible to existing forms of critical analysis. The 'figure' of dance, as the second epigraph suggests, is a space within but not reducible to the space of language. Theatre, from the Greek 'Theatron' means 'seeing space'. To take time and space as self-evident phenomena, as so often happens in dance, is to fail to perceive that movement creates its own time and space, that time and space are not containers which movement fills to varying degrees. What interests me here in terms of *affect* in criticism, is that I suspect most criticism rests on too simple a binary opposition between the intellect and the senses. Nietzsche, writing on Carmen, has a lovely account of the interpretative movement which is both thought, and entirely without thought:

> I tremble before the dangers which this daring music runs. And, strange to say, at bottom I do not give it a thought, or am not aware how much thought I readily do give it. For quite other ideas are running through my head all the while. Has anyone observed that the more one becomes a musician, the more one is also a philosopher? The grey sky of abstraction seems thrilled by flashes of lightning.[18]

III

> Word spoken and note sung both enter the mind through that whorled and delicately fleshy gateway the ear. Poem written or song written come through that crystalline receiver of quanta the eye, in search of the inner, the mental ear. In music, this eye detour is a convenience, an adjunct only; music goes on being what is sounded and what is heard. But the written

13. *Ibid.*, pp2-3.

14. Quoted in Nancy Miller, *Getting Personal*, 1991, p81. I am indebted to Nancy Miller for drawing my attention to the link between theory and metaphors of performance in the draft of the 'Dreaming, Dancing and the Changing Locations of Feminist Criticism' chapter of this book.

15. See also Le Guin, *op.cit.*, pp182-3: 'Originally music was recited just as verbal text was (and we still say "recital" for a solo performance of music). It was performed from memory, by imitation and rote learning, more or less exactly repeating an original, with considerable latitude for variations, or else improvised according to strong, guiding conventions of structure and technique.

Notation – the writing of music and the means of printing it and now the photoreproduction technology that makes even manuscript infinitely reproducible – had a huge effect on both the composition and the performance of music. Yet there is a lot of music that actively resists or evades notation, including some of the liveliest contemporary music (jazz, synthesizer composition). And written music in this case did not replace performance. We don't go to the symphony or the rock concert and each

word found a detour past both outer ear and inner ear to nonsensory understanding. A kind of short-circuit, a way round the body. Written text can be read as pure sign, as meaning alone. When we started doing that, the word stopped being an event.[19]

Ursula Le Guin, *Dancing At the Edge of the World*

As the curtain goes up on *Shelf Life*, the dancers' costumes resemble the torn pages of a printed book. The text is narrated and sung by Eckert in a marvellous counter-tenor voice, as he strolls about the stage. The music is by Dreiser. The gritty narrative concerns a man who breaks up with his girlfriend, and takes off in a 1966 Buick, a stack of paperbacks on the backseat, whose contents melt together as he drives along.

> Six novels packed between the big books. Question. If the paperbacks spend long enough time together, will they share secrets, will they bleed like new clothes in the first wash.[20]

Eckert is mixing and matching the characters from six books to tell of the break-up of his disastrous four-year affair. Or, another way of interpreting the action would be to ask, as did the *Ham and High* reviewer of the first British performance of *Shelf Life*: 'Have you ever muddled up characters from different novels, put them in each other's plots and let them take the consequences?' It is 'an impenetrable thriller', he concludes.[21]

In *Shelf Life*, the movements are as eclectic as the texts. This lends another dimension to the word, and to the notion of *performance*, in 'performance art'. Many would say that *Shelf Life* is not a dance but should be contained under the rubric of this new genre.[22] Drawn from 'gymnastics, oriental dance, pantomime, various moves from the martial arts, religious and spiritual movements and floor-stretching exercises, the movements also include abrupt gestures and unusual lifts and carries. The choreographic emphasis on hand movements – quick staccato gestures constantly brought into play – accompanies rhythmic steps to minimalist music.' As the narrative proceeds, the dancers and narrator converge and collide on stage.

The result is certainly bizarre. Most reviewers express more or less complete bafflement. The following response, from the *Chattanooga Times*, is characteristic:

> However, while stimulating the imagination and the intellect of many in attendance, they left still others gasping for words to describe the experience.[23]

At the same time, however, the *Chattanooga Times* reviewer succinctly poses the question behind my paper: why do we feel the need to describe? Is this because words are the only possible medium for criticism?

The genesis of *Shelf Life* is perhaps relevant in this respect. The

sit there reading a printed score in silence.

But that's exactly what we do in the library.

Why did it happen to words and not to music? A dumb question, but I need an answer to it. Which, I guess might be that the note is purely a sound, the word impurely a sound. The word is a sound that symbolizes, has significance; though it is not pure information, it is or can function as a sign. Insofar as it is a sign it can be replaced by another sign, equally arbitrary, and this sign can be a visual one. The note, having no symbolic value in itself, no "meaning", can't be replaced by a sign. It can only be indicated by one.

Word spoken and note sung both enter the mind through that whorled and delicate fleshy gateway the ear. Poem written or song written come through that crystalline receiver of quanta the eye, in search of the inner, the mental ear. In music, this eye detour is a convenience, an adjunct only; music goes on being what is sound and what is heard. But the written word found a detour past both outer ear and inner ear to nonsensory understanding. A kind of short-circuit, a way round the body. Written text can be read as pure sign, as meaning alone. When we started doing that, the word stopped being an event.'

choreographer, Jenkins works 'collaboratively' with her dancers. Her programme notes emphasize that 'the dancers play an essential role in suggesting, adapting and shaping the overall structure of each work'. Whilst working on *Shelf Life* Jenkins asked each of the dancers to choose a favourite novel and a single character from that novel. The final list comprised: *A Taste of Time*, by Ferol Egan; *Death is a Lonely Business*, by Ray Bradbury; *Even Cowgirls Get the Blues*, by Tom Robbins; *Places in the World a Woman Could Walk*, by Janet Kauffman, *Sometimes a Great Notion*, by Ken Kesey; and *Valley of the Horses*, by Jean Auel.[24] Movement was composed from each dancer's unique temperament and point of view. The script and the soundscript (by Eckert and Dreiser) were generated around this.

In the end what is significant, however, is that the final image is indeed 'impenetrable'. 'It is as dissonant and as discontinous as Dreiser's electronic sound-score. The images are set up as signposts that point, but never tell the way.' There is no traditional plot or structure. The viewer is made to feel increasingly introspective about the processes of seeing. 'How we frame questions about what is happening on stage shapes our answers.' Each detail breaks down into the next. 'As the narrative proceeds, we are forced to relinquish the relative security of a single vision, the desire to see it all.' But at the same time, *Shelf Life* forces us to pay attention to the tiniest details of our own perceptions.

Like Cunningham, Jenkins has democratized the stage space, 'forcing us to decide *independently* whether we will follow simultaneous actions that occur in the foreground, background, left or right.'[25] Jenkins's work is less about form and content, than about *how* we see. The dancing is 'sharp, angular and proceeds in explosive spurts, as if the movements were illuminated and captured for one intense millisecond by a blinding strobe light.' The fragmented surface detail even extends to the costumes. Sarah Woodall describes how she wanted the audience to respond to the idea of books as objects. She designed all the costumes in creamy, raw silk rolled in colour 'like the edges of the pages in some mass-market paperback', and she silk-screened the fabric with a collage of words xeroxed directly from the covers of the books, to convey a sense of their 'surface quality'.[26]

The effect of *Shelf Life* is similar to Greenberg's conception of modernist and some postmodern art:

A repudiation of all symbolism and intellectual interpretation ... rather the significant qualities that are immanent in the purely sensuous structures of perceptual experience ...

To render substance entirely optical, and form, whether pictorial, sculptural or architectural, as an integral part of ambient space – this brings anti-illusionism full circle. Instead of the illusion of things, we are now offered the illusion of modalities; namely, that matter is incorporeal, weightless and exists only optically, like a mirage.[27]

16. Adorno, quoted in Subotnik, p104.

17. See Adam Smith, 'Of the Imitative Arts', in W.P.D. Wightman and J.C. Bryce (eds), *Essays in Philosophical Subjects*, 1980.

18. T.N. Foulis (ed.), *The Case of Wagner: A Musician's Problem*, (1888), 1911, pp2-3.

19. *Ibid.*, p193.

20. Quoted in David Gere, 'The Making of a New Dance', p19.

21. Review by Keith Watson, *Ham and High*, 9 November 1990, p95.

22. Noel Caroll, 'Performance'.

23. Review by Nikki C. Hasden, *The Chattanooga Times*, Vol CXVIII, no 261, 17 October 1987.

24. See programme notes for the first performance in 1987. The dancers were James Aarons, Susan Chilcote, Martin Gould, Ellie Klopp, Anne Kraus and Jesse Traschen.

25. See reviews by Rita Felciano, *The San Francisco Bay Guardian*, Vol 24, no 49, 12 September 1990; by Kathrine Sorley Walker, *The Daily Telegraph*, 7 November 1990; and by Paul Hertelendy, *San Jose Mercury News*, 3 April 1987. I have quoted from these reviews to 'translate' *Shelf Life* in interpretation.

26. Quoted in David Gere, *op.cit.*, p19.

Postmodern literary theorists (I'm thinking of Barthes, Derrida, Foucault here) have been concerned to break down texts into what Barthes calls 'useless details', in order to rearrange subject, object and space. Barthes' image for the graphic distribution of the text is the *haiku*:

> Neither describing, nor defining, the haiku diminishes to the point of pure and sole designation ... permanently alienated definition ...
>
> The haiku, articulated around a metaphysics without subject and without God, is apprehension of the thing as event and not as substance.[28]

Like Derrida's *Grammatology*, Barthes' is a reading that accepts the spatial, the figurative, the fragmentary. Both reject the *linearity* of the sentence, paragraph etc. Accordingly, a Derridean reading (Hortense Spillers', for example) would participate in the dance of language itself.[29] This would be similar to the kind of 'creative' criticism often demanded *within* modern and postmodern texts as described by Naomi Schor. If interpretation is something done *in* rather than *to* texts, Schor argues that:

> It is a 'creative' rather than a critical activity; in *In the Cage* the young woman is not content merely to encode and decode, rather she delights in filling the gaps, piecing together the fragments, in short adding something of her own to the faulty, often trivial texts in hand ... The results of this unbridled imagination are 'stories and meanings without end'.[30]

It is a reading which doesn't try to privilege any single or individual element by fusion, or by placing it in a hierarchy, but which exists in the gaps between the different elements.

To stay with Barthes for a moment. Barthes' 1968 essay 'The Reality Effect' is one of the earliest theoretical attempts to show that interpretation need not be equated with translation:

> As soon as discourse is no longer guided and limited by structural imperatives ... nothing could indicate why we should halt the details of the description here and not there; if it were not subject to an aesthetic or rhetorical choice, any 'view' would be inexhaustible by discourse; there would always be a corner, a detail, an inflection of space or colour to report ...
>
> When, under the influence of the von Frisch's experiments, it was assumed that bees had a language, it had to be realized that, while these insects possessed a predictive system of dances (in order to collect their food), nothing in it approached a *description*. This description appears as a characteristic of the so-called higher languages, to the apparently paradoxical degree that it is justified by no finality of action or communication.[31]

27. Quoted in David Michael Levin, 'Balanchine's Formalism', p34.

28. Roland Barthes, *Empire of Signs*, 1982, p83.

29. See note 14 above.

30. Naomi Schor, 'Fiction as Interpretation/ Interpretation as Fiction, in Susan Suleiman (ed.), *The Reader in the Text*, 1989, p171.

31. Roland Barthes, 'The Reality Effect', *The Rustle of Language*, 1989, pp142-3.

Elsewhere, Barthes call this the 'unreal reality' of language ('Not that which resists meaning, but rather that which remains after meaning has been excavated'), a linguistic model in which to interpret is not to impoverish by setting up a shadow world of meanings.[32]

In *Grammatology* Derrida's focus is on the microscopic and the marginal. Foucault too examines the play of discontinuities, and the textual non-sequiturs, as it were. Detail, as Alan Liu points out,

> is the very instrument of the anti-foundational and the anti-epistemological imperative in high cultural criticism: its contention is that there is no reason why contexts of discretely perceived particulars should resolve into culture as a single, grounded and knowable order. The emperics, pragmatics and dialogics of high cultural criticism are finally methodologies as much against knowledge – a methodical antimethod.[33]

In terms of detail, the kind of visual perception demanded by the advent of video (with its emphasis on individual moments, not the *flow*) is useful here as a metaphor for a new way of seeing the detail/whole. This is not to say that we weren't capable of seeing in 'deconstructive' ways before, just that it makes it harder to avoid thinking in this way (i.e., as a methodological tool not a shift in perception – its use is metaphorical not institutional). Yvonne Rainer, in conversation with Trisha Brown, describes the analogous processes of deconstruction and bricolage commonly associated with postmodern dance, in Brown's *Glacial Decoy* (1979):

> The costumes bring in another dimension of not exactly a persona, but an association with personae created elsewhere and earlier somewhere between *Les Sylphides* and *Primitive Mysteries*, maybe even *Antic Meet* which has that take-off on *Primitive Mysteries*. And it is the dress that produces the association. There's a recurrent, fleeting transformation from a body moving to a flickering female image. I think that because the dress stands away from the body the image is never totally integrated or unified, so one goes back and forth in seeing movement-as-movement, body-inside-dress, dress-outside-body, and image-of-woman dancer, which is not the same thing as seeing or not seeing your work in terms of being a woman. Femaleness in *Glacial Decoy* is both a given, as in your previous work, and a superimposition.[34]

Another media analogy may be helpful here, this time from television. The impact of television indicates the limits of the esoteric theories of spectatorship derived from film theory ('the gaze'). 'I have never thought of the female spectator as synonymous with the woman sitting in front of her screen munching popcorn,' says Mary Ann Doane. The point is that the spectator doesn't exist. She emerges as a function of a discursive strategy at a particular historical moment, and the way we watch television is indicative of

32. Roland Barthes, *Roland Barthes by Roland Barthes*, 1977, p27. See also Naomi Schor, *Reading in Detail*, 1987, pp87-8.

33. Alan Liu, 'Local Transcendence: Cultural Criticism, Postmodernism, and the Romanticism of Detail', *Representations*, Vol 32, Fall 1990, p81.

34. Trisha Brown and Yvonne Rainer, *A Conversation About Glacial Decoy*, 1979, p32.

what Barbara Creed calls the 'messy realities' of the critical situation:

> Television conceptualised as a piece of furniture within a domestic scene, an event, an entertainment, a family pastime, a diversion – as well as a 'text', promised to open up to enquiry new considerations about criticism and its processes.[35]

35. Barbara Creed, *Camera Lucida*, Vols 20-21, 1990, p23.

36. Quoted in Cook, *op.cit.*, p160.

37. *Ibid.*, p161.

38. *Ibid.*, pp66-7.

The same would be true of listening to music. 'The listener,' writes Alfred Schutz, 'responds neither to sound waves, nor does he perceive sounds; he just listens to music.'[36] We're talking here about a different kind of viewing, listening or reading, in terms of overlaps and discontinuities – the random aspects of the viewing process, the flickering of attention spans. This has nothing to do with linguistic self-referentiality. This kind of reading would represent a criticism for the pleasure of reading, the sheer *physical* enjoyment of the text. And this is the kind of criticism that asks 'What is it like to read/watch/listen?', which is not the same as an (essentialist) description of content. Eric Blom coined the term 'overhearing' to refer to this kind of involvement with music. He called it a 'delicious sense of effortless absorption' and described it as 'a blessed state ... The only trouble is that overhearing cannot be cultivated.'[37] In his chapter entitled 'The Perception of Form: Some Tests', Nicholas Cook points out that it is impossible to listen equally intently throughout a piece of music. He adds:

> Refraining from clapping in the course of an extended work is intended as a recognition of the aesthetic unity of the whole. Someone who claps half-way through a performance of Beethoven's String Quartet Op. 130, for instance, reveals himself as incapable of appreciating this unit and, what is worse, disrupts the enjoyment of other listeners who do have this capacity. Or at least that is the idea; but how far it has a foundation in people's aesthetic experience – rather than in snobbery – is another matter.[38]

IV

> Come now, this won't do. I'm too clear-sighted this evening, and if I don't pull myself together my dancing will suffer for it. I dance and dance. A beautiful serpent coils itself along the Persian carpet, an Egyptian amphora tilts forward, pouring forth a cascade of perfumed hair, a blue and stormy cloud rises and floats away, a feline beast springs forwards, then recoils, a sphinx, the colour of pale sand, reclines at full length, propped on its elbows with hollowed back and straining breasts. I have recovered myself and forget nothing. Do these people really exist, I ask myself? No, they don't. The only things are dancing, light, freedom and music. Nothing is real except making rhythm of one's thought and translating it into beautiful gestures. Is not the mere swaying of my back, free from any constraint, an insult to those bodies cramped by their long corsets, and enfeebled by a fashion which insists that they should be thin?

But there is something more worthwhile than humiliating them; I want, for one moment only, to charm them! It needs only a little more effort; already their heads, under the weight of their jewels and their hair, sway vaguely as they follow my movements. At any moment now the vindictive light in all those eyes will go out, and the charmed creatures will give in and smile at the same time.

Colette, *The Vagabond*

The fourth epigraph, from *The Vagabond*, suggests a syntax of modern dance so presented that it is aesthetically accessible neither as purely literal movement, nor as wholly figurative movement, but rather as both simultaneously. This involves the creation of forms of bodily inscription in which the dance is not subject to, but subject of multiple representations. The passage records the progress of the dancer's movements from being the object of the watching audience/the spectators, to the subject of her own dance. For the spectators as well, she abolishes the distance between subject and object, she *inverts* the gaze. The possibility of this new dynamic of the literal and the figurative derives from the fact that the human body is caught between the objectively real and the inwardly virtual (and because, by contrast with literature and literary criticism, the physical body cannot be reduced to pure sign, and ignored, in dance). The kind of new formalism I am describing here heightens this tension to the degree that it achieves the impact of the body that demonstrates the dancer's objective spatialization, suspending, or obliterating this condition through the expression of pure self-reference.

But perhaps all this is over-optimistic? What about the dangers of dancing? I'm thinking particularly of Jane Marcus' formulation: 'In criticism dancing shoes will not do. We still need our heavy boots and mine detectors.'[39] Thus pure Derridean linguistic self-referentiality is insufficient (because of the presence and demands of bodies, and the physical demands of reading, writing and spectating).

The trope of the detail, and of the 'unreal reality' of language, meanwhile, are seductive. But these too readily become a metaphysic. Despite the dance of detail, it is arguable that lack of form is itself a form. In the *Aesthetics* Hegel saw music as the locus of the emergence of the tension always present between a drive towards unity, articulation and wholeness, and an equally strong countervailing drive towards fragmentation, disjunction and particularization.[40] Alan Liu argues in 'Local Transcendence: Cultural Criticism, Postmodernism and the Romanticism of Detail' that the local is always threatening to go transcendental:

The method of antimethod can at times seem too dogmatic ... The picture of great detail, as it were, threatens to become A GREAT PICTURE of detail ...

We are for a moment again a child shaking one of those globed,

39. Jane Marcus, 'Storming the Toolshed', in N.O. Keohane, M.Z. Rosaldo, and B.C. Gelpi (eds), *Feminist Theory: A Critique of Ideology*, 1982, p218.

40. See G.W.F. Hegel, *The Phenomenology of Mind*, (trans. and intro. J.B. Baillie), 1974.

> water-filled landscapes filled with miniature snowflakes. The flakes of detail fall into place, and we are charmed by both their slow suspense and the crystal clarity of the scene when all has settled into mock reality.[41]

The problem is perhaps summed up in what Lyotard calls 'the continuation of romanticism' in his analysis of the *differend*:

> The differend is a feeling for the unspeakability of any truth about final solutions, a noncognitive reaching after unspeakable words ... Incommensurability, heterogeneity, the differend, the persistence of proper names, the absence of a supreme tribunal? Or, on the other hand, is this the continuation of romanticism etc.[42]

I would argue that we have not yet achieved a mode of attention which, in Elizabeth Bowen's words, is careless enough. At the end of Elziabeth Bowen's novel *The Little Girls*, we read of 'Chance, and its agents, time and place'. 'Chance is better than choice,' Bowen says. 'In its carelessness it is more lordly. Chance is God. Choice is man.'[43]

In the end, deconstruction is always interpretative, on the side of mind, not matter. This is what Derrida calls the inter-view in *Choreographies*:

> In French, to take a glimpse is to look into the spaces between things, ENTREVOIR, that is inter-view, the desire to invent incalculable choreographies would remain.[44]

In the new forms of criticism required by and in dance, however, perhaps we have glimpsed the space between linguistic self-referentiality and the new metaphysic, between interpretation and expression, abstraction and emotion. Keats called this knowledge proved upon the pulses; Kipling, a miraculous weaving which can't be described, but can only be transferred from one art form to another. Here we would find the aesthetics of the first reading of a text, or of the experience of watching a dance. As Eryimachus says in Valery's *Dance and the Soul*, which I used as one of my epigraphs, the problem is that these are 'steps ... so easy and familiar to us that they never have the honour to be considered in themselves, and as strange acts'.[45]

41. Alan Liu, *op.cit.*, pp81, 91.

42. Jean-François Lyotard, *The Differend*, p135.

43. Elizabeth Bowen, *The Little Girls*, 1980, pp235-6.

44. *Ibid.*, p66.

45. Paul Valery, 'Dance and the Soul', *An Anthology*, 1977, p302.

The Public and Private Lives of T.E. Lawrence

Modernism, Masculinity and Imperial Adventure

Graham Dawson

The image of the post-Enlightenment man [is] tethered to, not confronted by, his dark reflection, the shadow of colonized man that splits his presence, distorts his outline, breaches his boundaries, repeats his actions at a distance, disturbs and divides the very time of his being.

Homi Bhaba, 'Foreword' to Frantz Fanon's *Black Skin, White Masks*[1]

In my case, the efforts of these years to live in the dress of Arabs, and to imitate their mental foundations, quitted me of my English self, and let me look at the West and its conventions with new eyes: they destroyed it all for me. At the same time I could not sincerely take on the Arab skin: it was an affectation only. Easily was a man made an infidel, but hardly might he be converted to another faith. I had dropped one form and not taken on the other ... Such detachment came at times to a man exhausted by prolonged physical effort and isolation. His body plodded on mechanically, while his reasonable mind left him, and from without looked down critically on him ... Sometimes these selves would converse in the void; and then madness was very near, as I believe it would be near the man who could see things through the veils at once of two customs, two educations, two environments.

T.E. Lawrence, *Seven Pillars of Wisdom*[2]

I The 'Lawrence of Arabia' Legend

In October 1918, his military role in the Arab Revolt at an end, T.E. Lawrence returned from the Arabian desert to London, 'the great city of modernity', to confront the image of himself represented there.[3] Stories of his adventures were already public knowledge in governing and intellectual circles, and from the moment of his return Lawrence found himself to be among the most sought-after men in the metropolis.[4] London was by this time

> the world's biggest city, still expanding with extraordinary rapidity, generating a remarkable cityscape and a fascinating technology ... [This] made for a sense of excitement and stimulus. London had now become the outright point of concentration for English national culture ... through it and from it came the newspapers, the books and the ideas of the country at large ... It was the capital of Empire and the centre of world trade ... a 'world city' with a world hinterland, an *entrepôt* for culture, publishing,

1. Homi Bhabha. 'Foreword' to Frantz Fanon, *Black Skins, White Masks*, Pluto Press, London 1986, p xiv.

2. T.E. Lawrence, *Seven Pillars of Wisdom* Penguin, Harmondsworth 1962, p30.

3. Malcolm Bradbury, 'London 1890-1920', in M. Bradbury and J. MacFarlane (eds), *Modernism 1890-1930*, Penguin, Harmondsworth 1976, p179.

4. Desmond Stewart, *T.E. Lawrence*, Paladin Grafton, London 1979, pp215-18. Hereafter referred to as *TEL*.

> finance and shipping, a magnet ... for migration ... [It] teemed with suggestions of indefinite and sometimes outrageous possibility, of hidden but magnificent meanings.[5]

Expanding national and international publics increasingly looked to London for the lead in new tastes, fashions and fads. This was the metropolitan centre to which in August 1919, Lowell Thomas brought his multi-media show *With Allenby in Palestine*, and launched the 'Lawrence of Arabia' legend.

Initially conceived as a celebration of General Allenby's overall campaign in the Middle East, covered by Thomas as a war correspondent, the most popular part of the show proved to be 'The Strange Story of Colonel T.E. Lawrence, the leader of the Arab Army', featuring film and slide material of Lawrence in Arab dress. Under a new title – *With Allenby in Palestine and Lawrence in Arabia* – it played for several months to packed houses at the Covent Garden Royal Opera House, the Royal Albert Hall and other major London venues before touring the provinces and the British Empire, eventually being seen by over four million people.[6] In Thomas' narrative commentary, later reworked for publication in magazine and book form, 'Lawrence of Arabia' is the romantic hero of an epic adventure, the 'blond Bedouin' who lived the life of the Arabs, became the commander of their guerrilla army and led them to freedom:

> He brought the disunited nomadic tribes of Arabia into a unified campaign against their Turkish oppressors ... Lawrence placed himself at the head of the Bedouin army of the King of the Hejaz, drove the Turks from Arabia, and restored the Caliphate to the descendants of the Prophet ... Lawrence freed Arabia, the holy land of millions of Mohammedans.[7]

In common with imperial adventure heroes of the pre-war tradition, this Lawrence is an idealized chivalric knight of omnipotent power and coherence. Combining the virtues of cleverness, physical strength and leadership, his seemingly effortless martial feats signify the imagined superiority of British imperial masculinity over that of other races.[8] By November 1919, the public image of Lawrence constructed by Thomas had made him a world figure – 'the first media legend' and 'the most celebrated soldier of the First World War'.[9]

II LAWRENCE OF ARABIA AND THE 'REAL' T.E. LAWRENCE

The relation between the Lawrence of Arabia legend and the 'real' T.E. Lawrence is a remarkably complex issue. From one perspective, the legend can be analysed as the product of Thomas' imaginative investment in the living soldier whom he encountered at work in Arabia, and represented as an idealized hero. In his narration of 'the Greatest Romance of Real Life', however, Thomas does not claim that his narrative will *make* Lawrence into a hero: but that Lawrence is already a hero, whose exploits need only to be recorded. The fantasy works to background or censor out any features which

5. Bradbury, *op.cit.*, pp179-83.

6. Jeremy Wilson, *Lawrence of Arabia: The Authorised Biography of T.E. Lawrence*, Heinemann, London 1989, pp622-6; *The Sphere*, 23 August 1919.

7. Lowell Thomas, ' "The Uncrowned King of Arabia", Colonel T.E. Lawrence, The Most Romantic Career of Modern Times', *The Strand Magazine*, Vol 59, Jan-June 1920, p42. For the whole serialization see pp40-53, 141-53, 251-61, and 330-38. See also Lowell Thomas, *With Lawrence in Arabia*, Hutchinson, London 1925.

8. For an analysis of the Thomas narrative, see Graham Dawson, 'The Blond Bedouin: Lawrence of Arabia, Imperial Adventure and the Imagining of English-British Masculinity', in M. Roper and J. Tosh (eds), *Manful Assertions: Masculinities in Britain since 1800*, Routledge, London 1991. For the Victorian tradition of imperial heroism, see Graham Dawson, *Soldier Heroes and Adventure Narratives: Case Studies in English Masculine Identities from the Victorian Empire to Post-Imperial Britain*, University of Birmingham PhD, May 1991, Chapter Two.

9. Stephen E. Tabachnick and Christopher Matheson, *Images of Lawrence*, Jonathan Cape, London 1988, dustjacket and p22. Hereafter referred to as *Images*.

contradict this idealizing investment, thus concealing its own existence as such, so that the romantic hero of Thomas' adventure narrative and the real Lawrence appear to fuse together into a 'living legend'. From another perspective, T.E. Lawrence's own contribution to the legend must be emphasized. His own fascination with the energizing myth of imperial adventure had brought him to the Middle East in the first place, in a series of journeys and sojourns made between 1909 and the outbreak of war. His admiration for the great traveller Charles Doughty, and the inspiration of Doughty's *Travels in Arabia Deserta* on Lawrence's own journeys and writing, are well documented. Martin Green suggests that 'Lawrence's vision of himself as hero' derived from mediaeval chivalric romance, and quotes Lawrence's own claims that as a youth, he had harboured 'chivalric' fantasies of leading the great but fallen Arab people in a 'crusade' for freedom. These investments in the 'otherness' of the Arabs were his personal appropriations of a common cultural imaginary shared with Thomas and his audiences.[10]

Lawrence's self-imagining clearly constitutes a significant dimension of the 'reality' which Thomas claims to record. While the adventure story plays free with the historical 'facts' of the Revolt and Lawrence's involvement with it, it nevertheless roots itself in that historical reality and produces a version of it that some later historians have continued to find broadly convincing.[11] Similarly, Thomas might have filmed Lawrence in Arab dress, but he did not ask him to put it on. As well as a form of 'power-dressing' to impress the Arabs, Lawrence's 'cross-dressing' can be located as a component of his homoeroticism in relation to both Arab and European young men.[12] It became an element, that is, in his own public self-representation, which he himself brought to the metropolis on occasions such as the party in January 1919 (on the occasion of the Emir Feisal's visit to London prior to the Paris Peace Conference), attended by Lawrence 'in full Sharifian white'.[13] Taken out of the desert and placed in this context, the wearing of Arab dress becomes a form of 'aestheticism' and 'dandyism' identified by Martin Green as the mark of revolt by the younger generation against the 'seriousness' of their elders; and as Bradbury points out, 'the dandy is an essentially urban figure, a style-maker standing out in the general display.'[14]

If Thomas' hero is produced out of an encounter with Lawrence's own self-imagining as 'Lawrence of Arabia', the latter is itself only one among many other of Lawrence's identifications: a single component in a lived masculinity that is necessarily more complex and multi-faceted, and is fashioned in the spheres of work, the family, friendship and sexuality as well as in the landscape of adventure. The legend is a result of Thomas 'recognizing' aspects of Lawrence in a particular, and highly selective way. The storybook hero which he composed from this encounter then becomes a kind of public mirror to Lawrence's own self-imaginings, and necessarily impacts back upon the ways that Lawrence sees himself and the ways he is (and likes to be) recognized by others.[15]

It is unsurprising, then, that the 'real' T.E. Lawrence would appear to have

10. Martin Green, *Dreams of Adventure, Deeds of Empire*, Routledge and Kegan Paul, London 1980, pp326-8. See also *TEL, op.cit.*, pp41, 64, 225, 246 on Doughty, and pp41-125 on Lawrence's pre-war visits. For key themes in the Arabian imaginary, see Richard Burton, quoted in Green, *op.cit.*, pp291-2; and Peter Mansfield, *The Arabs*, Penguin, Harmondsworth 1978, pp491-8.

11. See *Images passim* for a concise review of the historical evidence. Tabachnick's own view is that 'the basic stories of Lawrence's leadership of the Arabs and his secret intelligence work are true' (p40).

12. 'If you can wear Arab kit when with the tribes, you will acquire their trust and intimacy to a degree impossible in uniform. It is, however, difficult and dangerous.' T.E. Lawrence, 'Twenty-Seven Articles' (of advice to political agents working with the bedouin), in the *Arab Bulletin*, 20 August 1917, quoted in Mansfield, *op.cit.* Lawrence's alleged homoeroticism is a theme developed at length in *TEL*, including his involvement with the 'Uranian' movement (pp20-2), his relationship with the young Arab, Dahoum (pp99-108), and his seductiveness in Arab dress (p191).

13. *TEL*, p218.

14. Martin Green, *Children of the Sun: A Narrative of 'Decadence' in England after 1918*, Constable, London 1977, pp69-74.

held intensely ambivalent views about Thomas' version of Lawrence of Arabia. This is evident in the contradictory accounts that have emerged about Lawrence's original collaboration with the journalist. Thomas claimed to have enjoyed his full co-operation when they met in Jerusalem and Akaba; that, indeed, 'He arranged for my jaunt to Arabia.' Lawrence, on the other hand, complained that Thomas had made 'a sort of public mountebank' out of him. He publicly distanced himself from the Covent Garden show, refused to endorse its authenticity and insisted on a disclaimer in Thomas' book that he, Lawrence, was not the source of its material.[16] The ambivalence emerges again over the show itself, for Lawrence 'quietly attended the show several times while stating his disdain for it to his friends'.[17] This suggests a secretive private fascination with an image of himself produced for the widest public consumption, co-existing with a public disavowal, a reluctance or antipathy to being recognized publicly in such a form, as such a hero.

These contradictory responses of the real man to the heroic image have given rise to a great deal of research and debate among Lawrence's many biographers. Thomas himself incorporated Lawrence's 'modesty' into the image of a reluctant hero who preferred archaeology to war, emphasizing a charming discrepancy between Lawrence's 'public' and 'private' selves which reinforced the fascination of his 'mysterious' hero.[18] Stephen Tabachnick, while broadly endorsing Thomas' positive view of Lawrence, considers it 'flawed' in parts and attributes this to Lawrence having fed Thomas falsehoods. 'In many cases Thomas was clearly repeating tall tales and propaganda, sometimes in garbled form, that Lawrence himself had told him in a spirit of mischief and mockery or in order to garner political support for Feisal.' Tabachnick finds no difficulty in distinguishing the 'true' from the 'false', nor does he consider Lawrence to have done. As these fictions subsequently assume a life of their own, Lawrence 'began to detest and hide from his own partially-created public image'.[19] In sharp contrast, Desmond Stewart sees Lawrence as a champion self-publicist who 'used mysteries' in order to 'creat[e] a myth about himself'. Stewart's Lawrence is himself responsible for constructing the Lawrence of Arabia legend, before disingenuously distancing himself from its most public form. This poses real problems for a biographer concerned with the 'truth' about Lawrence; which Stewart resolves through his psychological interpretation of Lawrence's character as a charlatan.[20]

III MASS MEDIA, STAR IMAGE AND PUBLIC RECOGNITION

These interpretations underline the extent to which T.E. Lawrence was caught up in the developing legend in complicated ways. Yet all of them remain overly psychological in approach, and fail to take full account of the conditions of cultural production that shape the telling of the narrative and organize its relation to public audiences. Thomas' 'Lawrence' depended upon the popular technology of slide projection, upon the crowd-pulling power of the exciting new medium of film, and upon a growing sophistication in publicity and

15. This concept of 'social recognition' is developed at greater length in Dawson, *op.cit.*, especially Chapter Four; see pp469-71.

16. *TEL*, p197, including quote from Thomas; Lawrence's letter to E.L. Greenhill quoted in *Images*, p22.

17. *Images*, p22. See also *TEL*, p232. Evidence that he attended the show at least once is given in Thomas, *op.cit.*, *With Lawrence* (p275).

18. *TEL*, p197; Thomas, 'Uncrowned King', *op.cit.*, p43.

19. *Images*, pp91, 22, 40.

20. *TEL*, pp52-4.

mass-marketing techniques.[21] The popular newspapers which seized upon Thomas' image, and continued to pursue T.E. Lawrence in the years after he had withdrawn from public life, were undergoing rapid transformation into mass circulation dailies competing fiercely for readers, and consequently giving more space to human interest stories and sensationalism.[22] When, in February 1929, Lawrence returned home from service with the RAF in India following (unfounded) allegations in the press about spying activities, audiences of millions in the several thousand cinemas then existing throughout Britain were able to watch him in person on newsreel films of his disembarkation.[23]

The dependency of the Lawrence of Arabia image upon the complex modern media of mass communication necessarily means that Lawrence himself could not possibly be 'in control' of it. As Richard Dyer has shown, any 'star image' is a complex construction produced by a variety of agencies, from the entertainment industry operating according to an increasingly rationalized division of labour, to reviews and commentators, to fans themselves. The outcome – a fabricated image of a real person – systematically blurs the distinction between itself as image, a product of representation, and the 'private' or authentic self of the person thought to be 'behind' it. The public image of the star feeds off real life events, as off the more clearly fabricated fictions, indiscriminately; and itself becomes 'real' insofar as the public identity of the real person is transformed by it. Any attempt by the star to distance him or herself from this public image, to deny aspects of it, or even to claim privacy, are likewise absorbed into it; locking the star into publicity.[24] A further repercussion of Dyer's argument may be that, in the blurring and 'leaking' between public and private, star image and real person, the real person may lose the ability to distinguish one from the other. Public recognition may lead to identification with the image, so that publicity becomes desirable and stimulating, and the star image an attractive and empowering way of imagining the self. The lack of personal control over these recognitions, however, makes this kind of investment fraught with psychic danger.

After Thomas' show, the Lawrence image was recognizable to an invisible mass public for whom he became a figure of fantasy: so, for example, T.E. Lawrence received hundreds of love letters from women he had never met, addressed to the hero of a film.[28] The already complex self-imagining which had generated the energy sustaining his activities throughout the Arab Revolt, was rendered even more complex by the necessity of negotiating this mass public recognition. To say this is not to fall back upon a clear-cut – and ultimately untenable – distinction between a 'real man' and a 'star image', between clearly demarcated 'facts' and 'fictions', or between 'private awareness' and 'public reputation'. The contradictions experienced by Lawrence – his ambivalence at being a soldier hero – concerned by own imaginative investments in different versions of himself (some of which were magnified as a public spectacle for audiences around the world) and his own desire for particular kinds of recognition.

Dyer suggests that the extraordinary situation of the star magnifies into a

21. John MacKenzie, *Propaganda and Empire: The Manipulation of British Public Opinion 1880-1960*, MUP, Manchester 1984, pp32-5, puts Thomas' show in the context of the widespread use of magic lantern slides with a lecturer to promote imperial themes, from the 1880s, and their gradual supersession by film from the early twentieth century.

22. James Curran and Jean Seaton, *Power Without Responsibility: The Press and Broadcasting in Britain*, Methuen, London 1985, pp52-74 on the interwar press, especially pp60-2. The *Daily Express* – the paper that in 1922 'discovered' Lawrence to be serving in the RAF – saw its circulation rise from under half a million in 1910 to nearly two and a half million in 1939. John Stevenson, *British Society 1914-45*, Allen Lane, London 1984, p402.

23. In 1926, there were 3000 cinemas in Britain, growing to nearly 5000 by 1938; and in 1934, 903 million tickets were sold; see Stevenson, *op.cit.*, pp395-6. Archive film of Lawrence can be seen in *Lawrence of Arabia* (BBC 1986, produced by Julia Cave and Malcolm Brown). On the India episode see *TEL*, pp285-6.

larger public stage what is actually a very ordinary, though disturbing, aspect of everyday life in modern Western cultures: namely, the difficulty of composing a coherent individual identity, given the proliferation of images and versions of the self (and of alternative, possible selves).[26] Seeking 'exemplary lives' for the modern world, we watch the public spectacle of stars negotiating this difficulty, and probe into their private lives to find out whether, and how, those images can be fitted together into some kind of coherence; or alternatively, whether and how it is possible to live with their multiplicity and fragmentation. So it is that even the most intimate of exchanges between T.E. Lawrence and his confidantes, the stories he told friends in domestic privacy or wrote in personal letters, are now available alongside Harry Chase's original photographs of Lawrence of Arabia, for our scrutiny and judgement.

In a diary entry recording a private conversation with Lawrence made by his friend Richard Meinertzhagen at the time of the Paris Peace Conference, for example, we can read that:

> He told me that ever since childhood he had wanted to be a hero, that he was always rushing into limelight and hiding in utter darkness but the limelight had always won ... He hates himself and is having a great struggle with his conscience. Shall he run away and hide, confess his sins and become hopelessly discredited – or carry the myth on into the limelight in the hopes of not being exposed ... He blames Hogarth, Lowell Thomas, Storrs and many others ... for making him a little War Hero.[27]

What emerges here, and in many other accounts of Lawrence in the diaries, memoirs and letters upon which his biographers have feasted, is a representation of a man not at all 'in control', but driven by a deep-rooted psychological conflict centring on the discrepancy between public identity and its recognition, and a sense of other hidden and unrecognized private selves. The hero, the myth, the limelight, all become simultaneously desirable and feared under a drive that has operated 'since childhood', but must now negotiate an intensified public scrutiny in which Lawrence's very conflict about the legend becomes incorporated into it and ensures its continuing vitality and interest.

The fascination exerted by such insights into the 'private moments' of Lawrence, where he appears 'really' to be a tortured soul, lies in its diametrical contrast to the heroic public image. Where Thomas' Lawrence is the figure of an omnipotently-powerful masculinity, the 'real' Lawrence revealed in these private (and therefore presumed authentic) moments is out of control, damaged, a man whose very identity as a man has been thrown into crisis: the subject of a narrative far more complex and contradictory than any adventure story.

24. Richard Dyer, *Heavenly Bodies: Film Stars in Society*, MacMillan, London 1987, pp8-14. On p50 he discusses Marilyn Monroe in terms of 'the person who inhabits and produces the sexy image ... the person who plays the fantasy'.

25. *TEL*, p249.

26. Dyer, *op.cit.*

27. Quoted in *TEL*, p226. Hogarth and Storrs were Lawrence's superiors at the Arab Bureau.

IV COMPOSING THE SELF: 'SEVEN PILLARS OF WISDOM'

Lawrence himself was the first of many to attempt that story. The outcome was *Seven Pillars of Wisdom*, his own self-consciously epic narrative about the Revolt, which he wrote between 1919 and 1922.[28] The contrast with Thomas' heroic adventure could not be greater, and indeed the book establishes a dialogue with the legend, in a kind of settling of accounts. It can be read as Lawrence's attempt to compose a public identity that he could live with more comfortably, and to elicit recognition of himself as a man more complex, than Thomas' adventure hero.

Seven Pillars is a vast labyrinth of a book, criss-crossed by Lawrence's journeys to and fro across the desert, back and forth to Cairo, away on raids. Narrative action is interspersed with lengthy passages of reflection upon his spiritual and moral, as well as physical vicissitudes; upon his Arab companions, their culture and his relationships with them; upon the landscape in all its stark and empty grandeur; and upon the diplomatic, political and military complexities of the Revolt. Adventure themes arise only to be displaced by some further shift in mood and tone. Most importantly, both the moral certainties and the hero's triumphal overcoming of obstacles that characterize Thomas' adventure quest are dissolved into an altogether equivocal and unsettling narrative in which Lawrence 'painfully works to construct the Arab Revolt, yet he ... shows himself falling apart in the process.'[29] This subjective fragmentation – the very antithesis of that complete masculine coherence imagined by Thomas – is shown to result from the profoundly disturbing, and indeed ultimately destructive quality of Lawrence's lived experiences in Arabia; fraught, as it must necessarily have been, with massive contradictions and dangers, which Thomas' omnipotent fantasy flattened out, ignored or whisked away with a wave of his magic wand.

28. T.E. Lawrence, *Seven Pillars of Wisdom: A Triumph*, Penguin, Harmondsworth 1962. Referred to hereafter as *SP*.

29. *Images*, p156. My discussion of *SP* is especially indebted to Stephen Tabachnick's succinct and suggestive reading, pp155-63.

V DISTURBING ADVENTURE

Several distinct although interconnected sources of disturbance can be identified in *Seven Pillars*. There are disturbances stemming from the contradictory nature of Lawrence's political role as British agent and his guilty awareness of British duplicity in dealing with the Arab leaders, by withholding from them knowledge of the secret Sykes-Picot agreement by which – contrary to promises made by Lawrence to Hussein and Feisal – agreement on the carving-up of the postwar Middle East was reached between Britain and France. Lawrence's guilty sense of having betrayed the Arab cause is made all the more devastating by his own recognition of the right to self-determination of the Arab people.

> The Arab Revolt had begun on false pretences. ... I could see that if we won the war the promises to the Arabs were dead paper. Had I been an honourable adviser I would have sent my men home, and not let them risk

> their lives for such stuff. Yet the Arab inspiration was our main tool in winning the Eastern war. So I assured them that England kept her word in letter and spirit. In this comfort they performed their fine things: but of course, instead of being proud of what we did together, I was continually and bitterly ashamed.
>
> In revenge I vowed to make the Arab Revolt the engine of its own success, as well as handmaid to our Egyptian campaign: and vowed to lead it so madly in the final victory that expedience should counsel to the Powers a fair settlement of the Arabs' moral claims. Clearly, I had no shadow of leave to engage the Arabs, unknowing, in a gamble of life and death. Inevitably and justly we should reap bitterness, a sorry fruit of heroic endeavour.[30]

30. *SP*, pp282-3. See also pp387, 565-9.

31. *Ibid.*, pp226-7, 85-6, 580, 560.

32. Jeffrey Meyers, *The Wounded Spirit: A Study of 'Seven Pillars of Wisdom'*, Martin Brian and O'Keefe, London 1973, p106. See, for example, *SP*, pp488-9 (weather), 387 (scorpion bite), 618 (wounded), 254 (travelling in the desert wind), 192 (dysentery fever).

Split loyalties of this kind, and the contradictory pull that they exert, are rendered invisible in Thomas' portrait of the omnipotent blond Bedouin.

This conflict exacerbates Lawrence's already difficult encounter with the 'otherness' of Arab culture. 'The Bedo were an odd people. For an Englishman, sojourning with them was unsatisfactory unless he had patience wide and deep as the sea.' Far from the smooth induction portrayed by Thomas, *Seven Pillars* dwells upon the physical hardships of Bedouin life, especially acute at the first encounter, for one not brought up to it.

> The long ride that day had tired my unaccustomed muscles, and the heat of the plain had been painful. My skin was blistered by it, and my eyes ached with the glare of light striking up at a sharp angle from the silver sand, and from the shining pebbles. The last two years I had spent in Cairo, at a desk all day or thinking hard in a little overcrowded office ... In consequence the novelty of this change was severe, since time had not been given me gradually to accustom myself to the pestilent beating of the Arabian sun, and the long monotony of camel pacing.

Elsewhere, Lawrence writes of 'the beastliness of living among the Arabs'; and at one point describes how 'a homesickness overcame me, stressing vividly my outcast life among those Arabs ... I was dead tired, longing as seldom before for the moody skies of England.'[31]

Lawrence's account charts the energy required to maintain the mental and physical endurance that underlies the achievements performed so effortlessly in Thomas' romance; and their human costs. *Seven Pillars* catalogues an endless sequence of physical pain and suffering – 'dysentery and delirium, thirst and starvation, boils and bruises, stings and bites, broken bones and bullet wounds, torture and degradation'.[32] Where Thomas attributes to Lawrence a playful enjoyment in killing, in *Seven Pillars* the excitement of 'train-blowing' is countered by his concern to prevent unnecessary loss of life. When required personally to execute an Arab murderer to prevent an inter-tribal blood feud:

> Then up rose the horror which would make civilized man shun justice like a

> plague if he had not the needy to serve him as a hangman for wages ... Afterwards the wakeful night dragged over me, till, hours before dawn, I had the men up and made them load, in my longing to be set free of Wadi Kitan. They had to lift me into the saddle.[33]

The responsibilities of command weigh heavily upon him with regard to loss of life. After a fierce engagement with the Turks, who 'astonished' Lawrence by their attack on the Wadi Hesa and the village of Tafileh, he agonizes that 'by my decision to fight, I had killed twenty or thirty of our ... men ... This evening there was no glory left, but the terror of the broken flesh, which had been our own men, carried past us to their homes.' The adventure ethos and his own 'heroism' are mocked in Lawrence's parody of a regulation military report on this engagement, which he considered a 'verbal triumph, for the destruction of this thousand poor Turks would not affect the issue of the war.'[34]

A different form of subversion occurs when he tells of failure. Where adventure involves a controlled risk of failure – operating as a *frisson* not a threat – here we find an account of Lawrence's failure to accomplish one of the most important missions given him by Allenby: the destruction of the railway bridge at the Yarmuk Gorge, which would 'isolate the Turkish army in Palestine ... from its base in Damascus, and destroy its power of escaping' when Allenby advanced into Palestine in November 1917. An accidentally dropped rifle alerts the Turkish troops, frightened Arabs dump the explosives into the ravine, and the guerrilla force hastily withdraws. The raiders ride home, 'our minds ... sick with failure', into a 'grey dawn' accompanied by a 'grey drizzle of rain ... so soft and helpless that it seemed to mock our broken-footed plodding.'[35]

Where Thomas' adventure hero enjoys effortless omnipotence, in Lawrence's own account the heroic persona crucial to his prestige among the Arabs has to be struggled for in the face of these disturbances, and is sustained only through a continual assertion of self-control and will-power. This forms the cohesive principle upon which Lawrence's masculine identity is constructed. In one sense, then, the difficulties encountered by Lawrence function as the necessary condition of his self-fashioning, comparable to the obstacles in an adventure quest. The most devastating source of disturbance in *Seven Pillars*, however, is sexuality, which precisely undermines the cohesive principle itself.

VI THE RAPE AT DERAA

Entirely absent from Thomas' romance, sexuality is here present from the first page, in Lawrence's description of the masculine brotherhood of the Arab army, where 'our youths began indifferently to slake one another's few needs in their own clean bodies.'[36] It assumes greatest importance in the famous 'Deraa incident', in which Lawrence narrates his capture on a spying mission whilst disguised as an Arab in the Turkish-controlled town of Deraa, leading to his sexual violation and brutal whipping by Turkish soldiers. The episode is pivotal in the book as a figure for risk gone wrong, envisaging the encounter

33. *SP*, p187. On 'train-blowing', see *SP*, pp371-90, pp434-43; and Thomas, 'Uncrowned King', *op.cit.*, pp141-2. See *SP*, p379 where Lawrence saves a prisoner.

34. *SP*, pp483-92. In Thomas, plans do not 'go adrift' like this.

35. *Ibid.*, pp396, 423. The intervening pages tell the full story of the raid.

36. *Ibid.*, p28.

with otherness in wartime conditions as being not only deeply threatening, but ultimately crippling to both physical and psychic coherence. Riding south after his escape, Lawrence feels

> curiously faint; my muscles seemed at once pappy and inflamed, and all effort frightened me in anticipation ... Now I found myself dividing into parts ... and my parts debated that their struggle might be worthy, but the end foolishness and a rebirth of trouble.

The lasting impact of the incident is his conviction that 'the citadel of my integrity had been irrevocably lost', and himself irreparably ruined.[37]

Jeffrey Meyers has usefully located the Deraa incident in the context of a series of symbolic oppositions running throughout *Seven Pillars*, in which masculinity, endurance and the will are correlated with cleanliness and spiritual purity. This gives rise on the one hand to Lawrence's idealization of Arab homosexual love, developed in his account of the pure affection of the two young Arabs, Farraj and Daud; while on the other, it produces a misogynistic association of femininity with weakness, corruption and filth, and with the carnality of the body, in a projective disavowal necessary to secure Lawrence's identification with the masculine. By violating his body and pushing it beyond its capacity to endure, the torture and rape at Deraa breaks Lawrence's will, and so throws into crisis the system of values upon which the coherence of his masculinity depends. Furthermore, in the brief description of how, after the flogging stopped, 'a delicious warmth, probably sexual, was swelling through me', Lawrence is forced to confront his own masochistic sexuality, a symptom of 'moral weakness' which operates like 'traitors from within'. Deraa literally 'shattered' him, leaving him exposed to self-persecution and destructive self-punishment from chivalric ideals of purity to which he no longer feels able to aspire.[38]

Since the publication of *Seven Pillars*, a debate has raged about whether or not the Deraa rape actually occurred. Edward Said, for example, has argued that it was a 'necessary fantasy' of Lawrence's in which he expiated personal and political guilt in a wished-for scenario of sexual punishment.[39] But in either case – whether as a response to a real traumatic event or as an entirely imagined scenario – the pivotal position of Deraa within Lawrence's narrative establishes its central significance for the public identity composed and seeking recognition there. An analysis of this significance is suggested by Jessica Benjamin's argument about the pervasiveness of sado-masochistic fantasies of erotic domination in modern Western cultures.[40] She explains sado-masochism in terms of a general splitting of the self – along the polarities of controller and controlled, violator and violated, assertive and yielding – brought about by partially successful efforts towards individuation. In this, the 'masculine' impulse towards differentiation (whereby the boundaries of the self are asserted, establishing its separateness and autonomy from others) is split off from the 'feminine' impulse towards recognition by a significant other

37. *Ibid.*, pp459-61, 456. For Deraa, see pp450-56.

38. Meyers, *op.cit.*, pp114-29; *SP*, pp454, 477. See also *SP*, p508 for Lawrence's hatred of sex and procreation, and p547 on the body and the will.

39. Edward Said speaking in *Lawrence of Arabia* (BBC 1986, produced by Julia Cave and Malcolm Brown). See also *TEL*, pp187-9, 244; *Images*, *passim*. For the continuing controversy, see Lawrence James, *The Golden Warrior*, Weidenfeld and Nicolson 1990, and the review article by Phillip Knightley, 'Was There Really a Rape at Deraa?', *The Independent on Sunday*, 19 August 1990, p6.

40. Jessica Benjamin, 'Master and Slave: The Fantasy of Erotic Domination', in Ann Snitow *et al.* (eds), *Desire: The Politics of Sexuality*, Virago, London 1984.

(prototypically the mother, in relation to whom the self experiences its own connectedness and dependence on others), with one or other becoming the dominant element in the psyche. Since differentiation and recognition are interdependent (with the self paradoxically needing to be recognized in its autonomy, and needing to be autonomous in order to recognize the other as different), the denial of either will tend to inhibit the capacity to give and receive recognition and feel connected to an other experienced as independent from the self.

Benjamin suggests that modern masculinities tend to be formed in a denial of the impulse to recognition, establishing gender difference through 'the repudiation of the mother' – a 'false differentiation' secured by overly 'rigid and tenacious' boundaries, at the price of a psychically deadening isolation. 'If the sense of boundary is established by physical, bodily separation, then sexual and physical violence (if not in reality, then in fantasy) are experienced as ways of breaking the boundary' and escaping from its 'numbing encasement'. Benjamin sees the masochist as one who is unable to relinquish control voluntarily, 'and must or wishes to be forced to do so'. Masochism is 'a desire for subordination to another person, rather than for the experience of pain as such ... a search for recognition of the self by another who alone is powerful enough to bestow this recognition'.[41] According to this argument, Lawrence's identification with the position of the violated in his account of the Deraa incident can be read as an impulse towards recognition which requires a breaching of the boundaries established by the masculine self. In the extremity of his self-control, Lawrence's own body, rather than that of another, becomes an object and instrument of his will. The breaking of his will occurs when Lawrence has temporarily abandoned the position of power he occupies as a British officer among Arabs and, in disguise, is subjected to the desire of the Turkish colonizer for a 'white' colonized Circassian Arab. The power relations between British, Turks and Arabs underpin a colonial fantasy in which the positions of violator and violated are now reversed. Once 'broken', however, Lawrence's renewed identification with the position of the master proves impossible.[42]

41. *Ibid.*, pp292-8, 303-8.

42. for a controversial account of Lawrence as a 'rabid masochist' (*sic*), see Anthony Nutting, *Lawrence of Arabia: The Man and the Motive*, Hollis and Carter, London 1961. Nutting was an adviser to the David Lean/ Robert Bolt epic film, *Lawrence of Arabia* (Horizon 1962), which explores masochism and colonial fantasy in relation to the Deraa incident. See Dawson, *op.cit.*, pp370-87. In 1968 the *Sunday Times* published interviews with a services colleague, John Bruce, who claimed to have administered to Lawrence periodic beatings with birch rods, at Lawrence's request, over a twelve-year period before his death in 1935. See Phillip Knightley and Colin Simpson, *The Secret Lives of Lawrence of Arabia*, Nelson, London 1969.

VII 'TIRED TO DEATH OF FREE WILL'

Where the adventure hero is an ideally unified being with ceaseless energy, the compounding, after Deraa, of the various disturbances narrated in *Seven Pillars* produces an overwhelming sense of Lawrence's personal and political exhaustion. Faced by a further setback promising 'the complete ruining of my plans and hopes', he returns to Allenby's headquarters confessing that 'I had made a mess of things', and asking to be relieved of his responsibilities.

> I complained that since landing in Arabia I had had options and requests, never an order: that I was tired to death of free-will, and of many things beside free-will. For a year and a half I had been in motion, riding a

thousand miles each month upon camels: with added nervous hours in crazy aeroplanes, or rushing across country in powerful cars. In my last five actions I had been hit, and my body so dreaded further pain that now I had to force myself under fire. Generally I had been hungry: lately always cold: and frost and dirt had poisoned my hurts into a festering mass of sores.

> However, these worries would have taken their due petty place, in despite of my body, and of my soiled body in particular, but for the rankling fraudulence which had to be my mind's habit: that pretence to lead the national uprising of another race, the daily posturing in alien dress, preaching in alien speech: with behind it a sense that the 'promises' on which the Arabs worked were worth what their armed strength would be when the moment of fulfilment came ... Chargeable against my conceit were the causeless, ineffectual deaths of Hesa. My will had gone and I feared to be alone, lest the winds of circumstance, or power, or lust, blow my empty soul away.[43]

43. *SP*, pp512-4.

44. *Ibid.*, pp651-5.

His request being turned down, Lawrence returns to the field to take part in a swirl of renewed activity on Allenby's eastern flank, which leads seven months later to the fall of Damascus.

In this final stage of the narrative, however, moral value and meaning inexorably drains away. This is epitomized by Lawrence's account of the Arab army's discovery of a Turkish massacre of Arab men, women and children at the village of Tafas. 'I said, "The best of you brings me the most Turkish dead", and we turned after the fading enemy, on our way shooting down those who had fallen out by the roadside, and came imploring our pity.' In the attack on the column

> By my orders we took no prisoners, for the only time in our war. ... In a madness born of the horror of Tafas we killed and killed, even blowing in the heads of the fallen and of the animals; as though their death and running blood could slake our agony.

The Arab army then find 'one of us' left to die with 'bayonets hammered through his shoulder and other leg into the ground, pinning him out like a collected insect'.

> When we said, 'Hassan, who did it?' he drooped his eyes towards the prisoners, huddling together so hopelessly broken. They said nothing in the moments before we opened fire. At last their heap ceased moving; and Hassan was dead; and we mounted again and rode home slowly ... in the gloom, which felt so chill now that the sun had gone down.[44]

In claiming responsibility for this massacre of Turkish prisoners and making no attempt to conceal or justify its immorality, Lawrence's account of Tafas, more than any other single episode in *Seven Pillars*, undermines both the idealized heroic image of Lawrence of Arabia and the moral nature of his quest. This chill landscape, weariness and deep sense of loss is the very antithesis of Thomas's romance world, figuring instead a nightmarish dystopia.

Subtitled 'A Triumph', *Seven Pillars'* ending is decidedly equivocal and can be read as an ironic commentary upon Thomas' legend. Despite the cheering crowds and dancing dervishes, Lawrence's arrival in Damascus is far from heroic: 'the won game of grab left a bad taste in my mouth, spoiling my entry.'[45] Lawrence's loyalties remain ambivalent to the end – one minute hopeful that 'we [sic] should be safe, with the Arabs in so strong a place that their hand might hold', the next celebrating the arrival of Allenby, 'fit representative of the Power which had thrown a girdle of humour and strong dealing round the world'. The end comes when Lawrence relinquishes to Allenby the burden of responsibility for public order and essential services in the city, which dominates the final pages.

> In ten minutes all the maddening difficulties had slipped away. Mistily I realized that the harsh days of my solitary battling had passed. The lone hand had won against the world's odds, and I might let my limbs relax in this dreamlike confidence and decision which were Allenby.

Even this, with its lapse into heroic posturing, is contradictory: requesting 'leave to go away ... In the end he agreed; and then at once I knew how much I was sorry.'[46]

VIII *SEVEN PILLARS* AND MODERNISM

Under the impact of the various disturbances that undermine the adventure story in *Seven Pillars*, the imagined coherence or Thomas' fantasy hero disintegrates into a multiplicity of competing identifications. 'In his self-portrait, Lawrence appears contradictory and unpredictable, a man ... able to assume many roles precisely because of the multitude of personalities he harboured within. ... Viewed objectively as a character in *Seven Pillars*, Lawrence *is* his contradictions.'[47] Where Thomas' adventure offers an imaginary flight from modernity into a romance world, the exploration of paradox, ambiguity and contradiction in *Seven Pillars* suggests that it can usefully be located within modernism, as a text charting a response to the uncertainties of modern existence.[48]

Marshall Berman has characterized the modern world as a 'dynamic new landscape' of constantly changing human environments and proliferating moral uncertainties, 'capable of everything except solidity and stability': a world of 'agitation and turbulence, psychic dizziness and drunkenness, expansion of experiential possibilities and destruction of moral boundaries and personal bonds, self-enlargement and self-derangement, phantoms in the street and in the soul'.[49] This description of modernity perfectly captures the atmosphere established in *Seven Pillars* from the very first page:

45. *Ibid.*, pp666-71.

46. *Ibid.*, pp670, 682-3. Lawrence's exclusion from the Arab national community and consequent feeling of isolation and sadness is graphically captured in an image (p674) of him listening to the calls to prayer from a nearby mosque after the fall of Damascus. 'The clamour hushed, as everyone seemed to obey the call to prayer on this first night of total freedom. While my fancy, in the overwhelming pause, showed me my loneliness and lack of reason in their movement: since only for me, of all hearers, was the event sorrowful and the phrase meaningless.' The world he is barred from is one in which providential design continues to operate.

47. *Images*, pp156-60.

48. 'To confront the decline, by the late nineteenth century, of religious, philosophical, and scientific certainties (of God, objective truth, historical progress etc), as well as the very notion of a fixed viewpoint, modernists explore the paradoxical many-sidedness of the world. Alarmed at the spectre of nihilism, the loss of meaning in transcendent imperatives and firm secular values, modernists view reality as necessarily constructed from relative viewpoints ... Instead of an omniscient and reliable narrator, modern writers develop either single

or multiple, but all limited and fallible vantages from which to view events ... the paradoxes may be heightened to the point of apparent irresolution, confronting the reader or audience with a 'Janus-faced' reality, impenetrable in its enigmas.' Eugene Lunn, *Marxism and Modernism*, Verso, London 1985, pp36-7.

49. Marshall Berman, *All That Is Solid Melts Into Air: The Experience of Modernity*, Verso, London 1983, pp18-9.

50. *SP*, pp27-8.

51. Berman, *op.cit.*, pp21-2, on Nietzsche. See *TEL*, pp239-40 on Lawrence's interest in Nietzsche.

52. Lunn, *op.cit.*, p37.

> Some of the evil of my tale may have been inherent in our circumstances. For years we lived anyhow with one another in the naked desert, under the indifferent heaven. By day the hot sun fermented us; and we were dizzied by the beating wind. At night we were stained by dew, and shamed into pettiness by the innumerable silences of stars. We were a self-centred army without parade or gesture, devoted to freedom, the second of man's creeds, a purpose so ravenous that it devoured all our strength, a hope so transcendent that our earlier ambitions faded in its glare.
>
> As time went by our need to fight for the ideal increased to an unquestioning possession, riding with spur and rein over our doubts ... we had surrendered, not body alone, but soul to the overmastering greed of victory. By our own act we were drained of morality, of volition, of responsibility, like dead leaves in the wind.
>
> We lived always in the stretch or sag of nerves, either on the crest or in the trough of waves of feeling ... Gusts of cruelty, perversions, lusts ran lightly over the surface without troubling us; for the moral laws that seemed to hedge about these silly accidents must be yet fainter words. We had learned that there were pangs too sharp, griefs too deep, ecstasies too high for our finite selves to register.[50]

Lawrence's staging of the self needs to be seen in parallel with other modernist narratives that attempt to fashion meaningful perspectives and articulate new sensibilities from within the maelstrom. In a world without God, human beings must imagine themselves anew; and in doing so, discover within the psyche the sources of creativity and destructiveness once mapped in terms of providential design. Subordination of the will to God is replaced with the liberating assertion of human will to fill the void. The power to create new worlds, to bring into being human dreams, is matched by its inverse: the power to bring about a nightmare. 'The possibilities are at once glorious and ominous. Our instincts can now run about in all sorts of directions; we ourselves are a kind of chaos.'[51] The coherence and moral integrity of individual human subjectivity imagined in both realist and romantic narratives of the nineteenth century fragments into a variety of modernist subjectivities, imagined as 'a psychic battlefield, or an insoluble puzzle, or the occasion for a flow of perceptions and sensations'.[52]

In this general 'crisis of individuality', the effort towards new forms of subjectivity produces comparable manifestations across the boundaries of national cultures. The move from Lawrence's original fascination with the ancient civilizations of the Middle East to *Seven Pillars*, for example, bears comparison with the shift in Yeats' poetry from romantic dreaming of the heroic cultures of 'old Ireland', through the endeavour to transform the modern world in their image, to ironic wisdom in the discovery of their dark and hollow antithesis. Similarly, the world of *Seven Pillars* has some striking affinities with German Expressionism: its source in feelings of self-contempt, guilt and unworthiness; its subordination of form to articulate an intense emotional and visionary experience; its powerful release of erotic and violent instincts; its tormented and apocalyptic language; its refusal of resolution and harmony, in the face of intense longing for regeneration and an end to suffering.[53]

The main difference between *Seven Pillars* and these more familiar modernist forms is that its imagining of the divided self is shaped, just as surely as Thomas' romantic hero, in the encounter with the otherness of Arabia and the Arabs. Lawrence's fractured sensibility is located not within the paradigmatic modern landscape of the metropolitan city, but instead within the once romantic 'natural' landscape of the desert.[54] This is now transformed through Lawrence's modern mode of inhabiting it, in those ceaseless journeys by camel, aeroplane and car, into a setting fit for a Western quest now governed by the 'will to power'. 'Self-overcoming and extreme freedom' are its promised rewards, to be accomplished in Nietzschean mode through denial of the body, the search for wisdom through excess, the assumption of a right to take exceptional actions, often extended to powers over life and death. The Western imaginary of the Arabian desert correlates with this landscape of the soul; the harshness of its climate and terrain providing conditions conducive to such a test, the Bedouin being its measure. 'It was precisely with a Nietzschean will that Lawrence created his world, a new Arab empire.'[55] Conversely, it is the disturbing encounter with Arab otherness – precisely Lawrence's '*efforts* to live in the dress of Arabs' – which 'quitted me of my English self, let me look at the West and its conventions with new eyes', and 'destroyed it all for me' [my emphasis].[56] *Seven Pillars* narrates both the assertive movement of modernist masculinity into the colonial periphery, and its unravelling and breakdown there.

53. Richard Ellmann, *The Identity of Yeats*, Faber and Faber, London 1964; Lunn, *op.cit.*, pp58-64.

54. 'Still another body of inherited belief that could no longer sustain the modernists was the idea of nature (developed by some of the romantics) as an effective counterfoil to modern urban and industrial society.' Lunn, *op.cit.*, p40.

55. Meyers, *op.cit.*, pp106-8.

56. *SP*, p30, quoted at the head of this article.

57. *Images*, pp160-3. See, for example, Lawrence's description of himself wearing Arab robes in the cold mountains as like a 'hard-iced Bridal cake', *SP*, p508.

IX WRITING, PUBLIC RECOGNITION AND AMBIVALENCE

When considering *Seven Pillars* as the search for a form of self-imagining, however, it is important to hold the distinction between the Lawrence engaged in the Arab revolt in 1916-18, and the Lawrence composing a narrative perspective back in the city in 1919-22. In his postwar writing, Lawrence worked at his *memories* of the war, and sought to compose them into a narrative that he could live with, in which the problematic and contradictory impulses to self-idealization and self-denigration might be transformed into a more integrated sense of self. Stephen Tabachnick has stressed the importance of humour and irony in Lawrence's efforts to establish a 'balance' between elements of the contradictory self-portrait. Humour is used to debunk and question conventional assumptions, to introduce an element of ironic relief into painful events, and to distance himself through self-mockery 'in any situation in which he threatens to become too proud of himself ... Time and again in *Seven Pillars*, his humour restores a sense of proportion when he begins to portray himself as a hero.'[57] However, this humorous, ironic voice can itself be seen as comprising yet another of Lawrence's many 'selves', rather than expressing a new-found authentic coherence.

For if the stake in Lawrence's search for a voice was the construction of an alternative public version of himself to set against Thomas', as a solution to this lived dilemma of public recognition, the writing of *Seven Pillars* only went half way. In one sense, the narrative operates as a confessional: a form of public self-revelation of problematic dark truths hidden behind the legend, designed to help assuage the guilt and allay the resulting self-punishment. As such, though, the writing itself becomes caught up with the shame attached to the Deraa incident in particular, producing an intense ambivalence. 'He came perilously close to a nervous breakdown as ... he could never seem to reveal exactly what had happened but could not conceal it either.'[58] The writing in a sense repeats the loss of integrity which it seems designed to counter, under the impact of that prevailing division between public and private life which was so central to contemporary masculinity: 'The sort of man I have always mixed with doesn't so give himself away.'[59] The narrative was rewritten twice in its entirety (once after Lawrence apparently lost the manuscript) and was extensively revised before publication. Its publishing history also tells a story of ambivalence: eight copies being printed for friends in 1922, and a lavishly produced limited edition in 1926 making it 'the decade's most talked about and least available book'. A heavily abridged version, *Revolt in the Desert*, appeared in 1927, but the first fully public edition was withheld until after Lawrence's death in 1935.[60] The writing and publishing of *Seven Pillars* registers the conflict within a masculinity seeking public recognition of its own disturbance and contradiction, but in crisis over the public form in which to appear; its strategies for coherence shattered, leaving it torn between the desire and the impossibility of telling the truth about the self.

58. *Images*, p156.

59. T.E. Lawrence, Letter to Robert Graves, quoted in Meyers, *op.cit.* p119.

60. *TEL*, p233. See pp231-55, 274-5, 290, for a sceptical account of the writing and publishing of *Seven Pillars*. Both books were instant bestsellers in English and other languages, and *Seven Pillars* has been continuously in print ever since. *Images*, p156.

Towards a New Aesthetics?
Some Reflections on the Christa Wolf Reception in West Germany

Daglind Sonolet

I

The fall of the communist regime in East Germany was a rapid and bloodless event carried out by a wave of massive popular support. Most intellectuals in East and West were stunned to watch not only the total capitulation of the regime, but also the people's passionate rejection of communism or any kind of socialist reformism. As the public was faced with more and more facts about corruption and privilege, police surveillance and harassment, economic and ecological disaster – facts that had been known, albeit not in their depressing proportions – questions were inevitably raised about continued loyalty to the regime. Indeed, what about the frame of mind and motives of those Eastern intellectuals who had supported the system to the very last, if not uncritically, among them Stefan Heym, Stephan Hermlin, Hermann Kant, Volker Braun, Günter Kunert and Christa Wolf?

East German intellectuals who had believed in a reformable state socialism were swept aside by popular verdict; yet Western leftists were no less caught out. Their confused reactions to the end of the German Democratic Republic show that, despite the Wall and communist dictatorship, many had credited the regime with the capacity eventually to install an alternative society to western capitalism, and now were either bemoaning the scrapping of non-capitalist 'advantages' in the GDR, or else indulging in breast-beating about their protracted blindness to the real situation.[1]

The public washing of the dirty linen of political rights and wrongs gave rise to the violent controversy about Christa Wolf's relation to the socialist regime and the evaluation – or re-evaluation – of her work in the light of the new ideological and historical situation. In this debate the work and person of Christa Wolf often stand for other GDR writers: Wolf was singled out as by far the best-known, nationally and internationally celebrated writer, in order to pose not only the question of the writer's privileged position under the former socialist regime and his or her 'intellectual honesty', but also the questions of the relation of the intellectual to power, of artistic production to ideas in German postwar cultural production and reception. As one critic put it: 'With the end of the division of Germany we have also reached the end of the literary division. The literatures of the GDR and the Federal Republic have been released for reviewing.'[2]

The immediate cause that sparked this debate was a short story published by Wolf in the spring of 1990, '*Was bleibt*' ('What is left'),[3] in which she relates the

1. See, for example, the debate in *Die Zeit* throughout 1990, with articles by Günter Grass (9 February), Wolf Biermann (2 March), Fritz J. Raddatz (29 September), Hans Joachim Schädlich (19 October); the interviews with Grass and Walser in *Der Spiegel* (16 July 1990 and 8 October 1990 respectively). Unless otherwise stated, all translations from the German are my own.

2. Ulrich Greiner, '*Die deutsche Gesinnungsästhetik*', *Die Zeit*, 2 November 1990.

3. Christa Wolf, *Was bleibt*, Luchterhand, Frankfurt 1990.

fact that some ten years earlier she had been for several weeks under the surveillance of the Stasi, the East German security police. This barely veiled autobiographical account drew a sharp reaction from two well known West German critics, Ulrich Greiner[4] and Frank Schirrmacher,[5] amounting to nothing less than a frontal attack on Wolf's whole work and personality. I shall summarize here the main arguments of this debate and then briefly relate them to the broad lines of the Wolf reception in the Federal Republic.

Greiner, though conceding that nobody must reproach Wolf with the 'error' of having held on to the last to the project of socialism – 'for we too (the literary critics) ... have erred' – nevertheless charges her with opportunism for having done so: she took the honours (literary prizes, membership of the Academy of the Arts) and the privileges they brought, and left the SED, the East German Communist Party, when it was no longer risky to do so; she published '*Was bleibt*' when its veiled critique of the Stasi presence carried no danger to her any more. By calling her *Staatsdichterin*, a state poetess, Greiner makes her into a mouthpiece of official political and cultural ideology. Wolf's immense success in the West seems to rest on the 'aura of danger' she managed to create. The 'real existing threat' looming over her was used by Wolf again and again for literary success 'just as masterfully as mendaciously'; her imprecise, veiled language and her 'gratuitous self-accusations' adding spice to the attractive picture of the intellectual living under a constant yet unnameable threat. Greiner suggests that Wolf's latter-day disappointed flight into the literary idyll is but a new edition of an old German problem: the intellectual's retreat into the realm of art and thought in order to avoid conflict with adverse political powers.[6]

In this angry awakening of a leftist to the consequences of his illusions, no new information about Wolf is offered. Therefore the argument that Wolf is late in publishing her critique of police surveillance applies equally to her critics, who could have run her down much earlier. Frank Schirrmacher is no less severe; however, he attempts to locate in Wolf's psychological make-up the contradiction between her insights into the shortcomings of GDR socialism and her filial loyalty to the very regime with which she became increasingly disillusioned. To Schirrmacher, Wolf's 'literary status [is] highly overrated'; what interests him is, rather, Wolf's 'in many respects exemplary biography' of a German intellectual of her generation. In his view, Wolf has never understood that she lived in a dictatorship, where citizens were locked up and civil liberties denied. Instead, she always comprehended conflict between GDR citizens and their state in terms of a personal crisis situation. Typical for intellectuals of her generation, Christa Wolf has 'built a familiar, quasi-intimate relationship to her State and its institutions'.[7]

The socialist state granted the intellectuals important privileges, but also subjected them to sharp repression, again and again testing their loyalty, not unlike a severe father, who encourages and reprimands. True, Wolf herself admitted that members of her generation had remained dependent upon authority, always afraid of being expelled from the group.[8] Schirrmacher remarks that while intellectuals in other European communist countries had

4. Ulrich Greiner, '*Mangel an Feingefühl*', *Die Zeit*, 1 June 1990.

5. Frank Schirrmacher, '*Dem Druck des härteren, strengeren Lebens standhalten*', *Frankfurter Allgemeine Zeitung*, 2 June 1990.

6. Ulrich Greiner, '*Mangel an Feingefühl*', *op.cit.*

7. Frank Schirrmacher, *op.cit.*

8. See Wolf's conversation with Therese Hörnigk, Christa Wolf, *Im Dialog*, Luchterhand, Frankfurt 1990, pp24-66.

usually 'seen through' Stalinism by the mid 1950s, the German comrades were permanently handicapped by the problem of national socialism. Indeed, the SED state's demand for unconditional loyalty rested on its moral claim to have built a society radically different from the national socialist one – a new Germany. Wolf's generation, born around 1930, was too young to have had any real responsibility for national socialism and its crimes; it was, however, old enough to have been incorporated into its youth organizations[9] and affected by its ideology, and to derive from these a lasting feeling of guilt and shame and a longing for 'reparation'. The communists who returned after the war from exile, prison and concentration camps, became the new father figures, who could win the young people's unwavering loyalty with the promise of absolution and the restoration of lost integrity. Christa Wolf hinted repeatedly at the near-impossibility of critically distancing herself from this moral authority, once it had dawned on her that it was also authoritarian.[10]

Schirrmacher sees this moral dilemma at the heart of Wolf's writing. It deflects or suffocates her incipient critique: it prompts her increasingly numerous outbreaks of helpless, tearful self-laceration: it colours her language, giving it the imprecise, resigned quality that Greiner also noted to be so insupportable. The interesting thing is, however, that Schirrmacher establishes here, in this contradictory attitude of bondage *cum* melancholic self-accusation, the link with the Wolf-reception in West Germany. Indeed, according to him, the key to Wolf's success in the Federal Republic lies in the fact that her self-accusatory and at the same time victimized attitude meets its mirror-image in the West, where it allows the same generation to belatedly and vicariously compensate for the resistance to national socialism that was not offered under the Nazi regime.

Though arguing in a more sophisticated manner than Greiner, Schirrmacher too constructs Wolf as a typical case of postwar German intellectual development, the production and reception of her work being wholly explicable in terms of the psychological and ideological needs of a generation. Literary aspects play no role. If Christa Wolf's work were as congruent with contemporary interests as is suggested here, it would indeed be quite worthless. The refusal to engage in a debate about Wolf's writing – in other words, the wholesale dismissal of her work as either the expression of GDR ideology (Greiner), or else as an 'all-German,' psychological problem (Schirrmacher) – inscribes itself in a periodically resurfacing unease with the relationship between cultural value and ideological content, between aesthetic value and ideal, between *Geist* and *Macht* – spirit and power.

A few months after charging Wolf with opportunistically clinging to the wrong kind of idealism, Greiner moves on to dismiss the whole of East and West German literature as a product of *Gesinnungsästhetik*, partisan or committed aesthetics, and thus devoid of cultural value. He directs his polemic against the self-congratulatory and, in his view, widespread opinion that literature in both Germanies was meritricious and therefore good. In East and West, literature gave itself the air of fighting 'with great moral integrity for

9. The parents of the postwar generation were former '*Pimpfe*', i.e. members of the Hitler Youth 'turned round'; Sascha Anderson, '*Das Prinzip Subversion und seine Folgen*', *Neue Rundschau*, no 1, 1990, pp94-8.

10. See Christa Wolf, *Im Dialog*, op.cit., pp24-66; I want to draw attention to Wolf Biermann's funny and conciliatory comment on the Eastern intellectuals' depression after the breakdown of communism. More or less courageous 'in the name of genuine Marxism and true socialism' they were more linked than separated by 'the same historical hope'. Wolf Biermann, '*Nur wer sich ändert, bleibt sich treu*', *Die Zeit*, 24 August 1990.

humane principles, of offering resistance against repression and restoration', while in reality it found a *modus vivendi* with the powers-that-be and bore mediocre products. The revelation of this obvious self-deception causes indignation because there had been a 'consensus that German writers (the left-wing, the committed, the critical ones) had wanted, said and written the good. And literary criticism had respected this consensus, by evaluating not according to aesthetic, but to moral and political principles.'[11] Now, however, with the full truth of the SED regime and its half-hearted opponents becoming known, one can say aloud that one had always had one's doubts about the quality of East German literature.[12]

Both Schirrmacher's and Greiner's explanations suggest that the reception of Christa Wolf's work, and of East German literature in general, could be so positive in the West, because it was rooted in a moral attitude towards literature common to all Germans. This view – far from being directly political – largely ignored a writer's political affiliations and the socio-political conditions of literary production, and rather saw in literature a vehicle for uplifting ideas. Unwittingly then, well-meaning left critique contributed to an atmosphere of literary continuity in a divided Germany.

It is true, of course, that for twenty-five years Wolf's work met with great success in West Germany, despite some critical voices, and that acclaim translated into a considerable number of editions of some of her texts. Christa Wolf received the important literary prizes and honours which the Federal Republic has to offer: Bremer Literaturpreis (1977), Georg-Büchner-Preis (1980), membership of the Akademie der Künste, West Berlin (1981), etc; she gave lectures and readings to great public acclaim, and her work has been studied assiduously. Abroad, Wolf is read for her commitment to topical problems, above all those of women's inequality and personal identity in modern, technological society.[13] In answer to Greiner's polemic, Volker Hage observes that Wolf is internationally appreciated not for having treated the problems of the 'supposedly really existing socialism' in the GDR, but for the way she posed the problem of the self, of the 'difficulty of saying I', which is 'not a problem specific to the GDR, but one specific to modern prose *per se*'.[14]

The communist breakdown released emotions and reflections pent up for years, explaining the polemic about a biased attitude towards Wolf's writing. Yet Schirrmacher and Greiner are certainly wrong in the way they reject Wolf's work, confounding personal morality and literary value, and making literature wholly dependent on the supposed moral and intellectual disposition of a certain German public, which – if nothing else – can't explain Wolf's international recognition. To take the German controversy beyond its present phase of breast-beating and *ad hominem* demonstration, one would have to reconsider the broad political and cultural context in which East German literature became available in the West, and where the evolving German-German relations played a role, as well as the cultural climate during the 1970s and 1980s (with the peace, ecology and feminist movements). And lastly, this context would also include the state of literary and cultural theory in the

11. Ulrich Greiner, '*Die deutsche Gesinnungsästhetik, op.cit.*.

12. Cf. the interview with Günter Grass in *Der Spiegel*, 16 July 1990, where the interviewer suggested that one tended to give the GDR a 'bonus', not knowing how much the colleague in the East could honestly say without having difficulties with the authorities.

13. Cf Myra Love, 'Christa Wolf and Feminism: Breaking the Patriarchal Connection', *New German Critique*, no 16, 1979, pp31-53; Anna K. Kuhn, *Christa Wolf's Utopian Vision: From Marxism to Feminism*, CUP, Cambridge, 1988.

14. Volker Hage, 'Kunstvolle Prosa', *Die Zeit*, 1 June 1990.

present revolt against humanism and modernity. It becomes evident that the West German reception of Christa Wolf's work assumed a great complexity over the years, with political, cultural and aesthetic aspects interwoven, so that one cannot simply speak of a 'partisan' aesthetic.

Schirrmacher and Greiner have diagnosed, in the West German appreciation of GDR literature, a displacement of interest away from the politics and ideology of the East German regime onto human and moral problems – a movement which seemed inscribed in the nature and evolution of the German-German relations. Indeed, relations between the two German states, though political, were in a strange way *a*political at the same time, particularly so in the case of the Federal Republic which initiated them. After years of cold war stalemate, a change of policy was introduced in the *Deutschlandpolitik* by the government Brandt-Scheel, in the early 1970s, profiting from, and contributing to, an atmosphere of East-West detente. Up to then, the aim of reuniting Germany in 'free self-determination', the non-recognition of the GDR and the claim to sole representation of the interests of the German people, had shaped the policy guidelines towards communist countries. In the *Ostverträge*, the treaties with the Soviet Union and Poland (1970), and the Berlin Agreement (1971), the Federal government bracketed these principles in order to improve relations with Central and Eastern Europe in bilateral accords, in the absence of an international peace settlement. The *Grundlagenvertrag* (1972) foundations treaty with the GDR initiated a policy of small steps, leading eventually to a bilateral network of treaties that allowed for an intensification of commercial, cultural and human relations between the two German states. This *de facto*, if not *de jure*, recognition of the GDR was used by the communist German state to achieve the long-coveted international status, at the same time as it apparently sealed the existing German division. But this accord also laid the foundations for an eventual rapprochement between the two Germanies, which ultimately bore its fruit in the final era of detente under Gorbachev.

Paradoxically, then, the *Ostpolitik* helped to depoliticize German-German relations. While the FRG clearly defined itself as a democratic state in the Western tradition, practising a 'social market economy', being a member of the EC and NATO, and defending Western democratic values against the Eastern bloc's communist dictatorship and state-planned economy, in its relations with communist Germany it increasingly papered over ideological differences and insisted on human relationships between the two states. In the 1980s, the central component of the *Deutschlandpolitik* had become freedom of movement and information; with the *Kulturabkommen* (1986) cultural agreement, the West German government hoped to further a sense of a united cultural nation. These improvements in the relations between the two states encountered their limits, however, in the FRG's refusal to renounce definitely the aim of reunification by changing its constitution, and in the aggressive-defensive attitude of the GDR.[15]

For East Germany, the Federal Republic remained the model of economic

15. For this discussion see Christian Hacke, '*Die Deutschlandpolitik der Bundesrepublik Deutschland*', in Werner Weidenfeld and Hartmut Zimmermann (eds), *Deutschlandhandbuch: Eine doppelte Bilanz 1949-1989*, Bundeszentrale für politische Bildung, Bonn 1989, pp535-50.

achievement. Under Honecker, from the 1970s onwards, the principles of pragmatism and efficiency replaced the ideals of the socialist utopia and caught the GDR in an ever-greater dilemma of how to found a separate German identity. The powerful anti-fascism argument that had originally helped to legitimize the East German state had worn itself out, and historicism – the dictum that socialism will triumph in the end – had relegated the socialist utopia to the distant future. Intellectuals were trapped in a contradictory situation, having to justify their loyalty to East German communism with threadbare and anachronistic arguments, while disregarding the manifest failings of 'real existing socialism' and hoping against hope.

The paradoxical nature of the relationships between the Federal Republic and the GDR finds a parallel in the contradictory attitude West German intellectuals adopted towards the communist state. To most non-socialist intellectuals in the West the two Germanies continued to represent the divided nation. Though rival siblings, the two countries shared the same history, culture and literature. The yardstick for evaluating literary excellence remained the German literary tradition and its development in terms of language and form; and most East German literature produced within the parameters of official ideology was judged wanting in this respect. The critic Marcel Reich-Ranicki observed that, in general, GDR literature, even when willing to come to terms with the defects of socialist society, shied away from a confrontation with ideology; for when serious critique was proffered, a 'high price' had to be paid – i.e., it had to be retracted.[16] Thus, he went on, literature created a secure world ruled by a 'pathfinder ethic'.[17] And Wolfgang Emmerich added the observation that in the international context, because of the long-imposed tradition of didactic-realist writing, GDR literature tended to appear provincial and untouched by the insights and techniques of modern writing.[18] However, the doctrine of two separately emerging German literatures that had gained ground during the Adenauer era seems to have given way, in the 1980s, to the more ambivalent view of 'convergence and divergence' between East and West German literary production.[19]

The Left – if one can make such a collective designation – displayed a more lenient attitude towards the socialist regime in East Germany, which, though a dictatorship, was not a rule of bloody terrorism. The attempt to create a socialist society was considered an interesting experiment in comparison to capitalist West Germany; it had to be given the benefit of the doubt and should be judged on its own terms. These 'own terms' were advertised by the GDR as anti-fascism, anti-capitalism, and the egalitarianism of the 'socialist human community', combined with the ambitious claim of founding a *Kulturnation* on the legacy of classical German culture. East Germany was in many ways considered more unspoilt, the better conserved Germany: less ravaged by rapid industrialization, still preserving old villages and towns; less materialistically oriented than the 'Americanized' West. According to Günter Gaus, from 1974 to 1981 head of the permanent representation of the FRG in the GDR, the GDR sported a petty-bourgeois egalitarianism; however, it

16. Marcel Reich-Ranicki, *Entgegnung: Zur deutschen Literatur der siebziger Jahre*, Deutscher Taschenbuch Verlag, Stuttgart 1982, p317. The book groups literary criticism from 1968 to 1979 that had appeared in *Die Zeit* and in the *Frankfurter Allgemeine Zeitung* – among others the articles on Wolf's *The Quest for Christa T.*, '*Eine unruhige Elegie*', pp240-8, and on *Patterns of Childhood*, '*Ein trauriger Zettelkasten*', pp249-54.

17. *Ibid.*, p160.

18. Wolfgang Emmerich, *Kleine Literaturgeschichte der DDR*, Luchterhand, Frankfurt 1989, p445.

19. *Ibid*, p449; Hans Mayer, who in the 1950s had been one of the supporters of the two literatures doctrine, contests it emphatically in the 1980s, speaking of an 'astounding convergence' of literary themes and tendencies. *Die Umerzogene Literatur: Deutsche Schriftsteller und Bücher 1945-1967*, Siedler Verlag, Berlin 1988, p158.

integrated its young people, provided everyone with work, and for that reason alone was more humane. Gaus also remarked that '(t)heir use of language is less uprooted than ours',[20] while another critic observed that East Germans can still write a 'Kleistian German'.[21]

Western intellectuals have always used the existence of communist Germany as a benchmark for the shortcomings of Western society. Fully aware of the restrictions imposed on their colleagues in the East, such as censorship, modest material circumstances and limited travel opportunities, many of them nevertheless accepted the commitment to a 'cause' as compensation for these deprivations and bewailed its absence in the West. Eastern writers, for their part, continued to affirm that a regulative idea, and the state's defence of it, were a severe but salutary cause of friction between the individual and authority, inculcating discipline and concentration – an argument to which Western intellectuals remained sensitive.[22] State-controlled cultural policy protected the arts from the laws of the market – from vulgarization and commercialization, as many intellectuals saw it.[23] Grass wrote that in 'cultures of oppression' writers play an important role; not so in the West, where social democracy produced parties hostile to culture.[24] And Hans Mayer, who has taught literature in both East and West Germany, observed that East German 'authors' vouchsafed with their existence what they published, and therefore were more likely to mean what they said: unlike the provocative 'scribes' in the West, they have no 'cynically granted carnival licence'.[25]

This rather sympathetic view of the socialist conditions of cultural production has affected the appreciation of Wolf's work in the West, insofar as their consequences for her writing have rarely been given serious consideration. For example, Manfred Jäger, one of the first to trace Wolf's remarkable path from party-line literary critic to independent writer 'in search of the truth', was also one of the first to caution Western critics not to underestimate the specific circumstances that condition this quest, which he identified as 'the conscious compulsion or unconscious seduction to compromise'. It would be presumptuous, he argued, to demand of East German authors that they 'disregard the circumstances under which, and the readers for whom, they write'.[26] In other words, Wolf should be evaluated on her own terms, as a believing socialist, whose efforts towards 'subjectivity' and 'truth' situate themselves within paramaters which, though given, are never expressly delimited. Jäger adds only that East German literature, far from following the prescriptions of the culture bosses or accepting imposed limitations, steadily pushed forward the limits of literary freedom.[27] There seems to have been an implicit assumption that the GDR offered the possibility of little by little realizing cultural freedom within the confines of socialism. Hans-Jürgen Greif affirmed that Wolf's main concern was the 'free development of the individual';[28] while another critic suggested that in the GDR, where a socialist infrastructure is already given, writing can become a 'utopian way of living', indicating the way forward.[29]

Against this broadly sketched background I will now consider some key aspects in the evolving reception of Wolf in the FRG.

20. Günter Gaus, *Wo Deutschland liegt: Eine Ortsbestimmung*, Hoffman & Campe, Hamburg 1983, p27.

21. Hans Mayer, quoted in Emmerich, *op.cit.*, p448.

22. Christa Wolf, *Im Dialog*, *op.cit.*, pp29ff.

23. See Antonin Liehm's 'Foreword' to his *The Politics of Culture*, Grove Press, New York 1970, pp72-82.

24. Aafke Steenhuis, 'After the Fall', interviews with Günter Grass, *New Statesman & Society*, 22 June 1990, pp35-8.

25. Hans Mayer, *op.cit.*, p170.

26. Manfred Jäger, *Sozialliteraten: Funktion und Selbstverständnis der Schriftseller in der DDR*, Bertelsmann, Düsseldorf 1973, p40.

27. *Ibid.*, pp100ff.

28. Hans-Jürgen Greif, *Christa Wolf: 'Wie sind wir so geworden wie wir heute sind?'*, Peter Lang, Bern 1978, p127.

29. Thomas Beckermann, '*Das Abenteuer einer menschenfreundlichen Prosa*', *Text + Kritik*, no 46 (special issue on Christa Wolf), München 1985, p38.

II

None of Christa Wolf's books has provoked a more unanimous reaction than *The Quest for Christa T.* (1968),[30] which overcame the socialist realist mode still limiting her previous literary work, *The Divided Heaven* (1963).[31] The book commanded great interest and admiration for recuperating for GDR literature modern devices such as free movement in time and the mixing of the narrator's reflections, dreams and past events, in 'the poetical defence of the individual against the claim of the "iron definitions" '.[32] *Christa T.* is organized around two central themes: the impossibility of actually knowing an individual, which leaves the reflection open-ended, the search for Christa T. incomplete; and that of a young woman's quest for a self-realization which was otherwise denied her in the GDR of the 1960s, where socialism had come to mean progress through scientific and technical efficiency, leaving no space for imaginative individualists.

These two intimately linked dimensions were further developed in the critical and poetological reflections, *Lesen und Schreiben* [*Reading and Writing*] (1971).[33] Rebutting the contemporary Western verdicts on the 'death of the author' and the 'execution of the narrator', Wolf is concerned rather with 'the realisation of "subjective authenticity" as the fourth, the real dimension proper to the work of art'. For Wolfgang Emmerich, 'Christa Wolf's work is ... of particular relevance to literary history in that it has set markers, encouraged development,' while being itself an example for new tendencies.[34]

This preoccupation with artistic subjectivity, long bracketed in East German literary theory and practice (which also became central to Franz Fühmann's, Günter Kunert's and Volker Braun's work at the same time), was eventually to lead Wolf back to problematical figures of German Romanticism, such as Hölderlin, Bettina Brentano, Kleist and Günderrode, who had been excluded from GDR literature during its socialist-realist period. With *The Quest for Christa T.* Wolf entered, formally and thematically, the arena of modern literature. More than that, 'she consciously and artfully makes sensibility the main element of her restless elegy,' a sensibility which revolts against 'a too narrow rationalism', thereby placing her novel in the eighteenth-century German tradition of the sentimental novel, whose pinnacle was Goethe's *Werther*.[35]

If *The Quest for Christa T.* had been greeted with near unanimous acclaim in West Germany, the reviews of *Patterns of Childhood* (1976)[36] were less consistent. Wolf was credited for the courage she demonstrated in taking up the topic of German fascism as a lingering problem of personal identity – which had been treated much earlier by Böll, Grass and Walser in the FRG – and for the serious intentions she pursued. Thus Heinrich Böll remarked that Christa Wolf was countering the amnesia=amnesty response which characterized East and West German attitudes to the Nazi period.[37] In accordance with the East German state's self-understanding as anti-fascist and socialist, the problem of fascism was seen as having been resolved in works of 'anti-fascist resistance literature' during the 1950s, in contrast to the capitalist Federal Republic which was

30. Christa Wolf, *Nachdenken über Christa T.* (1968), Luchterhand, Darmstadt und Neuwied 1969. *The Quest for Christa T.*, Farrar, Strauss & Giroux, New York 1970.

31. Christa Wolf, *Der geteilte Himmel* (1963), Rowohlt, Reinbek 1968.

32. Marcel Reich-Ranicki, *op.cit.*, p248.

33. Christa Wolf, *Lesen und Schreiben: Aufsätze und Betrachtungen* (1971), Luchterhand, Darmstadt und Neuwied 1972.

34. Wolfgang Emmerich, *op.cit.*, p198.

35. Marcel Reich-Ranicki, *op.cit.*., p248.

36. Christa Wolf, *Kindheitsmuster* (1976), Luchterhand, Darmstad und Neuwied 1977. *Patterns of Childhood*, Farrar, Straus & Giroux, New York 1984.

37. Heinrich Böll, '*Wo habt ihr bloss gelebt?*', in Klaus Sauer (ed.), *Christa Wolf Materialienbuch*, Luchterhand, Darmstadt und Neuwied (1979) 1983, pp7-15.

generally portrayed as heir to the defeated Nazi Reich. In *Patterns of Childhood*, Wolf thematizes the 'ordinary' fascism of 'ordinary' people, using her own experience of growing up in a shopkeeper's family to describe opportunism, fellow-travelling and not wanting to know too much of what was going on. Wolf anchors 'ordinary' fascism in the authoritiarian structure of the personality, in obedience to authority and blind faith in ideology. The central concern of the book is to uncover the processes which formed these lasting psychological patterns in a childhood and youth spent under the Nazi regime. However, it is precisely the *leitmotiv* question of the book, 'How have we become what we are today?' that remains unanswered.

The positive critical response to *Patterns of Childhood* consists mainly of descriptive comments on Wolf's supposed intentions. To Ingeborg Drewitz, Christa Wolf has written 'a beautiful and difficult book, which shows ... the relation of private experience to historical reality'.[38] Uwe Wittstock, reviewing Wolf's and Fühmann's[39] books on fascism, locates the achievements of both authors in their success in freeing themselves from the official socialist position and overcoming the stage of self-pity and victimization which inhibits the capacity to mourn. Both authors thereby contributed to *Trauerarbeit*, the 'work of mourning' for the victims of German fascism, whose general absence Alexander and Margarete Mitscherlich had observed in their pathbreaking study.[40]

The readiness which many critics displayed in accepting Wolf's treatment of the topic betrays a certain unease and fear of contact vis-à-vis both German fascism and communism. Indeed, West German critics have noted the relation between an inconsequential treatment of German fascism and the prolongation of the fascist personality structure in (authoritarian) socialist East Germany. However, few dared challenge Wolf on this count, either to spare her problems with the authorities in her own country, or from an unwillingness to confront the possible parallels between the dictatorship character of Nazi Germany and the GDR socialist system.

Heinrich Böll is content with the hints at certain traits of fascism persisting in the GDR of the 1970s that Wolf disperses throughout her book: the unwillingness of schoolbooks to discuss national socialism in other than stereotyped terms; the occupation mentality young East Germans display towards Slavic countries; an indifference to Auschwitz as a special place of Nazi barbarism; the readiness to dispense global, unshakeable truths – i.e., the axioms of socialist ideology – as a cure-all for national socialism.[41] Yet, despite Böll's friendly inclination to accept the cautious mention of fascist remnants in the GDR as 'sufficient' proof of Wolf's critical distance from the regime, the fact remains that the author does not probe the reasons why these traits continue to exist. Notwithstanding important differences, the similarities between Nazi and socialist totalitarianism are strong enough that a treatment of daily fascism should be bound to provoke a debate about the SED regime. It is, ultimately, Wolf's unwillingness to attack the roots of the GDR malaise – the disempowerment and disciplining of the population, the disregard for

38. Ingeborg Drewitz, '*Stil und Existenz gehören zusammen*', *Text + Kritik*, *op.cit.*, p13.

39. Franz Fühmann, *22 Tage oder die Hälfte des Lebens* (1973), Fühmann's Hungarian war diary.

40. Uwe Wittstock, *Uber die Fähigkeit zu trauern: das Bild der Wandlung im Prosawerk von Christa Wolf and Franz Fühmann*, Athenäum, Frankfurt 1987, p185; Alexander and Margarete Mitscherlich, *The Inability to Mourn*, Grove Press, New York 1975.

41. Heinrich Böll, *op.cit.*, pp7-15.

individual freedom and responsibility – that prevents her from establishing the link between the two systems and, as Reich-Ranicki observes, prompts her to retreat into the 'lovingly described' petty-bourgeois milieu largely untouched by the crucial questions of national socialism.[42]

Alexander Stephan has noted that Wolf's 'allusions' do not add up to an 'analysis of daily fascism in the land of "real socialism" '. Also, Wolf wears 'blinkers' when associating contemporary fascism with the Greek regime of the Colonels, the fall of Allende's government, the war in Vietnam, yet leaving unmentioned the suppression of the revolts in Czechoslovakia in 1968 and in Poland in 1970. However, Stephan does not link these observations to the rest of his analysis.[43] Likewise Wolfgang Werth, who states that Wolf has 'shied away from the consequences of her own premises' by letting the book end with the arrival of the Red Army, omitting the introduction of socialism in the Russian-occupied zone. He retreats from his own critique, however, when he adds that only those who don't know the conditions under which the book was written can make such a reproach.[44]

What goes unnoticed here is that in accordance with GDR usage, Wolf does not distinguish fascism from national socialism but, using the one for the other, conflates the terms in a way that has also become endemic in the West. The consequences are important: it becomes impossible to recognize antisemitism as an inherent feature of national socialist ideology. That Wolf has actually not understood the specificity of national socialism at all, is obvious from her comparison of black ghettoes in the United States with the Warsaw Ghetto, where Jews were massed before being transported to the death camps, and her comment that in both cases escape is impossible for the inmates. As Reich-Ranicki pointed out: 'With such comparisons Christa Wolf has prettified the national socialist crimes.'[45] This point is important, because as the violent debate about the American TV series *Holocaust*, and the historians' controversy have shown, in East and West Germany people were actually very willing to deceive themselves about the uniqueness of the Holocaust – the systematic pursuit and extermination of the Jewish people – which is the particularity of national socialism and not that of all fascisms. The confusion of national socialism and fascism allows for the assimilation of Nazi crimes to the bulk of horrendous twentieth-century crimes against humanity. Thus Ingeborg Drewitz calls *Patterns of Childhood* a 'book of honest debate about the seductions of the century, especially national socialism'.[46]

One could of course object that Wolf did not intend to write the history of national socialism, but an account of one girl's childhood in the eastern provinces of the Third Reich. It is, however, Wolf, who sets herself the task of examining the topic of a German fascism which still lingers on in GDR psychological patterns, and who cannot but treat it in a half-revealing, half-disguising way.

Characteristic of Wolf's work after *Patterns of Childhood* is a resignation before the inevitable which is nonetheless castigated. The central event bringing about this important change of emphasis was certainly the expulsion from the GDR

42. Marcel Reich-Ranicki, *op.cit.*, p250.

43. Alexander Stephan, *Christa Wolf*, Beck Verlag, München 1987, pp124ff.

44. Wolfgang Werth, '*Wie sind wir so geworden wie wir heute sind?*', *Süddeutsche Zeitung*, 5-6 March 1977.

45. Marcel Reich-Ranicki, *op.cit.*, p253.

46. Ingeborg Drewitz, *op.cit.*, p13.

of the singer Wolf Biermann in 1976, which had important consequences for cultural politics and the cultural climate in the following years. Between 1976 and 1989, close to one hundred writers left, or had to leave, East Germany, often after having served prison sentences, and having been deprived of publication and exposed to many humiliations. The Honecker government, by means of temporary or indefinite expulsion, got rid of troublesome critics and hoped to pressure into conformity those who wished to stay.

If Wolf had understood literary creation as a critical contribution to the building of socialism, the Biermann case and its consequences taught her that, for the time being, art would have no influence on social development. Having contemplated leaving the country, she decided to stay, even though her isolation became considerable over the years, and her motivation for remaining – belief in the final superiority of GDR socialism – must have seemed increasingly dubious. She justifies her staying on by suggesting that the place of residence is finally not important, as long as work can provide 'inner freedom' in the face of uncomprehending political forces and an increasingly hostile society.[47]

In the 1980s, Wolf's interest definitely turned away from the debate with contemporary GDR society and focused on the 'human condition', by taking on the problems of women, peace and the environment. *Cassandra: A Novel and Four Essays*, *Accident*, and *Sommerstück* (*Summerpiece*),[48] shuttle between the themes of utopia, the threat of global destruction, and the fleeting happiness found in private life. There is a difference in tone: the melancholy, reflective language of *Christa T.* gives way to a lament about present unbearable conditions with little hope for change. The terms 'sorrow', 'grief' and 'pain' assume central importance in Wolf's texts in the 1980s.

The Cassandra project, first given as the 'Frankfurt Lectures in Poetics' in 1981, was undoubtedly a triumph for the author. They thematize the physical and emotional threat posed to humankind by Western rationality and technology as the expression of a male-dominated culture. In the fate of the prophetess Cassandra, Wolf evokes the brutal destruction, by male violence, of a budding alternative social project, based on love and understanding. Much of West German critique went along with this indictment of Western civilization and culture. What Wolf had to say about social alienation in contemporary East Germany was felt to apply perfectly to the West: 'the separation of the human and social from the economic process'; the 'alienation between the sexes'; the 'yawning gap that divides the domains of spirit and power, thought and action'. The conclusions Wolf drew from the particular situation in the GDR after the Biermann expulsion are generalized: a 'redefinition of the function of literature' becomes necessary; literature should now present for discussion 'alternative forms of living', it should be *Friedensforschung* – research into peace.[49] With her concern for peace, Wolf became a national figure: 'Especially as a German writer she feels threatened by a nuclear catastrophe that will [*sic*] wipe off the map the two parts of Germany first.'[50]

The Cassandra texts were published in a particular politico-cultural climate,

47. Christa Wolf, *Ansprachen*, Lucther-hand, Frankfurt 1989.

48. Christa Wolf, *Kassandra: Erzählung* and *Vorraussetzungen einer Erzählung: Kassandra*, Luchterhand, Darmstadt and Neuwied 1983. *Cassandra: A Novel and Four Lectures*, Farrar, Straus & Giroux, New York 1984; *Störfall: Nachrichten eines Tages*, Luchterhand, Darmstadt und Neuwied 1987. *Accident: A Day's News*, Farrar, Straus & Giroux, New York 1989; *Sommerstück, Luchterhand, Darmstadt und Neuwied 1989.*

49. Sonja Hilzinger, *Christa Wolf*, Metzler Verlag, Stuttgart 1986, p107.

50. Ulrike Strauch, *'Literatur muss heute Friedensforschung sein', in Jochen Neuberger (ed.), Materialien zu Christa Wolf Kassandra*, Lyon, Goethe Institut, no date available.

which certainly account to a large extent for the deep interest they aroused. The West German peace movement, at its height in the early 1980s, shared the conviction that the two Germanies, by virtue of their geo-political position, would be the first victims of a nuclear 'super-holocaust', given the fantastic nuclear arsenal then deployed on their soil by the United States and the USSR, and over which Germans had no control. The two superpowers were perceived as forces of foreign occupation, as two imperialisms which imposed unwanted and un-German political systems: communism and capitalist democracy, understood above all as de-individualizing mass societies, geared towards technological progress. In this amalgam of ideas, the understandable concern about security, the environment and a humane society is mixed with a familiar German critique of rationalism and politics, industrial society and urbanism. The preservation of peace becomes the chief priority, and the political shape which should be given to peace hardly plays a role. The peace movement and government policy, though in total disagreement over the Federal Republic's Western alliances, did coincide in the priority they gave to peace, i.e. the maintenance of the status quo, over freedom in Central Europe. Revolts in Central Europe were unwelcome, as they would jeopardize the FRG's *Deutschlandpolitik*.[51]

In West Germany, Cassandra has been widely interpreted as a 'figure of resistance' to male-dominated society, where abstract thought and the suppression of feeling foster a culture of violence and destruction: in the women's community at the Skamandros river Cassandra joins a 'resistance movement'. The dramatization of the security situation in East and West after the 1979 NATO decision to deploy Pershing missiles was taken so far, by the West German critique, as to locate the only hope of 'resistance' to the imminent nuclear threat in literature – not in political processes.[52] However, the need to resist, which Schirrmacher sees in the nervous reaction to the Wolf texts, is less of a generational problem as he would have it. According to reports on the audience for Wolf lectures and readings, a fascination had seized the young especially, indicating their existential fear and political disorientation.[53] The feminist-pacifist reception largely accepted the hopeless historical perspective developed in *Cassandra*: passive resistance to war-mongering male rationality would inevitably be crushed leaving 'no issue, no possibility, no hope', only 'mourning'.[54]

Not only are the notions of dominance and resistance shifted from the general domain of politics to specific field of gender power relations, making them immune from political mechanisms and opposable only by a ready-made vision of a new society, but also the term 'mourning' is removed from the precise historical context of expressing sorrow for the victims of Nazism, with which it had been associated in the reception of *Patterns of Childhood*, and becomes inflated. If the only possible reaction to looming destruction is mourning, the destruction is an inevitable fate brought on through no fault of the mourners: it is the result of the fatal history of humankind. This reasoning absolves Germans from their actual historical responsibility for the Nazi crimes.

51. Symptomatically, neither the peace movement, nor groups of the extra-parliamentary left, protested when in 1981 martial law was declared in Poland. See the discussion by Peter Bender, '*Die Notgemeinschaft der Teilungsopfer*', in Sven Papcke and Werner Weidenfeld (eds), *Traumland Mitteleuropa? Beiträge zu einer aktuellen Kontroverse*, Wissenschaftliche Buchgesellschaft, Darmstadt 1988, pp76-86.

52. Ulrike Strauch, *op.cit.*, pp315-8.

53. Horst Krüger, '*Der Hang zum Allgemeinen*', *Die Zeit*, 4 October 1988.

54. Sonja Hilzinger, *op.cit.*, p143.

These are instead inscribed in the inevitable and *ir*rational progress of Reason, which – what is more – did not reach its peak with national socialism, but with the competitive nuclear armament which threatens humanity as such. History and rationality are readily confounded here.

Although Wolf's work of the 1980s was not received uncritically, it remains true that critique, harsh or well-meaning, has generally been overruled by a consensus about Christa Wolf as a great writer. In the West she became a 'poetess', the 'grand lady', the 'first lady' of German letters, and so on.[55] The question was inevitably asked why it is that Wolf could draw such a devoted constituency in the West, when her message was gloomy and her tone reproachful? Why is she a 'cult figure', when her prose 'has become rather thin and bloodless over the years',[56] when nobody could dispute that she is 'Germany's most humourless writer',[57] that her prose lacks 'perspicacity', 'charm' and 'sensuality'?[58]

The answer to the attraction of this mixture was sought in a certain German cultural tradition, where the poet(ess) dispenses the sacred word in solemn. In Wolf's texts 'elegiac and melancholic, plaintive and accusing, suffering and compassionate tones alternate.' Wolf is in this sense 'a very German poet'.[59] Reich-Ranicki puts her overwhelming success down to a continuous German longing for 'the solemn and the sacred, elegiac pathos and priestly seriousness, sublime clichés and edifying banalities'. But the poet, like the priest, is also allowed – indeed expected – to reprimand: 'Wolf does not tire to lecture that in the West life is rather abominable and terrible, in the GDR, by contrast, despite all faults and shortcomings, it is rather lovely and hopeful.'[60] West Germans, then, snug in their material abundance, appreciate the thrill of an elevating sermon.[61]

The extent to which these qualities are particularly German shall remain open to discussion, and could only be decided by an analysis of the literary climate in postwar Germany. Indeed, if the West German public associates a need for repentance, sentimentality and mourning with the work of Christa Wolf, it has the choice to do so, unlike its East German counterpart, as Reich-Ranicki makes abundantly clear. In his critique there is a sense of the historical conditions underlying the development of literary life, of the dialogic relation of literature to the surrounding culture, a relation which makes writing into more than just an occasional piece, that qualifies it for re-interpretation. It is the relation of literary form to politics – to Christa Wolf's own and to those informing her texts – that I now want to address, an issue implicit in much of West German critique which is, however, rarely made explicit.

III

During the 1980s, as Jürgen Busche reminded us recently,[62] pro- and anti-Wolf factions appeared in different German newspapers, and Wolf – both her person and her work – have received sharp criticism. Several critics, Marcel

55. Cf. Fritz J. Raddatz, '*Ein Rückzug auf sich selbst: Christa Wolfs 'Sommerstück*', *Die Zeit*, 24 March 1989; Volker Hage, *op.cit.*; Uwe Wittstock, '*Christa Wolf und der fremde unbekannte Gott*', *Frankfurter Allgemeine Zeitung*, 14 April 1987.

56. Horst Krüger, *op.cit.*.

57. Marcel Reich-Ranicki, '*Macht Verfolgung kreativ?*', *Frankfurter Allgemeine Zeitung*, 12 November 1987.

58. *Ibid.*; cf. Uwe Wittstock, *op.cit.*

59. Uwe Wittstock, *op.cit.*

60. Marcel Reich-Ranicki, '*Macht Verfolgung kreativ?*', *op.cit.*

61. Michael Ignatieff commented that Germans have an old problem reconciling material success and quality of cultural products: the ideal (GDR socialism) must not be abandoned for money (FRG living standards) – one does of course, hence the bad conscience. See his '*Unheimliche linke Träume*', *Die Zeit*, 19 October 1990.

62. Jürgen Busche, '*Der Patzer des peinlichen Datums*', *Die Neue Gesellschaft – Frankfurter hefte*, no 8, August, 1990, pp 750-3.

Reich-Ranicki, Uwe Wittstock, Horst Krüger, Wolfgang Emmerich, Christel Zahlmann,[63] identify a decisive loss of control over literary form. If Wolf had deployed her own principle of 'subjective authenticity' successfully in *Christa T.*, where the protagonist takes shape as a distinct personality, her later production is said to suffer from the abolition of distance between author, narrator and main characters, resulting in a dissolution of form; 'subjective authenticity' declines into a less and less veiled autobiographical style relating selected details from daily life, without any justification of their formal necessity. A dichotomous world-view continues to dominate Wolf's thought: formerly it was capitalism vs socialism, now it has become the rationalist male vs holistic female conception of life. Emmerich, though an admirer, observes that Wolf relies more and more on direct 'non-literary' narration of fact, and that her 'omnipresent morality' and the 'steady appeal character' of her writing have started to strain readers' patience.[64] In Reich-Ranicki's view, the decline of literary quality in Wolf's work stems from the refusal to enter into conflict with GDR ideology and political power, a refusal for which Wolf is not to be blamed, though it has indubitably stifled her talent.[65]

The discussion of *Patterns of Childhood* first made evident that the handling of literary form – both by Wolf and by her appraisers – plays a crucial role in the understanding of historical relations. The West German critique dealt with the formal question of the book mostly at the level of writing and style, understanding both as the expression of the author's extenuating, perhaps overly complicated, but nonetheless finally successful struggle with memory for the release of fact and feeling, and the corresponding struggle for the narrative means to translate this effort. On this view, the problem of the narrator's identity, of 'who is speaking', central to the book, fully justifies three levels of narration and of time. Alexander Stephan explains that while the 'essayistic insertions' and the 'imbrication of the levels of time' induce a loss of 'immediacy', they yield 'objectivity' and 'moral integrity'.[66] It seems that the devices of modern, open writing – though 'complicated' – are totally justified by the result.[67] Even Fritz Raddatz, who laments that the book is a 'noble essay' and not a novel, resignedly separates formal failure from Wolf's moral intention: he calls her writing method the 'morally most unassailable' though 'most questionable as literature'.[68]

Yet, the substantial objections to the book have associated the failure to develop a penetrating analysis of Nazism with a dissatisfactory handling of the novel form. In Marcel Reich-Ranicki's view, the fact that the book is not a novel testifies to the dissolution of Wolf's thought: *Patterns of Childhood* remains a 'sad box of notes'. In the GDR, the book was published without this generic specification, which – Reich-Ranicki supposes – was added for commercial reasons when sold in the West. With very few exceptions the numerous characters populating the book gain no depth, 'remain shadows without life'. The formal constraints of the novel would have favoured a development of the characters according to their own logic, would have sharpened the focus and helped to operate an integration of the three different levels of time and

63. Reich-Ranicki, '*Macht Verfolgung kreativ?*', *op.cit.*; Uwe Wittstock, *op.cit.*; Horst Krüger, op. cit.; Wolfgang Emmerich, *op. cit.*; Christel Zahlmann, '*Mit ihrem Latein am Ende: Christa Wolfes "Sommerstück"*', *Frankfurter Rundschau*, 18 March 1989. Interestingly, Zahlmann points out that Wolf's piece raises the problem of diminishing self-confidence, but fails to give it a broader dimension by linking it to the problems of the motivation to write and of the usefulness of literature, remaining instead purely in the private sphere, bordering on self-pity and kitsch.

64. Wolfgang Emmerich, *op.cit.*, p322.

65. Marcel Reich-Ranicki, '*Ein trauriger Zettelkasten*', *Entgegnung, op.cit.*; '*Macht Verfolgung kreativ?*', *op.cit.*

66. Alexander Stephan, *op.cit..*, pp129ff.

67. Ingeborg Drewitz, *op.cit..*, pp11-6.

68. Quoted by Norman Schachtsiek-Freitag, '*Vom Versagen der Kritik*', in Klaus Sauer (ed.), *Christa Wolf Materialienbuch*, *op.cit.*, p126.

narration.[69] Instead of interpreting the complicated structure of the book as an expression of the masterful handling of a complex topic, both Hans Mayer, whose critique bears the title 'The Courage to be Dishonest', and Marcel Reich-Ranicki suspect that behind the formal non-integration of the book lie the inhibitions of socialist self-censorship. Mayer observes that 'most characters ... are ... hindered by self-control from freely developing.'[70] With characteristic conciseness, Reich-Ranicki draws the conclusions even more clearly. Though conceding that *Patterns of Childhood* is 'well-intentioned', he considers it a failure in every respect: in the domains of form, historical grasp and, lastly, ethics. The book contains passages of lacerating insights into the self-imposed limits to knowledge, that read like a desperate appeal to the reader for understanding and absolution. Reich-Ranicki quotes some of these: 'the complex problem of self-censorship', of 'shadowing and spying on oneself'; 'the elementary fear of learning too much and being pushed into a zone of non-agreement'. And, instead of relativizing them, like Werth, he assigns them a key importance: 'It is this elementary fear which caused the failure of *Patterns of Childhood*.'[71]

Greiner and Schirrmacher are right when they point to a confusion of ethical and aesthetic criteria in the reception of Wolf's work in West Germany, betraying an attitude of regret *cum* victimization; yet this confusion cannot be exclusively rooted in the dilemmas of a Left commitment. It seems to me rather that it testifies to the embarrassed and broken relation of East and West Germans to their own history, the Nazi past, and the recent past of the dictatorial GDR, as well as to a great insecurity concerning standards of literary judgment.

In most cases the approach to Wolf remains eclectic, while her development as a writer is separated from literary tradition and cultural policy and accepted as self-evident. For example, in the Cassandra lectures, Wolf attempted to circumscribe the possibility of an alternative form of writing to those models she considers 'closed', such as the rules laid down by French classicism, German classical aesthetics with their underlying 'philistine' ideology, and the 'linear narrative' of the nineteenth-century novel. However, as Stephan noted, she stops short of establishing firm rules for 'female writing'. Nevertheless, her preoccupation with nineteenth- and twentieth-century women's writing, her search for the literary expression of feeling and the activities of ordinary life, her remark that literature has to be '*Friedensforschung*', have all been seized upon as viable pathways to a new, open, peace-oriented literature, as a legitimate attempt to oppose 'the Western aesthetic of domination, horror and destruction with an aesthetic of resistance'.[72]

If the summarily defined notions of closed and open writing offered in the Cassandra essays have not been challenged, the story *Cassandra*, however, has generally been criticized as a failure in relation to Wolf's declared intentions, but without the attempt to establish a link with writing traditions, which would have allowed for some critical distance.[73] The figure of Cassandra is considered too 'sublime and stylized' to convey contemporary women's

69. Marcel Reich-Ranicki, *Entgegnung*, *op.cit.*, pp249-54.

70. Hans Mayer, '*Der Mut zur Unaufrichtigkeit*', *Der Spiegel*, 11 April 1977; incorporated in Hans Jürgen Greif, *op.cit.*, pp140-1.

71. Marcel Reich-Ranicki, *Entegegnung*, *op.cit..*, p254.

72. Sonja Hilzinger, *op.cit.*, p145.

73. Cf. Reinhard Baumgart, '*Ein Marmorengel ohne Schmerz*', *Der Spiegel*, 4 April 1983, pp229-30; Sybille Cramer, '*Cassandra, eine weibliche Widerstandsfigur: Christa Wolfs episches Antikenprojekt*', *Frankfurter Rundschau*, 22 May 1983; Sonja Hilzinger, *op.cit..*; Werner Ross, '*Kassandra Kämpft für die Frauen*', *Die Welt*, 23 April 1983; Alexander Stephan, *op.cit.*

situation and concerns, to testify to the 'idea of a female counterproject' to the 'world history of men'. Far from coming close to her new open writing, Christa Wolf resorts, in *Cassandra*, to typification: not only is the discourse *not* pacifist but it is 'rather murderous', the 'worst' example being the Greek enemies characterized by 'Achilles the beast',[74] while the description of the vengeful Amazon, Penthesilea, is considered 'one-dimensional and typified'.[75] The conclusion could have been drawn that *Cassandra*, with its stereotyped characters, signifies in Christa Wolf's development as a writer a return to pre-*Christa T.* socialist realist writing.

None of the monographic studies published in West and East Germany[76] attempt to establish a critical relation between Wolf's ideas, her 'arrangement' with GDR socialist ideology and reality, and the development of the form and language of her work. Alexander Stephan proceeds in a typically descriptive way, noting Wolf's tendency in the 1980s to formulate 'decisive opinions in essays and lectures', while her prose takes on an increasingly essayistic style; and while her growing interest in women writers coincides with her move away from the novel to 'intermediary forms' favoured by women, such as letters, diaries, travel accounts, fragments.[77] Is this the whole explanation? There seems to be a reluctance to relate Wolf's renunciation of the novel form to the *modus vivendi* of 'critical loyalty' which she found for herself in the GDR of the 1980s; a reluctance, too, to explore the suggestion that the novel form offers possibilities of expression which essayistic writing does not hold, and that the adoption of the essayistic form and style reflect restrictions of expression to which Wolf has conceded consciously or unconsciously. Wolf's critics have never deemed it necessary to discuss the novelistic genre and its literary and philosophical achievements. Mayer, Raddatz and Reich-Ranicki have been dismissed as wedded to old-fashioned criteria of 'great literature',[78] when they point to the organizing qualities of the novelistic genre which oblige the author to set in motion different characters, to concern him/herself concretely with the social reality and cultural climate of a particular place (such as Wolf did in *The Quest for Christa T.*). To simply oppose a 'traditional', 'closed' nineteenth-century novel form to an 'open', 'modern' handling of the novelistic genre means to avoid the crucial question of the extent to which a writer like Wolf, considering the situation she found herself in, could apply modern devices to the effect of open writing. Mayer and Reich-Ranicki suggest that in Wolf's work the free use of time, the uncertainty of the narrator's identity, the insertion of essayistic and reflexive passages, often serve to escape the treatment of certain psychological and moral problems raised. They suggest therefore that Wolf enacts a kind of self-censorship; by interfering in the capacity of author-narrator, she undercuts with counter-arguments questions that are flowing from the narrative.

A reappraisal of Wolf's work remains to be done and it might be helpful to take into consideration Mikhail Bakhtin's reflections on the social nature of literature. Bakhtin made the point, in his essay on the European reception of Dostoevsky's work, that literature certainly does fulfil a social function, which

74. Reinhard Baumgart, *op.cit.*

75. Sonja Hilzinger, *op.cit.*, p142; cf. Werner Ross, who calls the form classicist and closed, the language stilted; the 'shere of intimacy' is felt to have been added on, often sliding into 'banality' and 'high kitsch', '*Kassandra kämpft für die Frauen*', *op.cit.*.

76. Besides the work by Manfred Jäger, Sonja Hilzinger and Alexander Stephan, already mentioned, see also Therese Hörnigk, *Christa Wolf*, Aufbau Verlag, Berlin 1989.

77. Alexander Stephan, *op.cit.*, pp155-73.

78. Norbert Schachtsiek-Freitag, '*Vom Versagen der Kritik*', in Klaus Sauer (ed.), *op.cit.*, p127.

can also be vicarious. However, literature cannot be reduced either to the varying associations made by the reading public, or to authorial intention, though both aspects are part of its essence. Literature is language, a social instrument of communication, and as such saturated with evaluation. In his polemic against the Formalists, who defined literary language as a material, but self-contained non-ideological domain, Bakhtin objected that all language, because it is *a priori* a means of communication, carries ideological value. In no literary genre is this social aspect of literary language more evident than in the novel, where diverse social 'voices' confront each other in unresolved dialogue. It is the (no doubt impossible) task of the novelist to keep this dialogue among the different voices permanently open.[79]

In Germany after 1945 grave psychological and moral problems had to be taken on board, and literature gave complex ethical and aesthetic dimensions to them, which can be grasped only in a combined historical and formal analysis. The debate about Wolf has thrown into sharp relief the present dilemma about the usefulness of sociological and historical analysis in relation to aesthetic value and the validity of 'classical' genres. The implications of this debate dovetail with the postmodern uncertainty about the relation of art to social life, where the humanism of modernity is often simply disposed of, instead of being re-evaluated and adjusted. The wholesale rejection of postwar German letters as 'committed' and therefore 'non-aesthetic' seems an ahistorical way of dealing with the question. In his combative account of the development of German postwar literature, Greiner contends that *Gesinnungsästhetik* subjected literature to a teleological perspective – 'bourgeois morals', the 'class standpoint', or 'humanitarian goals' – that in the past 'definitely had its necessity', but which has lost its justification in the new era of a common German history.[80] Not only is it a dangerous practice to want to rid oneself of the historical past by dismissing it; it also suggests that 'true' German literature, and a 'true' aesthetic, can only issue from a 'whole' Germany. A strange idea, considering the vigour and astounding variety of German literature over the past forty years.

79. Mikhail Bakhtin, *Problems of Dostoevsky's Poetics*, Ardis, Ann Arbor, 1973; *The Formal Method of Literary Scholarship*, Johns Hopkins University Press, Baltimore 1978; *The Dialogic Imagination*, University of Texas Press, Austin 1983.

80. Ulrich Greiner, *op.cit.* Greiner is inspired here by Karl-Heinz Bohrer's renewed attempt to establish aesthetics as the 'history of self-liberation from ... ideological and historico-philosophical tutelage'. See Karl-Heinz bohrer, '*Die Ásthetik am Ausgang ihrer Unmündigkeit*', *Merkur*, nos 10/11, October-November 1990, pp851-65.

TECHNO-ORIENTALISM

FUTURES, FOREIGNERS AND PHOBIAS

David Morley and Kevin Robins

I

> Every western politician has either actual or cinematic experience of the brutalities of Japan inflicted on its prisoners-of-war. No one, whether in Asia or beyond, has fond memories of Japanese expansionism. Which is why, as Japan's economic power expands anew, the Japanese would do better to face up to the dark aspects of their past.
>
> Leader in *The Economist*, 24 August 1991

> Today, the modern era is in its terminal phase. An awareness of its imminent demise has made Americans, the most powerful Caucasians since World War II, increasingly emotional, almost hysterical, about Japan.
>
> Ishihara Shintaro

What concerns us is what has been called 'the problem of Japan', that is to say Japan as a problem for the West. Our interest here is in tracing a set of discursive correspondences that have been, and are still being, developed in the West between 'Japan', the 'Orient' and the 'Other'. More specifically, we want to explore why, at this historical moment, this particular Other should occupy such a threatening position in the western imagination. The French Prime Minister, Edith Cresson, publicly declares her belief that 'the Japanese have a strategy of world conquest.' The Japanese, she says, are 'little yellow men' who 'stay up all night thinking about ways to screw the Americans and Europeans. They are our common enemy.' Most tellingly, Madame Cresson likens the Japanese to 'ants'.[1] Her fear is that these 'ants' are colonizing the world and taking possession of the future. What are these fears and anxieties that Japan arouses in the western psyche?

1. See *The Economist*, 1 June 1991, p67; Garth Alexander, 'Japanese "Ants" Take the Fight to the Foreigners', *Sunday Times*, 23 June 1991.

II THE JAPAN THAT IS SAYING NO

For nearly five centuries now, Japan has been among the West's Others. It has been seen as the exotic culture (zen, kabuki, tea-ceremonies, geishas) of aesthetic *Japonisme*. And it has been seen as an alien culture, a dehumanised martial culture (kamikaze, ninjutsu, samurai) to be feared. Its difference has been contained in the idea of some mysterious ambiguity. Japan is both 'the chrysanthemum and the sword':

> The Japanese are, to the highest degree, both aggressive and unaggressive, both militaristic and aesthetic, both insolent and polite, rigid and adaptable,

submissive and resentful of being pushed around, loyal and treacherous, brave and timid, conservative and hospitable to new ways.[2]

It is this complexity and ambiguity in the image of Japan that has given it a particular resonance in western fantasies. But, if it has been complex, it has always been possible symbolically to control this image of Japan. As Mark Holborn writes:

> The dialogue between Japan and the West is frequently described in terms of Japan's absorption of the West. The pattern of imitation, absorption and finally reinterpretation of Western ideas is explicit ... In contrast, the West's absorption of Japan is inconclusive and rarely described. *Japonisme* was the first stage in the imitation of a Japanese aesthetic. It was primarily decorative and involved the borrowing of Japanese motifs and design elements. Oriental views provided the West with spectacle ...[3]

Japan absorbed the culture of the West because this was its 'destiny'. This was the logic and the nature of history, development, progress. The West's absorption of Japan is 'rarely described', or is only described in a displaced and sublimated way, through the discourse of exotica and aesthetica. The dialogue between Japan and the West was not one between equals, and the integrity of the West was never challenged by Japanese culture.

But no more. That integrity is now being assaulted by a Japan that is no longer content only to provide the West with spectacle. This has become apparent in the recently translated book, *The Japan That Can Say No*, by the Liberal Democratic politician and former Minister of Transport, Ishihara Shintaro.[4] Ishihara directly accuses the United States of adopting a racist attitude towards Japan, even suggesting that American planes used atom bombs against the Japanese, and not the Germans, 'because we are Japanese' [p28]. He also suggests that the bases of western economic and cultural supremacy are being undermined. If it is the case that 'Caucasians deserve much credit in the creation of modern civilziation' [p107] it is also true that their creative energies are being exhausted. Japan has a growing lead in new technologies, to the extent that the US nuclear weapons industry is dependent on Japanese suppliers. Technology is the key to the future:

> Technology gives rise to civilization, upon which, in time, culture thrives. Nations decline when they self-indulgently let life-styles become more important than workmanship and neglect their industrial and technological base. That is the lesson of history. [p57]

According to Ishihara, Japanese technological superiority now puts it 'on the verge of a new genesis' [p29]. Europe and the United States, in contrast, are on the verge of decline. The modern era that was shaped by the West is now in its terminal phase:

2. Ruth Benedict, *The Chrysanthemum and the Sword*, Meridian, New York 1974 [1946], p2.

3. Mark Holborn, *Beyond Japan*, Jonathan Cape, London 1991, p18.

4. Ishihara Shintaro, *The Japan That Can Say No: Why Japan Will Be First Among Equals*, Simon and Schuster, New York 1991. The original Japanese version was co-authored by Sony Chairman, Akio Morita. See also, Ian Buruma, 'Just Say No', *New York Review of Books*, 7 December 1989 , pp19-20.

5. Ishihara, *op.cit.*, p28.

> Americans should realize the modern era is over. Their cherished beliefs in materialism, science, and progress have borne bitter fruit. The defeat in Vietnam, despite raining Napalm and Agent Orange on the countryside for ten years, showed the futility of military power. America harnessed science and technology and spent a fortune to get to the moon, only to find a barren rock pile. All that money and effort and what does the nation have to show for it? [p123]

Japan is the future, and it is a future that has transcended western modernity. 'How preposterous,' Ishihara suggests, 'to assert that somehow modern Japan sprang full-blown from Western seeds!' [p107] He appeals to 'our national gift for improving and refining everything from Buddhist art to semiconductors' [p58], and celebrates Japan's 'Eastern ways and values' [p123]. 'We are,' writes Ishihara, 'in and of the Orient.' [p124] According to Ishihara, Japan is of the future; it is riding on the crest of a great historic wave and will shape the next age, a more human age beyond western modernity.

III STEALING AMERICA'S SOUL

Japan is calling western modernity into question, and is claiming the franchise on the future. And this has provoked a defensive response from the West. As Akio Morita points out, 'They have the feeling that strangers, or something foreign, has entered their midst. This gives them strong feelings of fear and anxiety.'[6] Anti-Japanese feeling grows strong as Japan seems to invade the symbolic strongholds of the West. Nippon TV Network paid around $3 million for the restoration of the Sistene Chapel ceiling, making it 'an unlikely symbol of the new balance of East-West power'.[7] Manhattan's Rockefeller Center has been acquired by Japanese real estate interests. And, most symbolically of all, Hollywood has now been 'invaded' by Japanese corporate capital. Having acquired CBS Records for $2 billion in 1988, Sony then purchased Columbia Pictures in 1989 for $3.4 billion (spending a further $600 million to bring on board the Guber-Peters entertainment company). Then, in 1990, followed Matsushita's 'copycat' purchase of MCA-Universal for a massive $6 billion. If there were other Japanese 'infiltrations' – $600 million of Japanese investment in Walt Disney Corporation; JVC's investment of $100 million in Largo Entertainment; Pioneer Electronics' acquisition of a ten per cent share in Carolco Pictures – the Sony and Matsushita manoeuvres were most symbolic.[8]

Both Sony and Matsushita were involved in a strategy to achieve global dominance in the new image industries through control over both hardware and software markets. Both companies use the term 'synergy' to describe their objective of controlling different media products (books, records, films, TV programmes) across different distribution channels (and particularly the new generation of High Definition TV products). As one commentator puts it:

> Now Sony can control the whole chain. Its broadcast equipment division

6. Akio Morita, from the Japanese version of *The Japan That Can Say No*, quoted in *The Sunday Times*, 29 October 1989.

7. Waldemar Januszczak, *Sayonara Michelangelo: The Cistine Chapel Restored and Repackaged*, Addison-Wesley, Reading 1990, p194.

8. See Asu Aksoy and Kevin Robins, 'Hollywood for the 21st Century: Global Competition for Critical Mass in Image Markets', *Cambridge Journal of Economics* Vol 16, no 1, March 1992. Most recently, Time Warner has made an alliance with Toshiba, the Japanese electronics company, and with C. Itoh, the trading house.

manufactures the studio cameras and the film on which movies are produced; in Columbia it owns a studio that makes them and crucially, determines the formats on which they are distributed. That means it can have movies made on high definition TVs, and videoed with Sony VCRs. It can re-shoot Columbia's 2700-film library on 8mm film, for playing on its video Walkmans.[9]

What Sony and Matsushita have both recognized is that a successful industry depends on having appropriate software to support hardware. They have also recognized that the industry is becoming a global one, and that economies of scale and increasing corporate integration are necessary to control world markets. Sony describes its strategy now as one of 'global localization', meaning that while it operates across the globe it aims to gain 'insider' status within regional and local markets.[10] They are set to conquer the world.

Europe and the United States have been put on the defensive. Herbert Schiller points to the irony of the situation:

> The buyout of MCA/Universal – one of the Hollywood 'majors' – by the Japanese superelectronics corporation Matsushita has already had one beneficial effect. It has caused the American news media, along with the government foreign-policy makers, to recognize a problem whose existence they have steadfastly denied for the past twenty-five years – cultural domination by an external power.[11]

Suddenly there is an anxiety about exposure to, and penetration by, Japanese culture. The fear is that Japanese investors are 'buying into America's soul'. There is a fear that, in contrast to western openness, Japan is characterized by a culture of self-censorship: 'It is not that any overt censorship takes place, but rather that the norms of a society well attuned to subtle signals make unnecessary rigid rules about what is acceptable discourse.'[12] Would Sony or Matsushita be prepared to make a movie about a taboo subject such as the war-time role of the late Emperor Hirohito? There is also a fear that Japan might turn 'cocacolonization' into 'sake imperialism'. What is apparent, too, is the sense that Japanese culture is incompatible with the Hollywood ethos. Whereas America is characterized by 'ethnic democracy' and pluralism, Japan is seen as a culture of 'ethnic purity' and homogeneity.[13] Japan is seen as a consensus and conformist society, the obverse of the individualistic and creative ethos that made Hollywood a world culture. Most vocal of all is Jeffrey Katzenberg, chairman of Disney Studios. 'Film-making at its essence,' he asserts, 'is about the conveyancing of emotion.' And what is clear about the Japanese is that they are lacking in emotion. The Japanese

> culturally err on the side of withholding emotion. In saying this, I am not simply offering an American perspective. The Japanese are the first to tell you this about themselves.

9. Nigel Cope, 'Walkmen's Global Stride', *Business*, March 1990, p56. See also 'Media Colossus', *Business Week*, 25 March 1991, pp42-8; Tim Jackson, 'Japan's Transistor Titans Gamble on the Big Picture', *Independent on Sunday*, 11 November 1990.

10. See Kevin Robins, 'Global Times', *Marxism Today*, December 1989.

11. Herbert Schiller, 'Sayonara MCA', *The Nation*, 31 December 1990, p.828.

12. David E. Sanger, 'Politics and Multinational Movies', *New York Times*, 27 November 1990.

13. James Fallows, quoted in Mark Tran, 'Hollywood Rides into Rising Sun', *The Guardian*, 30 November 1990.

> This sense of discipline and self-control has no doubt been a major factor in achieving the Japanese economic miracle that has turned a small island nation into one of the world's pre-eminent industrial powers.
>
> But it is also why I firmly believe that the recent marriages between Japanese hardware makers and American moviemakers may not be ones made in entertainment heaven.
>
> There will be a chasm in the fundamental understanding of the movie business that will likely prove exceedingly frustrating for Japanese and Americans alike.[14]

If the Japanese are investing in western popular culture it is, according to a vice-president of Disney, because 'they respect us for our ability to create magic – I think they admire something about the American spirit of ingenuity – almost a wildness or recklessness, a sense of fun – that the more conservative cultures aren't capable of.'[15] Respect – respect from an inferior culture – is one thing. The 'invasion of Hollywood' and the loss of a 'national heritage' are quite another.

At one level, the response is obvious, and it is made forcefully by Ishihara: 'The sentimental attachment to a Hollywood institution like Columbia Pictures and a New York landmark like Radio City Music Hall is understandable. But the American public ... should realise that it takes two to make a deal: Americans put these properties on the market.'[15] What is made clear is that Japan is not in the business of making movies, but in the business of making money. Within the United States, too, there has been criticism of cultural and economic protectionism. 'Bruce Springsteen doesn't lose his value because he's working for Sony Chairman Akio Morita instead of CBS Chairman Larry Tisch', says economist Robert Reich.[17] According to Reich, this kind of defensive cultural chauvinism and techno-nationalism is no longer appropriate to an era in which frontiers and borders are being eroded. In the context of rapid globalization, the question 'who is "us"?' is increasingly problematical and perhaps even irrelevant.[18]

At one level, perhaps, this is true. But at another level America still believes it has a 'soul', a national soul, and to see Japan as the enemy now is one way to bring the identity of that soul back into focus. Despite the apparent logic of both Ishihara and Reich, what seems clear is that the West both needs and wants its Japan problem. The idea of 'the coming war with Japan' seems to meet a desire of some kind.

14. 'The Teachings of Chairman Jeff', *Variety*, 4 February 1991, p26.

15. Jack Myers, quoted in John Huey, 'America's Hottest Export: Pop Culture', *Fortune*, 31 December 1990, p54.

16. Ishihara, *op.cit.*, p89.

17. Quoted in Tran, *op.cit.*, p53.

18. See Robert Reich, 'The Rise of Techno-Nationalism', *Atlantic Monthly*, May 1987; Robert Reich, 'Who Is Us?', *Harvard Business Review*, January-February 1990. See also Ishihara's criticisms of American Techno-Nationalism, Ishihara, *op.cit.*, p69.

IV JAPAN RISING?

At the psychic level, the question 'who is "us"?' arouses profound disquiet. That the Japanese are unlikely to hijack Bruce Springsteen or Michael Jackson is beside the point. What is so disturbing is the manner in which Japanese interests appear to work behind the scenes, remotely manipulating Western concerns, operating through the chameleon-like strategy of global localization.

Japanese economic strategies appear to be unfair and adversarial. Rather than buying American or European products, they prefer to buy raw materials or even whole businesses. And they operate with an unnerving dedication to this cause. James Fallows sees this in terms of 'Japan's lack of emotional connection to the rest of the world', in terms of a kind of asceticism and dedication that is almost inhuman.[19] In *You Only Live Twice*, Bond's police contact, Tiger Tanaka (who had hoped to be a kamikaze pilot during the war), describes the martial art of *ninjutsu*:

> My agents are trained in one of the arts most dreaded in Japan – *ninjutsu*, which is, literally, the art of stealth or invisibility. All the men you will see have already graduated in at least ten of the eighteen martial arts of *bushido*, or 'way of the warrior', and they are now learning to be *ninja*, or 'stealers-in', which has for centuries been part of the basic training of spies and assassins and saboteurs.[20]

More recently, Shredder, in *Teenage Mutant Ninja Turtles*, hidden away in the darkness of the sewer system, operates by the same ninja principles to erode and undermine American civilization. What these popular cultural expressions reflect is an anxiety about the 'stealth' of Japanese corporations. The Japanese stealers-in are perceived as having a robot-like dedication to achieving world hegemony and to undermining the principles of western modernity.

These anxieties must be seen in the context of an increasing sense of insecurity about European and American modernity. Modernity has always been that 'mysterious and magical word that puts a barrier between the European [and American] ego and the rest of the world'.[21] If it was the West that created modernity, it was also modernity that created the imaginary space and identity described as 'western'. As Agnes Heller and Ference Feher argue, however, the very dynamism of modernity also worked to undermine its western foundations.[22] The modernization project was cumulative, future-orientated, based upon the logic of technological progression and progress. Its various elements were also designed to be exported and to transcend their European origins and exclusiveness. Modernization and modernity, with their claims to universalism, could be transposed to other host cultures. In Japan this project found a fertile environment. The technological and futurological imagination has now come to be centered here; the abstract and universalizing force of modernization has passed from Europe to America to Japan. 'In the future,' Jean Baudrillard writes, 'power will belong to those peoples with no origins and no authenticity, who know how to exploit that situation to the full': 'Look at Japan, which to a certain extent has pulled off this trick better than the US itself, managing, in what seems to us an unintelligible paradox, to transform the power of territoriality and feudalism into that of deterritoriality and weightlessness.'[23] Japan has now become modern to the degree of seeming postmodern, and it is its future that now seems to be the measure for all cultures. And, thereby, the basis of western identity is called into question.

19. James Fallows, 'Containing Japan', *Atlantic Monthly*, May 1989. Cf. Karel van Wolferen, *The Enigma of Japanese Power*, Macmillan, London 1989); and 'The Japan Problem Revisited', *Foreign Affairs*, Vol 69, no 4, Fall 1990.

20. Quoted in Sheila K. Johnson, *The Japanese Through American Eyes*, Stanford University Press, Stanford 1988, p108.

21. Georges Corm, *L'Europe et l'Orient*, La Découverte, Paris 1989, p14.

22. Agnes Heller and Ferenc Feher, *The Postmodern Political Condition*, Polity Press, Cambridge, 1988.

23. Jean Baudrillard, *America*, Verso, London 1988, p76.

From 1848 to 1914 Great Britain was the leading creditor nation in the world. Then the United States assumed that role for the next seventy years. In 1985, it became the turn of Japan. It is the largest creditor and the largest net investor in the world, and its surplus on current and capital accounts is the highest ever recorded. Half the world's goods and services and half its population now come from the fifty countries that rim the Pacific – and the world's economic centre of gravity has begun to shift, from the Atlantic to the Pacific – from the Greenwich Meridian to the International Date Line.[24]

The roles have been reversed in other spheres, too. In the nineteenth century, Europeans and Americans regarded Japan as an exotic playground, while the Japanese regarded Europe and the United States as disciplined, group-orientated societies possessing the secrets of efficient industrial production. Today, it is the Japanese who flock to the United States and to Europe for exotic tourism, and it is the Americans and Europeans who regard Japan as an austere and disciplined society with frighteningly efficient industries. In a reversal of the traditional asetheticized image of Japan, its people are now increasingly seen as workaholics, as 'economic animals' under the governance of a 'Japan Inc.' pursuing GNP growth at the expense of everything else, spreading pollution, and spawning intimidating futuristic megalopolises.[25]

If the 'Pacific era' is finally coming into being, then it has been long and anxiously anticipated. In 1903, its imminence was announced by President Roosevelt: 'The Mediterranean era died with the discovery of America; the Atlantic era is now at the height of its development and must soon exhaust the resources at its command; the Pacific era, destined to be the greatest of all, is just at its dawn.'[26] This geo-economic and geo-political ascendancy of Japan has always seemed an awesome prospect. The (potential) rise of Japan has always threatened to put 'us' in danger. From the late nineteenth century onwards, fears of the 'Yellow Threat' have constantly resurfaced in the popular imagination. At its most fantastic, there is an image in which 'Japanese and Chinese hordes spread out all over Europe, crushing under their feet the ruins of our capital cities and destroying our civilizations, grown anaemic due to the enjoyment of luxuries and corrupted by vanity of spirit.'[27]

The early years of the twentieth century saw the growing popularity of Fu Manchu and Yellow Peril-type literature in Europe and the United States. The basic fear has long been of a Japan that is seen as being engaged in an inexorable struggle with the West, whether by military means, or, more recently, through trade wars (cheap, 'shoddy' goods from Japan have been a persistent source of anger and anxiety). The image of 'Japan Inc.' can readily be seen as an echo of the West's age-old fear of 'Oriental Despotism' – a phrase first used by the ancient Greeks to describe the Persians, but one which still provides the inherited script according to which the West now imagines (post)modern Japan.

24. See, Endymion Wilkinson, *Japan Versus the West: A History of Misunderstanding*, Penguin, Harmondsworth 1983; Masahide Shibusawa, Zakaria Haji Ahmad and Brian Bridges, *Pacific Asia in the 1990s*, Routledge, London 1991; Arthur Zich, 'Japan's Sun Rises Over the Pacific', *National Geographic*, Vol 180, no 5, November 1991.

25. Recent press coverage refers to a new disease afflicting the Japanese – *karoshi*, literally 'death from overwork'. See Frances Williams, 'All Work and no Play Taking its Toll of Japanese', *The Independent*, 31 August 1991.

26. Quoted in Philip Knightley, 'Spider's Web Across the Ocean', *The Guardian Weekly*, 17 March 1991.

27. Réné Pinon, quoted in Wilkinson, *op.cit.*, p59.

V SEMITES AND ORIENTALS

Edward Said's premise in *Orientalism* was that:

as both geographical and cultural entities – to say nothing of historical entities – such locales, regions, geographical sectors as the 'Orient' and the 'Occident' are man-made ... Therefore as much as the West itself, the Orient is an idea that has a history and a tradition of thought, imagery and vocabulary that have given it reality and presence in and for the West.[28]

Naoki Sakai develops the point further:

the Orient does not connote any internal commonality among the names subsumed under it, it ranges from regions in the Middle East to those in the Far East. One can hardly find anything religious, linguistic or cultural that is common among these varied areas. The Orient is neither a cultural, religious or linguistic unity. The principle of its identity lies outside itself: what endows it with some vague sense of unity is that the Orient is that which is excluded and objectified by the West, in the services of its historical progress. From the outset the Orient is a shadow of the West. If the West did not exist, the Orient would not exist either.[29]

The 'Orient' exists because the West needs it; because it brings the project of the West into focus.

Up until the Renaissance, Europe belonged to a 'regional tributary system' that included Europeans and Arabs, Christians and Muslims. Until then, the countries of western Europe only occupied the north-western edge of a geographical complex whose centre was at the eastern end of the Mediterranean basin. Subsequently, however, a 'North-South split, running through the Mediterranean – which only replaced the East-West division at a late date – [was] falsely projected backward' and was 'presented as permanent, self-evident and inscribed in geography (and therefore – by implicit false deduction – in history)'.[30] In this transition, northern Europe became redefined as the centre of the system, and all other regions were relegated to the status of its peripheries. In all of this, history is rewritten: Christianity is annexed arbitrarily to Europe, and becomes one of the central terms by which Europe understands itself (despite the fact that Christianity is middle-eastern in origin). A further crucial step involves the arbitrary annexation of Hellenic culture to Europe. As Samir Amin emphasizes, the history of 'Western thought' is conventionally traced back to Ancient Greece, and it is generally considered to come of age with the Renaissance (re)appropriation of Greek culture and philosophy.[31]

It has become a commonplace to observe that, from the time of the Crusades, and then, more dramatically even, from the moment of the Ottoman army's arrival at the gates of Vienna in 1683, it has been the 'threat from the East' which has produced attempts at European unification, both as a defensive response and as a rationalization for aggressive policies of expansion and the consolidation of white, Christian, 'civilized' Europe against its Other. However, the 'East' is not always or necessarily 'outside'. It can also designate the 'Other within'. German writers referred to Jews as 'Asiatics' or 'Orientals' right up to

28. Edward Said, *Orientalism*, Penguin, Harmondsworth: 1985, pp4-5.

29. Naoki Sakai, 'Modernity and its Critique', *South Atlantic Quarterly*, Vol 87, no 3, 1988, p499.

30. Samir Amin, *Eurocentrism*, Zed Books, London 1989, p93; cf. Corm, *op.cit.*.

31. *Ibid.*, pp90, 94. The problem with this 'fabrication of Ancient Greece' is that the Ancient Greeks themselves were quite clear about their Oriental roots, claiming significant Phoenician and Egyptian cultural ancestries quite at odds with the 'Aryan' definition of Greek culture constructed by nineteenth-century 'Hellomania'. See, Martin Bernal *Black Athena*, Free Association Books, London 1987.

the present century, and both Samir Amin and Edward Said stress the way in which the category 'Europe' – through the category 'Aryan' – has, at least since the time of Renan, been defined by contrast with the category 'Semitic' (a category which includes both Jew and Arab). We are, as Robert Young argues, forced to consider the relation of anti-Islamic and anti-Arab feeling to its 'dark shadow', anti-Semitism: 'In this context the Jews came to represent the Orient within, uncannily appearing inside when they should have remained hidden, outside Europe: thus the logic of their expulsion, or extermination, becomes inextricably linked with Orientalism itself.'[32] Within the terms of European racism, both Arab and Jew are subsumed together in the figure of the Orient, against which the western world struggles to differentiate itself.

As if all that were not enough, there are yet further complications. To speak of 'the Jews' is not only to specify a particular racial or ethnic group. It is also to invoke a figure of suspicion within western culture. In fact, it identifies a symbolic space that can be occupied by different groups at different times. A number of commentators have recently shown that it is the Japanese who are now coming to occupy that space in the imagination of the West. In a short discussion of the new European nationalism, Ian Buruma quotes from a disturbing piece of recent racist propaganda: 'With the wholesale appropriation of western ways, Jewry struts about in borrowed plumage, as does foremost Japan in the world at large.'[33] Slavoj Žižek draws attention to the dangers:

> Our perception of 'real' Jews is always mediated by a symbolic-ideological structure which tries to cope with social antagonism: the real 'secret' of the Jew is our own antagonism. In today's America, for example, a role resembling that of the Jew is being played more and more by the *Japanese*. Witness the obsession of the American media with the idea that the Japanese don't know how to enjoy themselves. The reason for Japan's increasing economic superiority over the USA is located in the somewhat mysterious fact that the Japanese don't consume enough, that they accumulate too much wealth.[34]

Similarly, Judith Williamson has pointed to the parallel between anti-Semitism and anti-Japanese racism: 'Anti-semitism fed off notions of "rich Jewish bankers"; anti-Arab mythologies blossomed in the seventies with the buying up of British landmarks by oil sheikhs. And now we have Japan take-over fear, alongside a popular fascination with inscrutable customs, currant-eyed criminals and bad guys on Suzukis.'[35]

In 1989, the Japanese overtook the Russians in opinion polls as the nation which Americans fear most. The 'official' explanation of this is in economic terms. As McKenzie Wark says, this scenario reflects the loss of American mastery: a scenario in which 'manifest destiny' turns out to lead 'from Fordism to Sonyism', and thereby to the premature end of the American century.[36] It is, however, not simply a matter of economic hegemony. More significant is the

32. Robert Young, *White Mythologies: Writing History and the West*, Routledge, London 1990, p139.

33. Ian Buruma, 'A Euro-Flag of Many Colours', *The Guardian*, 28 September 1991.

34. Slavoj Žižek, 'Eastern Europe's Republics of Gilead', *New left Review*, no 183, September-October 1990, p156. For a highly unusual Japanese-Jewish perspective on this relationship, see Isiah Ben-Dasan, *The Japanese and the Jews*, Wetherhill, New York 1972. Ben-Dasan writes of how 'the position of being a middleman or go-between invites persecution.' 'The Japanese,' he argues, 'known to the great masses of the non-white peoples of the world for the excellence of their products and services, are in a position similar to that of the Alexandrian Jews. They are honorary white men as the Jews were once, in a sense, honorary Greeks in Alexander's city'. [pp164-5] The Japanese, Ben-Dasan, says 'may one day find themselves facing a general hostility that will differ little from that which has inspired persecution of the Jews in many lands.' [p166] From our point of view the crucial question is not so much whether the category 'Jewish' and the category 'Japanese' share some common substance or display any essential similarity;

racism and paranoia evoked when the Japanese are seen to be buying up things – Hollywood studios, record companies, the Rockefeller Center and so on – that are somehow felt to be properly or quintessentially 'American'. It is a question of strangers 'stealing in' on the American Dream. And the Japanese are, as Waldemar Januszczak says, now the 'ultimate twentieth century strangers'. As he observes:

> If the Canadians (rather than the Japanese) had bought Columbia Pictures or Mickey Mouse or the Rockefeller there would have been no point in an outcry. Canadians, after all, are just like Americans, only less so. The Japanese, according to the occidental popular imagination are aliens from the East who are probably trying to take over the West.

(Remember Madame Cresson's outpourings.) This, as Januszczak goes on to argue, is 'a position in the Caucasian imagination that has hitherto been occupied by freemasons and foreign agents and Rosecrucians and little green men from outer space cunningly disguised as humans; and, of course, Jews. Like the Jews, the whole Japanese nation seems to add up to one huge secret society, bent on making money out of Christians.'[37]

Contemporary expressions of anti-Japanese feeling incorporate a long tradition of racist fascination and fear, one whose language and imagery is being reforged in contemporary political and cultural rhetoric. As Judith Williamson notes, by way of example, at the centre of Ridley Scott's highly successful film *Black Rain*, there is the antagonistic interplay of American cultural imperialism and Japanese 'economic' expansion. Michael Douglas complains: 'You Japanese sit on what you've got so tight I can't even pull it out of your arse.' His Japanese co-star, Ken Takakura, dismissively retorts: 'Music and movies are all your culture is good for ... We make the machines.'[38] There is, of course, a specificity to American-Japanese relations. When *The Japan That Can Say No* was officially published in English in 1991, one of the most contentious (and most often cited) passages was that in which Ishihara claims that there was a 'virulent racism' in the American decision to drop nuclear bombs on Hiroshima and Nagasaki.[39] It is hardly incidental, in this context, that the motive for *Black Rain*'s chief villain swamping America with counterfeit dollars is revenge for the 'black rain' which fell on Hiroshima.

VI MODERNITY AND ETHNICITY

We must recognize how abruptly and dramatically the histories and geographies of the dominated were fissured by their encounter with the West. National and regional geographies were disrupted by this contact, and histories and stories of the past had to be retold in a new light:

> It is as if the pre-contact time had been wrenched off and replaced by an unfamiliar temporal system that would efficiently dissolve the residual old.

it is, rather, that they increasingly occupy a comparably unfavourable position.

35. Judith Williamson 'Butch Ridley and the Sunrise Kids', *The Guardian*, 1 March 1990.

36. McKenzie Wark, 'The Tyranny of Difference: From Fordism to Sonyism', *New Formations*, no 15, 1991.

37. Waldemar Januszczak, 'The New Jews', *The Guardian*, 29 December 1990.

38. Williamson, *op.cit.* This is not, however, an exclusively American-Japanese dynamic. Judith Williamson notes that Yorkshire TV's recent (1990) police series, set in Hong Kong, was 'only one letter off being called "Yellow Threat Street" '.

39. Ishihara, *op.cit.*, p28.

> Peoples were also displaced from their sundry geographic centralities to the peripheral positions assigned by the Western metropolis: thus appellations like the Middle East and the Far East ... A new history and [a] new geography combined to produce the magical peripheries of the primitive.[40]

40. Masao Miyoshi and H.D. Harootunian, 'Introduction', *South Atlantic Quarterly*, Vol 87, no 3, 1988, p388.

41. Sakai, *op.cit.*, pp498-9.

42. *Ibid.*, pp476-7.

43. Ronald Dore describes this as the 'reverse convergence hypothesis'. See Ronald Dore, *British Factory – Japanese Factory*, University of California Press, Berkeley 1973.

Naoki Sakai stresses the involuntary nature of modernity for the non-West: modernity for the 'Orient' was primarily about subjugation to the West's political, economic and military control. The modern Orient was born only when it was invaded, defeated and exploited by the West; only when the Orient became an object for the West did it enter 'modern times'. For the non-West, 'modernity means, above all, the state of being deprived of its own subjectivity'; it is possible, then, 'to define the Orient as that which can never be a subject'.[41] What is clear is that the 'West' is not simply and straightforwardly a geographical category: 'It is, evidently, a name always associating itself with those regions, communities and peoples that appear politically or economically superior to other regions, communities and peoples.'[42] Onto the geography of 'East' and 'West' is directly mapped the distinction between the 'pre-modern' and the 'modern'. The category 'West' has always signified the positional superiority of Europe, and then also of the United States, in relation to the 'East' or 'Orient'.

It is on this basis that we can begin to understand the contemporary hysteria and panic about Japan. Japan has come to exist within the western political and cultural unconscious as a figure of danger, and it has done so because it has destabilized the neat correlation between West/East and modern/pre-modern. If the West is modern, Japan should be pre-modern, or at least non-modern. That is the case if it is to fit the terms of the established scheme by which 'we' order our sense of space and time and allocate their place in it to 'them'. The fact that Japan no longer fits throws the established historico-geographical schema into confusion, creating a panic of disorientation (if not yet, to be sure, of dis-orientalism).

Western social science has understood 'modernization' as a unilinear process of economic and social transformation, stretching from the cultural and intellectual world of seventeenth-century Europe to the post-1945 United States. It finds the emergence of Japan as an economic superpower hard to reconcile with this model (based as it is on a Euro-American definition of modernity). The scandalous and unthinkable possibility is raised that the West may now have to 'learn from Japan' – that is, to 'orientalize' itself in order to become economically competitive with the emerging economies of a 'Confucian zone' in the twenty-first century.[43] The unpalatable reality is that Japan, that most Oriental of Oriental cultures, as it increasingly outperforms the economies of the West, may now have become the most (post)modern of all societies.

What Japan has done is to call into question the supposed centrality of the West as a cultural and geographical locus for the project of modernity. It has also confounded the assumption that modernity can only be articulated through the forms the West has constructed. Indeed, what it has made clear are the racist foundations of western modernity. If it is possible for modernity to find a home in the Orient, then any essential, and essentializing, distinction between East and West is problematized. Japan can no longer be stereotyped as the 'Orient'; it is not possible to marginalize or dismiss Japanese modernity as some kind of anomaly. Its distinctiveness insists that we take it seriously. And, at the same time, it insists that we seriously consider the implications of this for the West's own sense of privilege and security.

VII ORIENTALISM AND OCCIDENTALISM

In this book, *White Mythologies*, Robert Young emphasizes 'the relation of the Enlightenment, its grand projects and universal truth-claims to the history of European colonialism'. 'The appropriation of the Other as a form of knowledge within a totalizing system,' he argues, 'can thus be set alongside the history (if not the project) of European imperialism, and the constitution of the Other as "Other" alongside racism and sexism.' Drawing on Derrida, he makes the point that, through the development of western culture, 'the white man [has taken] his own mythology, Indo-European mythology, his own *logos*, that is, the *mythos* of his idiom, for the universal form of that he must still wish to call Reason.'[44] In the deconstruction of this Europeanization of culture and knowledge, the work of Edward Said has clearly been of particular importance. *Orientalism* offers a cogent analysis of the process through which the 'Orient' has been produced as an object, not only of knowledge, but also of power, inscribed in both the discourses and the institutions of imperialism and colonialism.

Said's work on the 'Middle East' is clearly of relevance in looking at the West's construction of a 'Far East', but as Richard Minear rightly stresses, 'the historical relation between "the West" and Japan was very different from that which obtained between "the West" and Said's Orient.'[45] Thus, whilst it did succumb to western force in the nineteenth century, and also in the middle of the twentieth, 'Japan did not become a colony.' 'Nor,' Minear adds, 'did the abiding cultural ties which bound the West to the Orient exist between Japan and the West. Japan held no special interest.' This meant that the particular relation between Orientalist knowledge and imperial and military power, which has been so important in the case of the Middle East, did not hold in the case of Japan: Japanese studies 'never experienced the naked "authority over the Orient" which Said sees an an integral part of Orientalism'. 'Nor,' Minear adds again, 'did Japan wait for the West to discover its own past, its history, its identity.' Japan was always a sophisticated and literate culture, and, indeed, some of the most widely read books on Japan in western languages were written by Japanese. What is clear is that 'the West had very little to teach Japan about itself.'[46] This apparent hermetic integrity of Japanese culture has been crucial to the way it has functioned within the Orientalist *imaginaire*.

Its irreducible difference has been the source of both fascination and

44. Young, *op.cit.*, pp9, 4, 7.

45. Richard H. Minear, 'Orientalism and the Study of Japan', *Journal of Asian Studies*, Vol 39, no 3, May 1980, p508.

46. *Ibid.*, pp514-5.

anxiety. Thus Far Orientalism – from Lafcadio Hearn's *Glimpses of Unfamiliar Japan* through to Roland Barthes' *The Empire of Signs* – has been seduced by the elaborate and arcane rituals of Japanese culture; this Orientalism has been one in which Japan functions as a locus of self-estrangement and cultural transcendence. In his account of *The Japanese Tradition in British and American Literature*, Earl Miner suggests that 'Japan, a civilization as highly refined as the West, is familiar and congenial in its modern conveniences, in addition to having the additional grace for a world-weary Westerner of new and idealized forms of behaviour and art.'[47] In contact with this refined exoticism, the world-weary Westerner has indulged in unashamed aestheticism, eroticization and idealization. Japan has been the 'proper meeting-ground of East and West', where western rationalism might seek fulfilment through its 'marriage' (Fenollosa) with eastern mysticism.[48]

Yet this uniqueness of Japanese culture, which makes it exceptionally seductive, may also provoke fear and anxiety. There is a fear of what lies behind the enigmatic facade of Japanese aestheticism and spiritualism. There is a fear that Japan's irreducible difference will remain aloof from, and impenetrable to, western reason and universalism. A fear, too, that western culture might itself be overwhelmed by the oriental other. This is now a fundamental issue in discussions of the 'Japan problem'. A recent leader article in the *Financial Times* symptomatically suggests that 'Britain, though not Britain alone, fears some emasculation.'[49] Bruce Cumings reveals the existence of an unpublished report, commissioned from Rochester Institute of Technology by no less than the CIA, which tries to address the question of how different the Japanese are from 'us':

> The report deems the Japanese 'creatures of an ageless, amoral, manipulative and controlling culture ... suited only to this race, in this place'. Which 'creature' do they most resemble, you might ask. Well, the Japanese get along 'as does the lamprey eel living on the strength of others'. The lamprey eel will not stop sucking the lifeblood of the rest of us, this 'treatise' implies, until it has devoured the entire world.[50]

It may be ludicrous, even comical, but it is racist. It may be extreme, but it reflects a prevailing attitude towards the Japanese 'Other'.

'The most consistently interesting questions caused by Japan,' according to James Fallows, 'involve its differentness.'[51] If difference can be seductive, it is always disturbing, dangerous, and ultimately intolerable. The 'Other' must be assimilated or excluded: within 'our' universe there is no place for difference as such. 'What is at issue,' writes Cornelius Castoriadis, 'is the apparent incapacity to constitute oneself as oneself without excluding the Other – *and* the apparent inability to exclude the Other without devaluing and, ultimately, hating them.' It is almost always the case in the encounter between cultures, Castoriadis argues, that the Other is constituted as inferior:

> The simplest mode in which subjects value their institutions evidently comes

47. Earl Miner, *The Japanese Tradition in British and American Literature*, Princeton University Press, Princeton 1958, p270. See also Michel Melot, 'Questioning Japanism', *Block*, no 13, 1987/88.

48. Miner, *op.cit.*, p271.

49. 'Learning More About Japan', *Financial Times*, 19 September 1991.

50. Bruce Cumings, 'CIA's Japan 2000 Caper', *The Nation*, 30 September 1991, p367. This represents a response to Ishihara's *The Japan That Can Say No*. What we have here, as Cumings puts it, is 'the America that can say yo!'.

51. James Fallows, 'The Crucial Difference', *Times Literary Supplement*, 27 September 1991, p7.

> in the form of the affirmation – which need not be explicit – that these institutions are the only 'true' ones – and that therefore the goods, beliefs, customs, etc., of the others are false. In this sense the inferiority of the others is only the flipside of the affirmation of the *truth proper* of the institution of the society-Ego.

The sole foundation of the institution of ('our') society 'being belief in it and, more specifically, its claim to render the world and life coherent, it finds itself in mortal danger as soon as proof is given that other ways of rendering life and the world coherent and sensible exist.'[52] Difference is not easy to live with. But what if another culture were to seem, and to claim itself, 'equivalent' or even superior to 'ours'? What if it will not be excluded or converted? What if, as is the case with the Japanese, it seems to flaunt its differentness?

The 'Japan problem' is, in one sense, the problem of Japan's irreducible difference. Japan's differentness is a very particular problem for the West. The Japanese Other plays the West at its own game. Western Orientalism seems to have found its match in what seems to be an 'Orientalism in reverse.' In his discussion of Said's *Orientalism*, Sadik Jalal al-'Azm addresses the question of Islamic revivalism and fundamentalism. Its discourses on the inherent superiority of Islamic culture, he argues, 'simply reproduce the whole discredited apparatus of classical Orientalist doctrine concerning the difference between East and West, Islam and Europe. This reiteration occurs at both the ontological and epistemological levels, only reversed to favour Islam and the East in its implicit and explicit value judgements.' The 'dichotomizing' tactic of Orientalism is by no means the hallmark of western thought alone, and 'Orientalism in reverse' is, in the end, 'no less reactionary, mystifying, ahistorical and anti-human than Orientalism proper'.[53]

In this case, however, the argument is posed abstractly and is divorced from the question of power – in this case the institutional power of the West, which has ensured the authority of its Orientalism. As Lata Mani and Ruth Frankenberg argue, 'It is within the context of a specific set of unequal economic, social and political relationships between West and East that Western descriptions are produced. It is these relationships that lend them strength and endurance. Until this world-historical context changes, it does not make sense to speak of a "reverse Orientalism".'[54] Where power is missing, it is not really meaningful to talk of 'Orientalism in reverse'. But what about the case of Japan?

In the case of Japan, it is worth interrogating the recent flourishing of what *might* actually be understood as a form of 'Orientalism in reverse'. We are referring to the rise of *nihonjinron* discourses of 'Japaneseness', 'Japanese uniqueness', 'Japanese superiority', and 'Japan as Number One'. *Nihonjinron* discourses are works of cultural nationalism concerned with the ostensible uniqueness of Japan. They display a number of assumptions, centered principally around the idea that the Japanese constitute a culturally and socially homogeneous racial entity, the essence of which is both unchanged throughout

52. Cornelius Castoriadis, 'Reflections on Racism', *Thesis Eleven*, (forthcoming).

53. Sadik Jalal al-'Azm 'Orientalism and Orientalism in Reverse', *Khamsin*, no 8, 1981, p22.

54. Lata Mani and Ruth Frankenberg, 'The Challenge of Orientalism', *Economy and Society*, Vol 14, no 2, May 1985, p187.

history and quite different from all other races. *Nihonjinron* discourses are by no means new: these 'discussions of the Japanese' (a literal translation of *nihonjinron*) have been going on for at least the last hundred years.[55] As Richard Minear observes, 'With or without power in its favour, Japan has a long tradition of racist and ethnocentric behaviour; what nation does not? Perhaps European and American ideas about the "non-Western" world are exceptional only in that during the past several centuries Europe and America have had the military power to put them into action.'[56] What is at stake now, however, is the changed function these discourses have in the new context of a shifting balance of power between Japan, Europe and the United States. As Japan comes to assume a hegemonic position in the spheres of technology, manufacturing and finance, and as the question of Japanese military capacity increasingly comes on to the political agenda, there are growing fears about whether Japan might now have power in its favour and might now be inclined to put its nationalistic ideas into action. In the context of these changing power relations, *nihonjinron* discourses are taking on a new significance, as are European and American reactions to them.

Historically, the West has provided the universal point of reference in relation to which others have been defined as particular. Thus Japan has existed 'as a particularity, whose sense of identity is always dependent upon the Other. Needless to say, this Other is a universal one, in contrast to which Japanese particularism is rendered even more conspicuous.'[57] If the discourse of *nihonjinron* has stressed innumerable cases of Japan's difference from the West, thereby defining Japan's identity in terms of deviations from the West, 'this is nothing but the positing of Japan's identity in Western terms, which in return establishes the centrality of the West as the universal point of reference.'[58] Nonetheless, the desire has been to change this situation so that the Japanese would occupy the position of the centre and of the subject which determines other particularities in its own universal terms. In more recent developments of *nihonjinron* discourse what we are seeing seems to be a series of 'tryouts in rewriting world history and geography with the first world and Japan as the joint master-narrators'.[59] Western anxieties about Japan are an expression of resentment at this emergence of a threat to what has been seen as the West's natural and proper claim on universalism.

Japanese culture has developed a kind of reverse Orientalism, what Roland Robertson describes as 'Occidentalism', based on claims about the selfish individualism, materialism, decadence and arrogance of westerners (particularly Americans), and also on an explicit pride in Japanese racial purity, which has been contrasted with the allegedly debilitating consequences of American racial and ethnic heterogeneity.[60] This kind of Japanese self-projection and self-assertion can assume highly provocative and confrontational forms. When, in the context of the Gulf War, one Japanese commentator described the Americans as 'our white mercenaries',[61] it was difficult for the western forces to take. When Ishihara throws out a warning to 'the Caucasians' that their creative energies are becoming exhausted and their civilization is in its terminal phase,

55. Peter N. Dale, *The Myth of Japanese Uniqueness*, Croom Helm, London 1987.

56. Minear, *op.cit.*, p516

57. Sakai, *op.cit..*, p484.

58. *Ibid.*, p487. Of course, in any specific instance, the locus of the 'West' is geographically variable. Up until the mid-nineteenth century, for example, China was the 'western' Other in opposition to which Japan's identity was defined.

59. Miyoshi and Harootunian, *op.cit.*, p390.

60. Roland Robertson, 'Japan and the USA – the Interpenetration of National Identities and the Debate About Orientalism', in Nicholas Abercrombie *et al* (eds), *Dominant Ideologies*, Unwin Hyman, London 1991, p192.

61. Quoted in Ian Buruma, 'The Pax Axis', *New York Review of Books*, 25 April 1991, p26.

this can be decidedly unnerving and destabilizing. To be warned that the future belongs to those who are 'in and of the Orient' exposes a raw nerve.

There have been two kinds of western response to these 'Occidentalist' challenges. The first has been defensive, reflecting a certain disorientation and loss of self-confidence. Perhaps Japan *has* become Number One? The 1980s saw a quite significant shift in American perspectives on Japan, especially following the publication of Ezra Vogel's widely read *Japan as Number One*, and the emergence of the question about what America could 'learn from Japan'. This has also translated itself into attempts to reassert national self-image and self-esteem by recovering the essence of American difference. Indeed, what one sees is 'something like an American equivalent of *nihonjinron*, with much debate about the ways in which American national culture could be enhanced and protected from global relativization. In certain respects the idea of American exceptionalism is the equivalent of the idea of Japanese uniqueness.'[62] James Fallows, for instance, has argued that America could be made great again by capitalizing upon the 'American talent' for disorder and openness and by rejection of the 'Confucianism' which he says has taken hold of American society in the form of credentialism, reliance upon educational testing, and so on.[63]

But if there have been such responses of adjustment, there has also been a more aggressive retaliation against what is seen as Japanese provocation. An outburst of 'Japan bashing' flared up around 1987, and it did so as an immediate consequence of the thawing relations between the West and the Soviet bloc. It is the transformation to the so-called New World Order that is now changing American and European attitudes to Japan. Now there is a growing hostility to what is seen as its ruthless and dedicated economic expansionism, anger at a corresponding insensitivity to global concerns (the environment, famine) and resentment about its lack of political solidarity (the Gulf War).[64] Two recent Japan-bashers, Michael Silva and Bertil Sjögren, suggest that we have to cast our minds back to the wartime period if we want to gain insights into 'the Japanese mindset'. In trying to understand Japanese economic strategy, these authors explicitly use Pearl Harbour as a reference point, one that 'more than vaguely parallels today's economic confrontations'.[65] And, in a much cited article, James Fallows points to 'Japan's ever-present fears that the rest of the world is about to gang up on it and exclude it'. The last time Japan felt like this, Fallows goes on, was the moment of Pearl Harbour, when the country's military leadership 'was convinced that the West had decided to choke Japan to death, with boycotts, so Japan might as well strike'.[66] Japanese 'narcissism', a 'weakness of universal principles', and a 'lack of emotional connection to the rest of the world', all add up to make Japan seem a powerful figure of danger. Japan is different – a natural enemy. The western mood is resentful and belligerent. The talk is of 'the coming war with Japan'.[67]

Orientalism and Occidentalism head to head – cultures in contestation. Who is to be the 'unmarked' (the natural) point of universal reference? Who is to occupy the 'centre' in relation to which the 'Other' must define its particularity

62. Robertson, *op.cit.*, p189. This is not to suggest that the idea of American exceptionalism is new – manifestly it is not. What is new is the centrality of Japan as the point of reference in relation to which (or against which) 'Americanness' is being defined.

63. James Fallows, *More Like Us*, Houghton Mifflin, Boston 1989.

64. Ishihara reports a conversation in which a US congressman said that 'US-Soviet ties have dramatically improved and it's quite possible that the partnership between Washington and Tokyo might be dissolved.' 'Do you mean that Americans and Russians have rediscovered their mutual identity as Caucasians?' Ishihara responded. The congressman nodded in agreement. *Op.cit.*, pp77-8.

65. Michael Silva and Bertil Sjögren, *Europe 1992 and the New World Power Game*, John Wiley, New York 1990, p156.

66. James Fallows, May 1989, *op.cit.*, p40. See also the recent editorial in *The Economist* which argues that 'to play its rightful role in the world, Japan must first confess its sins.' 'Redemption's Reward', *The Economist*, 24 August 1991, p15.

67. George Friedman and Meredith LeBard, *The Coming War With Japan*, St Martin's Press, New York 1991.

and marginality? 'West' against 'East'. We could say that it should not, need not, be like this. In the words of Ihab Hassan, Occident and Orient 'have "comtaminated" one another, and this is, mainly, to the good'. These interactions, we might say, 'hint at the possibilities of human understanding, an understanding neither universal nor stubbornly local'.[68] And yet what we have is mutual paranoia: 'This idea that the others are quite simply others, which in words is so simple and so true, is a historical creation that goes against the "spontaneous" tendencies of the institution of society.'[69] There are powerful psychic investments in the desire to exclude the other.

68. Ihab Hassan, 'The Burden of Mutual Perceptions – Japan and the United States', *Salmagundi*, no 85-6, Winter-Spring 1990, pp74, 83. See also Ihab Hassan, 'Alterity? Three Japanese Examples', *Meanjin*, Vol 49, no 3, Spring 1990.

69. Castoriadis, *op.cit.*

70. James Fallows, 'Is Japan the Enemy?', *New York Review of Books*, 30 May 1991, p34.

VIII TECHNO-ORIENTATALISM AND THE FUTURE OF MODERNITY

In one sense, then, the West's 'Japan problem' is about the confrontation between cultural narcissisms. But to leave it at that would be too easy. There is something that is even reassuring about the possibility that Japan's phenomenal economic and technological success is attributable to 'the Japanese mind'. To invoke oriental conformity, stealth and ruthless dedication is to suggest that Japan does not play by the rules. The comparative lack of success of the European and North American economies must then be a consequence of abiding by universal principles and moral codes. Through such reasoning, it is possible, even in the face of competitive failure, to reaffirm the essential (that is, civilizational) supremacy of western culture.

Differentness is functional: it cannot be willingly or easily relinquished. Through the manic assertion of difference, the identity of western culture and identity can be sustained. And if the encounter with difference is painful, what it averts – what it represses, denies or disavows – is something that is more painful still. What it defers is the encounter with western self-identity and self-interest, as well as the recognition of what is common in both the Japanese and western experiences of modernity.

The functioning and the significance of technology in western identity is crucial to understanding what this means. What would the West be without its vaunted technological supremacy? Technology has been central to the potency of its modernity. Technology is held to be the key to the future, and Japan now has a growing lead in key areas of technological development. Consequently the West fears that the loss of its technological hegemony may be associated with its cultural 'emasculation'. Symbolizing this new relationship of weakness, as we have seen, American military capacity is increasingly dependent on Japanese high-tech components. The Japanese rise to power has been a perfectly conscious strategy: from the nineteenth century, 'Japan's leaders knew the country would be colonized, like Malaya or China, if it did not haul itself into the modern age'; and, following defeat in the Second World War, 'Japan's tattered postwar leadership understood that technology and industry were the only means of recovering independence of any kind.'[70] Akio Morita has described how he deliberately set out to make Sony's image synonymous with 'technical quality'. This was necessary in order to avoid the negative connotations of products being perceived as 'Japanese', given the level of anti-Japanese feeling in the immediate postwar period. In an interview in the mid 1980s, Morita recalled the task that faced him: 'When I first visited Europe in 1953, I discovered that Japan had a very bad image in Europe because of the war ... and I thought "unless we make a real high technical quality product we cannot sell anything here." So we have been trying to change our image, to concentrate on quality in technical standards.'[71] Through its strategies of technological innovation, Japan has more than recovered its independence, and has now hauled itself perhaps even beyond the modern age.

'This,' it has been argued, 'is the society where technology and rationalization have fused perfectly.'[72] Technological prowess has become associated with Japanese enterprise (Sony, Nissan, Matsushita, Panasonic, Toshiba, Toyota etc.). In Don DeLillo's *White Noise*, Jack Gladney's daughter utters two clearly audible and haunting words in her sleep, 'Toyota Celica':

> How could these near-nonsense words, murmured in a child's restless sleep, make me sense a meaning, a presence? She was only repeating some TV voice. Toyota Corolla, Toyota Celica, Toyota Cressida. Supranational names, computer-generated, more or less universally pronounceable. Part of every child's brain noise, the substatic regions too deep to probe.[73]

High-technology has become associated with Japaneseness. Out of this a new techno-mythology is being spun: Japan can be projected as 'the greatest "machine-loving" nation of the world', a culture in which 'machines are priceless friends'.[74] Japan has become synonymous with the technologies of the future – with screens, networks, cybernetics, robotics, artificial intelligence, simulation. What are these Japanese technologies doing to us? The techno-mythology is centered around the idea of a postmodern mutation of human experience. 'The Japanese are not altering the way we see the real world, they are doing something far more radical,' writes Charlie Leadbeater. 'They are taking us further and further into a different world of electronic images and sounds .. In future, the line between the real and the electronic will probably blur even further to the extent that it may not be fully recognizable.'[75] The Japanese are creating a new domain of artificial reality. Karaoke, computer games, *pachinko*, virtual reality – Japanese technologies are 'blurring the line between the real and the simulated ... producing the sensation that reality is only part of a world of simulation'.[76]

If the future is technological, and if technology has become 'Japanized', then the syllogism would suggest that the future is now Japanese too. The postmodern era will be the Pacific era. Japan is the future, and it is a future that seems to be transcending and displacing western modernity. Insofar as a nation's sense of identity has become confused with its technological capability, these developments have, of course, had profoundly disturbing and destabilizing consequences in Europe and the United States. The West has had to try to come to terms with everything that this technological 'emasculation'

71. Akio Morita, interviewed in Julian Temple's *It's All True*, BBC 2, 1984.

72. Charles Lummis, 'Japanese Critiques of Technological Society', *Canadian Journal of Political and Social Theory*, Vol 8, no 3, 1984.

73. Don DeLillo, *White Noise*, Picador, London 1985, p155.

74. Hidetoshi Kato, 'The Machine Cult', in *Visions of Japan*, Victoria and Albert Museum, London 1991.

75. Charlie Leadbeater, 'Masters of the Interior Universe', *Financial Times*, 3 September 1991.

76. Arata Isozaki, '*Wayo* Style: The Japanization Mechanism', in *Visions of Japan*, Victoria and Albert Museum, London 1991.

entails. As the dynamism of technological innovation has appeared to move eastwards, so have these postmodern technologies become structured into the discourse of Orientalism. Through these new technologies, the contradictory stereotypes of Japaneseness have assumed new forms; the new technologies have become associated with the sense of Japanese identity and ethnicity.

One response is to see *pachinko* and computer games simply as the postmodern equivalents of zen and kabuki. Like 'traditional' forms of Japanese culture, they too embody the exotic, enigmatic and mysterious essence of Japanese particularism. This is apparent in the postmodern romanticization of Japan as a space somewhere between the real and the imaginary. Tokyo is the centre for a new phenomenon of 'postmodern tourism': 'the paradigm of the modern decentered metropolis. It's not so much that it disorientates you – rather that you never get orientated in the first place.'[77] In cyberpunk fiction this aestheticism and exoticism becomes quite apparent. William Gibson's *Neuromancer*, as Yoshimoto Mitsuhiro observes, combines 'futuristic high-tech images of contemporary Japan and anachronistic images of feudal Japan still widely circulating in the popular American imagination'.[78] The same can be said of Ridley Scott's *Blade Runner*. Stephen Beard describes this as 'the reinvention of Japan as a land of high-tech enchantment' – 'manga, techno-porn, high-density urbanism, mobile fashion, hyper-violent movies, video-phones, fax cameras, hand-held televisions, video-games, disposable buildings, even a new breed of "radically bored" teen information junkies, *otaku*, who shun body contact and spend all their waking hours gathering data on the most trivial bit of media'.[79] Through the projection of exotic (and erotic) fantasies onto this high-tech delirium, anxieties about the 'impotence' of western culture can be, momentarily, screened out. High-tech Orientalism makes possible 'cultural amnesia, ecstatic alienation, serial self-erasure'.[80]

But there is another – a more resentful and more aggressively racist – side to this Techno-Orientalism. The association of technology and Japaneseness now serves to reinforce the image of a culture that is cold, impersonal and machine-like, an authoritarian culture lacking emotional connection to the rest of the world. The *otaku* generation – kids 'lost to everyday life' by their immersion in computer reality – provides a strong symbol of this. These children 'despise physical contact and love media, technical communication, and the realm of reproduction and simulation in general'; they are characterized by a kind of 'vacuousness' and by 'self-dissociation in hyperreality':

> In the age of cyber-medialism with its emphasis on simulation, the hi-tech media become the condition for survival. The media cyborgs in their electronic womb are also called *aliens* ... it's an empty, content-less joy of technology that drives them.[81]

These kids are people mutating into machines; they represent a kind of cybernetic mode of being for the future. This recreates in a new dimension the image of the Japanese as inhuman. Within the political and cultural

77. John Thackara, 'Seeing is Disbelieving', *The Listener*, 23 March 1989, p35.

78. Yoshimoto Mitsuhiro, 'The Postmodern and Mass Images in Japan', *Public Culture*, Vol 1, no 2, 1989, p18.

79. Stephen Beard, 'Blade Runner Boys', *The Modern Review*, Autumn 1991, p25.

80. *Ibid.*

81. Volker Grassmuck, 'Otaku: Japanese Kids Colonize the Realm of Information and Media', *Mediamatic*, Vol 5, no 4, 1991, pp199, 201, 207, 213. See also, Gabin Itoh, 'Godda Light? The Invasion of Dragon Quest in Japan', *Mediamatic*, Vol 5, no 3 1990.

unconscious of the West, Japan has come to exist as the figure of empty and dehumanized technological power. It represents as an 'ideal type' the alienated and dystopian image of capitalist progress. This provokes both resentment and envy. The Japanese are unfeeling aliens; they are cyborgs and replicants. But there is also the sense that these mutants are now better adapted to survive in the future. The *otaku* are *the* postmodern people. To use Baudrillard's phrase, the future seems to have shifted towards artificial satellites.

There is something profoundly disturbing in this Techno-Orientalism. Following Castoriadis, we have suggested that western xenophobia and racism are motivated by the apparent incapacity of a culture to constitute itself without excluding, devaluing and then hating the Other. That the Others must be instituted as inferior, Castoriadis describes as the 'natural inclination' of human societies. This is the logic of a kind of self-love that constructs itself in terms of a cultural and national narcissism. But there is something more, something deeper, something we might even describe as 'unnatural' in this logic of Techno-Orientalism. As Castoriadis goes on to suggest, hatred of the Other can also be seen as the 'other side of an unconscious self-hatred' – a hatred that is 'usually for obvious reasons intolerable under its overt form, that nourishes the most driven forms of the hatred of the Other'.[82] To explore this possibility speculatively, and perhaps only metaphorically, we might suggest that the resentment expressed against Japanese technology (rationality, development, progress) reflects an unconscius and primal hatred of this aspect of western maturity. There is perhaps a (delirious) refusal, rejection, detestation of that modernity into which our own culture has been transformed; of that (totalitarian) element of modernity that threatens some deep-seated aspect (or cultural monad) in western society.

82. Castoriadis, *op.cit.* On this question of self-hatred, see also Žižek, *op.cit.*, pp56-7.

Perhaps Japan is just a mirror of our own modernity and of its discontents. Maybe Japan simply reflects back to us the 'deformities' in our own culture. As it asserts its claims on modernity, and as it refuses the investment of western Orientalist fantasies, there might just be the real possibility to 'learn from Japan'. We shall increasingly be compelled to take seriously this Japan that can say no. Perhaps we should be less concerned with what we think it reveals about 'them', and more attentive to what it could help us to learn about ourselves and our own culture. Japanese no-saying is important because of the radical challenge it now presents to our understanding of modernity and of the cultural and ethnic conditions of its existence until now. Japan is significant because of its complexity: it is non-western, yet refuses any longer to be our Orient; it insists on being modern, yet calls our kind of modernity into question. Because of this Japan offers possibilities. It potentially suggests to us a way beyond that simple binary logic that first differentiates the modern and the traditional, and then superimposes this distinction on West and Orient. In so far as Japan complicates and confuses this impoverished kind of categorization it challenges us to rethink our white modernity.

This kind of intellectual and imaginative challenge cannot, and will not, obviate conflicts between Europe and America and Japan, but it could make it possible to handle real differences of interest in more complex ways. What Japan tells us is that we have to move beyond a worldview that confronts western modernity with its (pre-modern) Other. Contrary to Ishihara's argument, the modern era has not entered its terminal phase with the displacement of 'Caucasian' modernity. Modernity is now, more than ever, the condition of all cultures in this world. The issue is on what terms they are inserted into that modernity, and on what terms they will co-exist. Japan's achievement is that it is now no different from Europe or the United States in terms of its modernity. What is significant about Japan is its ethnicity, and the fact that it is the first non-white country to have interpolated itself into modernity on its own terms. In so doing it has exposed the racist foundations of modernity as it has been constructed until now.

SUNDERLAND
POLYTECHNIC

MA in Cultural and Textual Studies . . .

This taught course provides an interdisciplinary framework for studying culture, text and society.

Options include: Modernism, Fiction and History, Drama, Autobiography, Feminism, Minimalism, Cinema (Hollywood, British, Soviet and European), Mass Media, Vietnam and Representation, Detective Fiction, Religion.
Modular and flexible, it offers students the opportunity to combine a range of options or to focus on one discrete area. The MA can be taken full-time (one year) or part-time (two years).

For further details, write to the **Admissions Officer, MA in Cultural and Textual Studies, School of Humanities, Sunderland Polytechnic, Chester Road, Sunderland SR1 3SD.**

MA and Diploma in Cultural Studies: History and Theory

(full-time and part-time)

Post-structuralism and critiques of ethnocentrism; feminism and subjectivity; psychoanalysis and Marxism ... recent developments in cultural theory have been breathtaking. But how do these theories affect how we think historically?

The MA and Diploma are constructed around this central question. The course investigates current theories of culture and explores issues such as historical imagination and popular memory; historical fictions; different genres of historical narrative; everyday histories; and discourses of Empire and nation.

We are looking for students prepared to work intensively as part of a larger intellectual project, contributing their own research in both core and options. Candidates with any background in the social sciences or humanities are welcome to apply. In exceptional circumstances people who have no first degree will be considered.

Course team: Sally Alexander, Andrew Blake, Robert Chase, Catherine Hall, Mica Nava, Alan O'Shea, Kenneth Parker, Bill Schwarz, Couze Venn.

MPhil/PhD supervision and BA(Hons) also offered.

Further information and application forms from: The MA Course Secretary, Department of Cultural Studies. Polytechnic of East London, Longbridge Road, Dagenham, Essex RM8 2AS. Tel. 081-849 3545.

POLYTECHNIC OF EAST LONDON

PART-TIME MA IN CULTURAL STUDIES

at Cheltenham and Gloucester
College of Higher Education

Starting October 1992, and lasting two years.
Topics discussed: **cultural theories; French and British cultural history; cross-cultural studies; women and culture.**

For further information contact
Dr S. Gemie
Admissions Tutor for MA in Cultural Studies
Department of Humanities, Dunholme Building
PO Box 220, The Park, Cheltenham
Gloucestershire GL50 2QF

Preaching to the Perverted

Are Transgressive Sexual Strategies Radical?

A **one day conference** on Saturday **11 July** at the **ICA**, The Mall, London SW1. **Box office** 071-930 3647
Tickets £15 (£10 concessions) including ICA day membership

What is perversity and who has defined it? Are cultural definitions about perversity, formulated in the nineteenth century, still relevant? Does a celebration of sexual diversity automatically mean accepting notions about sexual perversity?

Writers about homosexuality, bondage, sado-masochism, fetishism and body modification have long been reformulating notions of sexual desire. Some have argued for a more positive image of perversity. But are all sexual transgressions radical? Or do critics, like those from psychiatry who still see perverse practices as regressive, have a point?

Speakers will include practitioners, analysts, cultural theorists and artists.

a *new formations* conference
to mark the publication of **Female Fetishism: A New Look**
by Lorraine Gamman and Merja Makinen (published by Lawrence & Wishart)

The Limits of Transgression

Elizabeth Wilson

Jonathan Dollimore, *Sexual Dissidence: Augustine to Wilde, Freud to Foucault*, Clarendon Press, Oxford 1991; £35 cloth, £9.95 paper.

I wrote this review shortly after watching Gore Vidal dispose of Michael Ignatieff on *The Late Show*.[1] 'Interviewers are so *cute* these days,' Vidal murmured wearily at one point. Impassively Buddha-like in the face of Ignatieff's anguished squeakings of 'conspiracy theory', he repeated with sublime urbanity his conviction that the United States is an empire – no republic, no democracy, no culture, just the world centre of barbarity and corruption. Michael Ignatieff looked as if he'd caught a sensitive part of his anatomy in his trouser zip when Vidal denounced the creation of the postwar 'red scare' by American governments, beginning with Harry Truman, and clearly found unbearable Vidal's insistence that the communist threat was entirely mythical, a demoniacal invention of American militarism. Ignatieff's bright-eyed, little boy liberalism was no match for Vidal's stony irony. He seemed out of his depth, uncomprehending – indeed at one point he appeared (unless I misunderstood him) to be attempting to turn what he saw as Vidal's hatred of 'macho culture' into an *effect* of homosexuality.

This encounter between postmodern man and what many of us might be tempted to dismiss as a now outdated American radical liberalism sheds light on Jonathan Dollimore's enterprise in a way I hope to clarify, for *Sexual Dissidence* in a sense itself contains opposing, or at least divergent, attitudes towards its subject(s). The postmodern and the oppositional work their way through this dense and very woven text, which draws together – or at moments simply juxtaposes – many strands of theory. Dollimore frequently uses one theory to interrogate another. Yet at the heart of the theoretical thickets gay activism and cultural politics keep a radical impulse in view.

It is a difficult text to summarize, and not until almost the last page does Dollimore tell us: 'My consideration of difference originated in a turn to history in order to repudiate … [the] theory … which construed homosexuality as an embrace of the same because of a fear of the different.'[2] This is a political and also a cultural agenda, for the theory to which Dollimore refers is psychoanalysis. Gay Liberation and the early women's movement would have no truck with Freud, but psychoanalysis has returned with a vengeance in recent years. Now, however, it dominates literary, film and art studies rather than regulatory practices such as social work. Who is to say whether it is more dangerous in this latest guise than in its former one? The problem with psychoanalysis as a theoretical tool of cultural studies is that some of it is

1. *The Late Show* is a nightly cultural and arts programme on BBC2.

2. Dollimore, p355.

indispensable – who could deny the importance of the unconscious in the creation of imaginative works and indeed any discursive text or other representation – yet its seduction may divert us from its lurking moral judgments which were easier to unmask when they resulted in attempts to cure homosexuals or stop mothers going out to work.

Jonathan Dollimore creatively addresses the tension for culturalists presented by psychoanalysis, acknowledging that he deploys psychoanalytic categories in order to reveal their inadequacies. This may be, as he concedes, inconsistent, yet itself creates an interesting dissonance.

He is, however, concerned with much more than psychoanalysis. One reading of *Sexual Dissidence* would be to see it as an extended meditation on the nature of sexual and cultural identity, and particularly in this case, homosexual identity. After all, contemporary lesbian and gay politics was quintessentially a politics of identity, and it is out of this politics that lesbian and gay studies has come. By the time lesbian and gay studies emerge, however, we are in a very different place: we find ourselves in an academic setting in which the crude certainties of 'Gay is Good' and other such embarrassing slogans have long since ceded to, and been superceded by, much more complex constructions and interrogations of identity, of what used to be called ideology, and of politics.

It is therefore appropriate that a discussion of essentialism should be positioned near the beginning of the book. Dollimore is, of course, aware of the critique of essentialism: the search for the 'true', 'authentic' self may lead to new, rigid categories: in *The Well of Loneliness*, for example, Radclyffe Hall resorts to ideas of Nature as a justification for the Third Sex, coupled with a romantic conception of the Invert as saintly martyr (an idea that Dollimore also finds, more surprisingly, in Rita Mae Brown's *Ruby Fruit Jungle*, albeit minus the martyrdom). Worse, essentialism reinvents or reinforces the very binary oppositions it would seek to subvert. Yet Dollimore to some extent defends the essentialist stance and rightly reminds us that it has at times significantly raised the visibility of the deviant, and can have progressive effects. It is nonetheless strange to find lesbians making more or less their only appearance in the book at this point – as bearers of essentialist ideology. I will return to the general absence of lesbians in *Sexual Dissidence* later.

Essentialism, notwithstanding its partially progressive potential, is not adequate to Jonathan Dollimore's definition of sexual *dissidence*. This he describes as a 'kind of resistance' which 'unsettles the ... opposition between the dominant and the subordinate'. Transgression and perversity are two terms which he explores and, I think, invites us to endorse.

The concept of transgression was explored by Michel Foucault in the 1960s in 'A Preface to Transgression',[3] in which he described a transgressive spiral. This constantly seeks to cross a limit – or *the* limit – of the permissible, but this act of transgression then sets up a further limit which then has to be crossed in its turn. One implication of this might be that the threshhold of what shocks is progressively raised. Contemporary culture, or aspects of it, are often

3. Michel Foucault, 'A Preface to Transgression', *Language, Counter Memory, Practice*, Donald F. Bouchard (ed.), Cornell University Press, Ithaca NY 1977. (Originally published as 'Hommage à Georges Bataille', *Critique*, no 195/196, 1963.)

described – and usually denounced – in this way. For example, anti-porn campaigners draw an apocalyptic picture of a descent from *Lady Chatterley's Lover*, through *Penthouse* and *Hustler* to hardcore violence and snuff movies. Once you are on the slippery downward slope there is no turning back. A similar course was predicted by Friedrich von Hayek in *The Road to Serfdom*, in which he argued that state intervention along Keynesian economic lines leads inexorably to totalitarianism. This is the conservative interpretation of transgression.

'Transgression' and 'transgressive' have become buzz words in cultural criticism in recent years, but with rather different meaning. To me, however, it is unclear just what this meaning is, and the initial discussion of it in *Sexual Dissidence* did not help. Dollimore refers to Oscar Wilde's 'transgressive aesthetic', and he relates it to the postmodern decentering of the subject, to the postmodern disappearance of the depth model, and to the debate as to whether the inversion of binary opposites 'subverts or on the contrary reinforces' the original binary order. The relationship of these to Wilde is not very clearly developed. However, the interesting issue is raised whether the very term transgressive – so seductive – is dangerous and self-defeating precisely because it is contained within that against which it rebels; this is what Dollimore refers to as 'containment theory'.

It is at least possible, of course, that the term transgression operates in cultural studies as little more than a new version of bohemianism, the negativity of revolt – that which Walter Benjamin saw in Baudelaire's stance to the world. (Baudelaire, says Benjamin, 'could ... have adopted Flaubert's statement, "Of all of politics I undertand only one thing: the revolt." '[4]) Such a possibility is implicit in the Foucauldian notion of 'resistance'. The problem is not that sexual and other regulatory discourses *produce* deviation; nor is it that these then produce their 'reverse discourses' of resistance. The problem is that the whole scenario confines us forever in a society of surveillance that we can never transcend. There may be a utopia beyond the prison house of discourse, but for sure we are never going to get there. All we can achieve is to be 'dissidents'.

Contemporary suspicion of utopian discourse is an unsuprising reaction to the perceived failures of Soviet utopianism, and has led to this recent preference for 'resistance' over any notion of the now discredited belief in revolutionary moments. The emergence of any truly new world order has been discursively ruled out, and is seen by radical cultural critics as almost rather offensive. Such pessimism – or should one call it discrimination, political refinement – is hardly surprising when the most 'revolutionary' event on the agenda is the return of the Romanoffs to St Petersburg, and of Nazism to Germany. Yet although Foucault's concept of resistance has been questioned, it is largely those such as Gillian Rose,[5] who tend to reject him outright, who have initiated an extended critique. Dollimore's discussion of Foucault is disappointingly brief, but he gives a lucid revised account of the historical emergence of the homosexual identity.

According to Dollimore, Foucault saw the Western construction of sexuality itself as a kind of utopia:

4. Walter Benjamin, *Charles Baudelaire: A Lyric Poet in the Era of High Capitalism*, Verso, London 1973, p13.

5. Gillian Rose, *The Dialectic of Nihilism: Poststructuralism and Law*, Basil Blackwell, Oxford 1984.

> What sustains our eagerness to speak of sex in terms of repression is doubtless this opportunity to speak out against the powers that be, to utter truths and promise bliss, to link together enlightenment, liberation, and manifold pleasures; to pronounce a discourse that combines the fervor of knowledge, the determination to change the laws, and the longing for the garden of earthly delights.[6]

6. Quoted in Dollimore, p223.

Dollimore contrasts the divergent accounts of perversity undertaken by Freud and Foucault, and then works them together to good effect. He argues that although Foucault's account contradicts Freud's, both perceive perversity – in this case homosexual perversity – as central to the binary constructions of sexuality and the workings of power. For Dollimore, perversity becomes an 'insinuating' presence, one which begins to undermine the binary oppositions that remain so dominant. In the end, we realize that essentialism and anti-essentialism are no longer binary opposites, rather they depend upon each other. Above all, heterosexual conformity is unstable, built on the quicksands of homosexual desire.

Jonathan Dollimore is at his best when disposing of the homophobic psychoanalytic accounts of homosexuality, and when retrieving a more 'perverse' Freud, and a psychoanalysis able to contribute towards a more complex understanding of homosexual perversity. The way in which contemporary theories and views of the homosexual originated in pre-modern, and certainly pre-Freudian discourse is also well brought out in some of the best sections of the book, on the early modern period.

Genet, Orton, and most of all Wilde, are interrogated, yet above all celebrated for their 'transgressive aesthetic', combining 'the anarchic and the political, the anger and the boredom'. This is one theme of the book, but there is an ever-present – indeed, an insinuating – counter-theme, an unresolved tension which turns into its opposite: instead of tension there is a sense of being muffled and smothered in the play of diverse theories. At times I felt I was treading a minefield of political correctness crisscrossed with theoretical tripwires.

For Jonathan Dollimore appears pulled in different directions. He wishes to incorporate the mass of recent theory concerning identity, cultural positioning, gender – the whole range of concerns addressed by cultural critique – and this leads him towards the 'postmodern' endless play of difference, fragmentation, the dissolution of opposites, the recognition that the 'transgressive' notion of 'gay identity' or 'gay sensibility' may be outdated or surpassed. At the same time, however, he wishes to proclaim and to insist on the importance of 'perverse' homosexuality as a radical challenge to the oppressiveness of Western bourgeois culture, to its racism as well as to its homophobia and its hatred of women. He is clearly aware that the one is in danger of contradicting the other, but for me he never managed quite to escape this dilemma. For all his critique of the psychoanalytic view of sexual difference, what does he offer in its place: a reassertion that we must 'eroticize the social' while liberating it from the imperatives of sexual difference. And as he himself immediately admits, 'Such theories have been plausibly criticized for their romantic and Utopian strains, also for the way they echo and sometimes invoke a post-Freudian version of the polymorphous perverse.'[7]

Dollimore disclaims both the intention and the very possibility of outlining a correct theory of difference. What is implicitly offered as an opposition to the oppressive norms reasserted – as he quotes – as recently as 1990 by Hanna Segal, one of the most respected *éminences grises* of British psychoanalysis, is the fragmented yet enduring figure of the Transgressive Pervert. This is consistent with the recent trend in lesbian and gay politics to reclaim the 'queer' and renounce the too-positive 'gay' – a move that has outrage potential; and gay has certainly come to seem rather twee. To what extent, though, does the transgressive mode take us beyond a sexualized version of Baudelaire's negative, bohemian revolt, mentioned above? Also, does it not reassert some kind of essential identity? This is the spiral in which Dollimore is entangled. His text is an exemplum of *différance* and deferral, an extended proliferation of texts to be explored which lead to further texts, and the many creative insights along the way do not quite compensate for the absence of a new synthesis.

As the author implicitly recognizes, lesbian writers have tended to exclude the lesbian from the role of sexual outlaw because they have been reluctant to give up an identity politics based on essentialism. For them the lesbian has remained *positively* heroic. The practice of lesbian sado-masochism and butch/femme positionings constitute an exception to this rule, but it is true that lesbianism has too often been celebrated and affirmed as a kind of manifestation of female oneness and wonderfulness, totally at odds with transgression. The best-known and most influential text in this tradition probably remains Adrienne Rich's 'Compulsory Heterosexuality and Lesbian Existence'[8] – lesbianism as universal female love and every woman's answer to the vileness of men. Yet at the same time lesbians are demonized in the dominant culture just as much as gay men. That they play such a marginal role in *Sexual Dissidence* may be partly because the lesbians who are not essentialists perhaps haven't written about it (this is only speculation). Even so, Dollimore could at least have considered the role played by the heroic lesbian as a mannish and unnatural figure in Benjamin's reworking of Baudelaire;[9] and the absence of lesbianism is alienating, and tends to reinforce a lurking suspicion that the Transgressive Pervert of sexual outlawry (male) gains centre stage only at the expense of consigning another group to the margins. This would tend to support the view that, much as one is inevitably and perennially attracted to the figure of the Transgressive Pervert (wouldn't we all like to be that glamorous), it is a romanticized construction, and that the usual condition of marginality is more often what we had always suspected: invisibility and negation.

Sexual Dissidence left me in many ways frustrated. Jonathan Dollimore attempts to retain the radical deviance, the protest of gay identity, but consistently hedges his theoretical bets. I grew weary of a sense of having it both ways. Of course we must recognize the complexities and the ironies, but

7. Dollimore, p355.

8. Adrienne Rich, 'Compulsory Heterosexuality and Lesbian Existence', in *Blood, Bread and Poetry: Selected Prose 1979-1985*, Virago, London 1986.

9. See Walter Benjamin, *op.cit.*, and Elizabeth Wilson, 'The Invisible Flâneur', *New Left Review*, no 191, January/February 1992.

we must also recognize the way in which their theoretical and discursive exploration has too often deprived them of any cutting political edge. Like, I imagine, Dollimore himself, I am attracted to the irony and richness of much in postmodernism; clearly he, like me, is only too aware of the brutal repression and violence meted out to homosexuals. Too often, he simply deploys them together, contiguously, and the figure of the Transgressive Pervert is inadequate to create the new synthesis: the combinatory of difference, complexity and oppression into a new moment of elucidation. Perhaps this ambiguity is inescapable. Yet, to return finally to *The Late Show*, I missed in *Sexual Dissidence* the uncompromising clarity of Vidal's denunciation of our world. This, paradoxically, for it supports Dollimore's thesis, seemed linked with his 'deviant' sexual identity. It is the clarity that Jonathan Dollimore lacks. It seemed to me – perhaps unfairly – that he has tried to inhabit the places of both Michael Ignatieff and Gore Vidal simultaneously. In the end this must be impossible. For my part, I shall have to side with Gore Vidal.

FREDRIC ON FILM THEORY

Warren Buckland

Fredric Jameson, *Signatures of the Visible*, Routledge, New York and London 1990; £35 cloth.

At the beginning and ending of 'The Imaginary Signifier' Christian Metz analyses the relationship between theory, film, and the theoretician. The primary aim of film theory for Metz is to 'disengage the cinema-object from the imaginary and win it for the symbolic', i.e. to produce a knowledge, or a little more knowledge, of film's discursive properties, rather than reify its imaginary pleasures (as do film critics and a large number of film theorists). But he points out that the cinema's imaginary dimension also instigates the film theoretician's very existence, which is based upon 'the desire to study the cinema'. Metz therefore warns against being 'swallowed up in the imaginary which is sustained by the cinema', but concedes that this is always 'a never-ending task'.[1] His solution consists in maintaining an ambivalent relation to the cinema: 'To be a theoretician of the cinema, one should ideally no longer love the cinema and yet still love it: have loved it a lot and only have detached oneself from it by taking it up again from the other end, taking it as the target for the very same scopic drive which had made one love it.'[2]

Fredric Jameson's very existence in the university is not dependent upon his 'desire to study the cinema' because he primarily writes and teaches about verbal narrative. What, then, can Jameson contribute to film theory? Part One of *Signatures of the Visible* consists of (what Jameson himself calls) 'occasional' essays on film (written between 1977 and 1986), while Part Two consists of one long essay, 'The Existence of Italy' (written in 1988), which Jameson describes as offering 'the most sustained rehearsal of the dialectic of realism, modernism and postmodernism that I have so far attempted'.[3]

In this long essay Jameson notes the simultaneous emergence of each aesthetic practice in this threefold logic with the three fundamental stages of capitalism – the emergence of realism with national capitalism, modernism with the break and restructuration of the monopoly period, and postmodernism with the multinational era. Although noting that the history of film does not coincide with these three stages of capitalism, Jameson nonetheless argues that film history 'recapitulates something like a realism/modernism/postmodernism trajectory at a more compressed tempo' [p156]. But what is remarkable is that Jameson argues for two separate film histories in terms of this threefold trajectory – one for 'silent' film and one for sound film:

> The two film species – silent and sound – each demand their own separate histories, and ... the threefold logic suggested here is observable in both, but

1. Christian Metz, 'The Imaginary Signifier', in *Psychoanalysis and Cinema: The Imaginary Signifier*. (trans. Ben Brewster *et al.*), The Macmillan Press, London 1982, pp3-5.

2. *Ibid.*, p15.

3. *Signatures of the Visible*, p6. All other page references will be cited in the text.

in unrelated and dialectically distinct ways. For one thing, silent film was never allowed to develop into its putative 'postmodern' version, although it might be interesting to entertain the hypothesis that the independent or experimental film in the post-World War II era (e.g., *Dog Star Man* [1959-64] of Stan Brakhage) developed in the empty space of a silent film postmodernism that never happened. [p157]

Wisely, Jameson does not discuss this contrived delineation of silent cinema any further (although he notes in passing that it developed from 'some inaugural realism of Griffith into the extraordinary modernisms of Eisenstein and Stroheim', [p157] with the American avant-garde conveniently filling-in as its postmodern phase), but instead concentrates on the articulation of the threefold logic in sound film.[4]

To this extent, Jameson covers some of the ground worked over by the 'contemporary' film theorists in the 1970s. The primary function of contemporary film theory was to develop a materialist knowledge of the ideology perpetuated by mainstream cinema and to map out the space for an oppositional cinema that would break the ideological hold of the mainstream. To achieve these goals, the contemporary film theorists sided with Brecht in the Lukács/Brecht debate between realism and modernism, as well as with Barthes in the Sartre/Barthes debate over the French literary avant-garde. For both Brecht and Barthes, the self-reflexive practices of modernism and the avant-garde aim to deconstruct the ideology perpetuated by nineteenth-century bourgeois capitalism, where this ideology is identified (as in Jameson) with the normative, representational practice of realism. To the modernist critique of realism the contemporary film theorists added the consideration of the subject addressed by each practice. They defined the classical narrative film as a realist practice that attempts to construct an illusory, coherent subject position – a position where meaning is realized. They then defined avant-garde/modernist film as a practice that disperses meaning and the illusory, coherent subject position through the deconstruction of narrative. In much the same way, Jameson defines realism as aesthetic representation, modernism as anti-representational, aesthetic (i.e. autonomous) art, and postmodernism as anti-representational anti-art. (Typically, Jameson represents these definitions schematically in the form of Greimas's semiotic square.) [p161][5] Furthermore, he identifies the third, postmodern, stage of sound film with video. [p157][6]

The contemporary film theorists conflated modernism with the avant-garde and established the generic division between realist and modernist texts exclusively in terms of form, resulting in the repression of an historical analysis of these texts. However, in *Signatures of the Visible* Jameson overcomes this formalism, as we have seen, by contextualizing aesthetic concepts within the various stages of the history of capitalism. To this extent, his work parallels the recent tendency in film studies to bring together film theory and film history (although Jameson rarely acknowledges this work). Two instances of this

4. Jameson's contrived delineation of early cinema is no doubt due to the fact that he fails to cite any research carried out on early cinema within film studies.

5. The fourth aesthetic practice remains undefined, although Jameson characterizes it as 'representational' and 'anti-art'.

6. Jameson doesn't write very much about video and postmodernism in 'The Existence of Italy' but confines himself largely to realism and modernism in the cinema. Jameson discusses video in 'Reading Without Interpretation: Postmodernism and the Video-text', in Nigel Fabb, Derek Attridge, Alan Durant and Colin MacCabe (eds), *The Linguistics of Writing: Arguments Between Language and Literature*, MUP, Manchester 1987. This paper is discussed in detail by Nicholas Zurbrugg, 'Jameson's Complaint: Video-art and the Intertextual Time-Wall', *Screen*, Vol 32, no 1, 1991, pp16-34.

tendency are Thomas Elsaesser's analysis of the historical preconditions of representation, spectatorship and visual pleasure in Weimar cinema[7] and Miriam Hansen's analysis of the emergence of spectatorship in American 'silent' film.[8] For Elsaesser a materialist history of Weimar cinema (and, indeed, other national cinemas) radically decentres its object of study: the historian goes beyond the histories of cinema's technological and economic practices, for 'one is faced with relations of power, control and pleasure which reach beyond film history.'[9] He goes on to say that:

> The materialist basis of Weimar cinema would in this analysis be less the overall political development of Germany on the brink of fascism, and more its part in another historical process – to which fascism is quite clearly a response – namely that which transformed, among other things, manufacture into administratively organized industrial production, and which engendered quite different demands on the human senses, faculties and skills, adding greatly to the overdevelopment of the eye. [*FHVP*, p78]

These remarks historicize one of contemporary film theory's primary assertions: that voyeurism is overdetermined in the cinema.

According to Elsaesser, moreover, historical explanation was marginalized from contemporary film theory, because it theorized filmic pleasure as being determined primarily by the immutable cinematographic apparatus, rather than by contingent narrative strategies. This means that, for the contemporary film theorists, 'different narrative strategies do not fundamentally alter the subject positions available to the spectator' which is why they '[did] not give a socially or nationally specific structure to the articulation of visual pleasure'. [*FHVP*, p65] But in his analysis of the specific social and historical structure of visual pleasure in films typical of Weimar cinema, Elsaesser stresses the way they foreground the act of narration through strategies such as framed tales, interlocking narrative voices, nested narratives, a high proportion of non-sutured point-of-view shots etc. These strategies address the spectator in a fundamentally different way to classical Hollywood cinema because 'visual pleasure appears as inseparable from anxiety and is inscribed in a network of power and loss of power, control and loss of control'. Furthermore, 'Weimar cinema' and its '*mise-en-scène* of the look fundamentally alters the relationship of the spectator to film and thus the question of identification'. [*FHVP*, pp73-4] Weimar cinema alters the spectator's relation to the film through a hyperbolic emphasis on looking, which splits the spectator's vision (between power/loss of power etc). This means that Weimar cinema does not perpetuate the illusory, coherent subject position the contemporary film theorists believed to be inherent in the cinematographic apparatus (a fallacy unchallenged by Jameson, as we shall see).

In part one of *Babel and Babylon* Miriam Hansen employs insights from both film history and film theory to locate in silent American film the historical emergence of the category of the classical spectator, a textual construct whose

7. Thomas Elsaesser, 'Social Mobility and the Fantastic: German Silent Cinema', *Wide Angle*, Vol 5, no 2, 1982; 'Lulu and the Meter Man: Louise Brooks, Pabst and Pandora's Box', *Screen*, Vol 24, nos 4-5, 1983; 'Film History and Visual Pleasure: Weimar Cinema', in Patricia Mellencamp and Philip Rosen (eds), *Cinema Histories/Cinema Practices*, University Publications of America, Los Angeles 1984, pp47-84.

8. Miriam Hansen, *Babel and Babylon: Spectatorship in American Silent Film* Harvard University Press, Cambridge, Mass 1991. All page references to this book will be cited in the text with the prefix *BB*.

9. 'Film History and Visual Pleasure', p78. All other page references to this essay will be cited in the text with the prefix *FHVP*.

function is to attempt to 'standardize empirically diverse and to some extent unpredictable acts of reception'. [*BB*, p16] Hansen charts the emergence of this standardized form of subjectivity through the analysis of a number of films (especially Porter's *Uncle Josh at the Moving Picture Show* [Edison, 1902] and *The 'Teddy' Bears* [1907] and the popular 'Peeping Tom' series of films) whose textuality is inscribed with ambivalent, transitional modes of address, in which the viewer's relation to the film oscillates between 'distraction' and 'absorption'. For Hansen, these distinct modes of address are not simply determined by the filmic text, but also by the context of exhibition: one-shot tableau films, shown predominately in vaudeville, variety shows etc., were assembled in random sequence and offered an unstructured mix of spectatorial pleasures, whereas multi-shot narrative films required their own distinct outlet – the nickelodeon (ensuring their own distinct audience). The exhibition space of tableau films constructed a mode of address 'predicated on diversity, on distracting the viewer with a variety of competing spectacles'. [*BB*, p34] But in the more specialized exhibition space of the nickelodeon, audience reception was gradually standardized. The live elements of the vaudeville exhibition space were internalized in the film itself by means of representational strategies, which 'aimed at suppressing awareness of the theater space and absorbing the spectator into the illusionist space on screen', [*BB*, p44] leading to the formation of the classical spectator. The enumeration of these representational strategies (continuity editing, image composition etc.) has been well documented by film historians, and it is well-known that the story, the imposition of a causal narrative logic from shot to shot, is the most important device for absorbing the spectator into the film. Hansen's main point is not to repeat these facts, but to emphasize that 'the display of diversity [in the tableau films and vaudeville exhibition space] also means that the viewer is solicited in a more direct manner – as a member of an anticipated social audience and a public, rather than an invisible, private consumer [as in narrative films].' [*BB*, p34]

Hansen goes on to discuss how early cinema transformed the gendered boundary between the public and private spheres. Noting that in nineteenth-century Europe and America public life was predominately a masculine sphere and the private realm of the family a feminine sphere, Hansen asserts that cinema at the beginning of the twentieth century functioned as an alternative *public sphere* for women (as well as immigrants), due to the social and cultural variations permitted in the live performances: 'The cinema catered to women as an audience, as the subject of collective reception and public interaction. It thus functioned as a particularly female heterotopia, because ... it "simultaneously represented, contested and inverted" [Foucault] the gendered demarcations of private and public spheres.' [*BB*, p118] The subsequent paradigmatic shift from early to classical cinema, involving the codification of film by means of narrative strategies and the development of the classical spectator based on the masculine psychic mechanisms of voyeurism and fetishism, is, for Hansen, a patriarchal defensive symptom which 'indicates the extent of the crisis unleashed by women's massive ascendence to a new horizon of experience [in the public sphere]'. [*BB*, p122][10]

In *Signatures of the Visible* Jameson develops his own historically informed film theory, which can be summarized as follows:

1) As we have seen, his theory does not duplicate such traditional problems as the gap between the formal and the historical, or the micro-text and the macro-structure, or the molecular and the molar. This gap in contemporary film theory tended to favour the formal, or the molecular – as in studies limited exclusively to the analysis of the specificity of the cinematographic apparatus, or in semiotic/psychoanalytic textual analyses. For Jameson, however, we must conceive the cinema as 'a historically new cultural apparatus, whose "material" structure may be expected to reflect (and to express), in its very formal structure, a particular moment or stage of capital and of the latter's intensified, yet dialectically original, reification of social relations and processes'. [p101] Here the perspective is historical at the outset: it conceives the cinema as a social practice, rather than starting with a formal framework and introducing history at a later stage.

2) Jameson defines the cinema as emerging from the capitalist process of *reification*, which he defines as a process whereby 'the traditional or "natural" [*naturwüchsige*] unities, social formations, human relations, cultural events, even religious systems, are systematically broken up in order to be reconstituted more efficiently, in the form of new post-natural processes or mechanisms.'[11] The process of reification simultaneously transforms both the mode of production of the economy into market capitalism and also reorganizes the division of labour in the psyche. The latter process constitutes the illusion that the individual in an isolated, free, coherent, and centred subject. Hence the concept of reification enables us to understand this centred subject as an historical construct emerging from capitalism's mode of production, and parallels Hansen's micro-history of the emergence of the classical spectator, also defined as an isolated, free, centred subject.

3) Jameson notes that reification privileges vision: '[Reification leads to] the fragmentation of the bodily sensorium and the "reification" of sight itself, the new hierarchy of the senses which in very uneven ways begins to emerge from Descartes and Galileo (the primacy of the "geometrical") until it becomes the dominant vehicle for the "will to power" of mature capitalism itself.' [p126] The reification of vision by the capitalist mode of production highlights one of cinema's *historical conditions of possibility*. Here, Jameson's explanation of the transfer of sense experience to sight is very similar to Elsaesser's, no doubt because both refer to Lukács' seminal paper on reification.[12]

4) A further effect of reification, as Jameson points out, is that it establishes the false belief that the imaginary (the realm of the private, the individual and the psychological) exists outside the symbolic (the realm of the public, the social and the unconscious). The problem this generates is 'to imagine that, sheltered from the omnipresence of history and the implacable influence of the social, there already exists a realm of freedom.' This in turn strengthens 'the grip of

10. Here I have greatly simplified Hansen's far more subtle and complex arguments and have also limited my discussion to the first section of the book, neglecting Hansen's monumental analysis of Griffith's *Intolerance* (1916), and of Valentino and female spectatorship.

11. Fredric Jameson, *The Political Unconscious*, Cornell University Press, Ithaca 1982, p63.

12. Georg Lukács, 'Reification and the Consciousness of the Proletariat', in *History and Class Consciousness*, (trans. Rodney Livingstone), Merlin Press, London 1971, pp83-222.

Necessity over all such blind zones in which the individual seeks refuge, in pursuit of the purely individual, a merely psychological, project of salvation'.[13] To liberate us from this false belief, Jameson argues, we must conceive the individual and the psychological as historical and political (as part of the symbolic) at the outset. Here, Jameson's comments parallel Hansen's micro-analysis of silent cinema's articulation of the public and private spheres.

5) Jameson notes that cinema emerged within the context of a historical dilemma in the arts, a dilemma that was the result of the artificial, reified division between the public and the private. With the emphasis focused on the illusory construction of the private domain, reception of the arts became nominalistic, in which shared motifs and values could no longer be taken for granted. Artists responded by producing private meanings and languages in their texts (a process of recoding pre-existing signifiers), and created open works of art which could be 'freely interpreted' by the individual consumer in any way s/he felt fit. Jameson writes:

> This is the point when film as an emergent cultural language and apparatus of the twentieth century assumes significant historical meaning. For it is, as Metz has instructed us, a very peculiar language indeed, a 'language without a lexicon' ('this does not mean that filmic expression lacks any kind of predetermined *units*, but such units, where they do exist, are patterns of construction rather than pre-existing elements of the sort provided by the dictionary.' [*Psychoanalysis and Cinema*, p212]) This is to say that the kinds of private language (special signifiers functioning as Lacanian 'upholstery tacks' [*points de capiton*]) we have become accustomed to in high modernist literature are here somehow authorized by the very nature of the cinematographic apparatus itself. [pp102-3]

In other words, Jameson is arguing that the *historical function* of the cinematographic apparatus is to promote the illusion of an individual, centered, coherent subject (as is cinema's function in Hansen's argument).

Jameson successfully identifies the historical determinations of contemporary film theory's findings (the construction by the cinematographic apparatus of an illustory, centered, coherent subject position etc.) but without challenging its essentializing tendency. This essentialism is manifest in both the contemporary film theorists' and Jameson's assertion that the cinema is inherently ideological at the outset. But for Elsaesser, it is 'a mistake to assume that the cinema was from the beginning 'ideological' in the accepted sense. On the contrary,' he continues, 'I believe that it is the task of film history to clarify the points and circumstances under which the cinema was appropriated as an instrument of ideology.' [*FHVP*, p69] In his recent anthology Elsaesser collects together a number of papers on early cinema which broach this issue.[14] As with Hansen's book, many of these papers attempt to determine how cinema developed a particular narrational logic, a problem Elsaesser sees as being tackled by film historians on three levels: the intrinsic development of early

13. Jameson, *The Political Unconscious*, op.cit., p20.
14. Thomas Elsaesser (ed.), *Early Cinema: Space, Frame, Narrative*, BFI Publications, London 1990.

film form; the industrial, economic, legal, demographic, and technological factors which determined the emergence of the narrative feature film, now conceived as a commodity (and therefore open to ideological exploitation); and finally, the simultaneous emergence of continuity cinema and its particular mode of address, one that turns a collective audience into isolated spectators (Hansen's 'classical spectator'). Because this historical research defines cinema's appropriation of narration, not as a 'natural', inevitable fact, but as a contingent, historical addition to the cinema (articulated differently by each national cinema), it avoids at the outset all tendencies to essentialize.

Jameson begins to tackle the problem of essentialism in an analysis of the films of Hans-Jürgen Syberberg. His analysis begins by noting that Syberberg reinvents the 'primitive' artist: 'What [Syberberg] produces is the low budget look of amateur actors, staged tableaux, and vaudeville-type numbers, essentially static and simply strung together … As in the other arts, the stance of the amateur, the apologia for the homemade which characterizes the handicraft ethos, is often a wholesome form of de-reification.' [p64] The static tableau images mimic those of preclassicial cinema, from a time before the capitalist process of reification systematically organized the cinema into a thriving, profitable industry – and correlatively, a time before the logic of the film's structure had been delimited and organized into an efficient, standardized discourse, one that attempts to address the spectator as an individual, unified subject.

Yet the 'originality' of Syberberg's films, for Jameson, lies beyond their destructive (or negative) impulses, for these films also aim towards a Blochian cultural revolution, a revolution that aims to detect and appropriate the 'Utopian (or positive) impulse' at work within negative impulses (ranging from fascism, to nationalism, and consumerism). This positive dimension of Syberberg's films constitute a narrative structure – a structure, however, that conflicts with the films' tableau format.

The purpose behind Syberberg's films is therapeutic – 'a psychoanalysis and exorcism of the collective unconscious of Germany'. [p70] They are made in accordance with a 'spiritual method', which Jameson characterizes as 'a forcible short-circuiting of all the wires in the political unconscious … an attempt to purge the sedimented contents of collective fantasy and ideological representation by reconnecting its symbolic counters so outrageously that they de-reify themselves'. [p73] But this process of de-reification does not lead, in the case of Syberberg, to a negative free play of signifiers, but to a positive attempt to come to terms with the real, historical significance of the subject matter of his films.

Jameson, however, remains sceptical (although not dismissive) of this positive, utopian impulse in Syberberg's films: 'The trouble is that … the realities with which Syberberg attempts to grapple, realities marked by the names of such real historical actors as Wagner, Himmler, Hitler, Bismarck, and the like, are at once transformed [or reified] into so many personal signs in a private language, which becomes public, when the artist is successful, only as an institutionalized sign system.' [p80] The only hope of a utopian impulse lies in the transitional period (an historical moment) between the destruction of the old forms of representation and the inevitable reification of the new forms. Incidently, Jameson also sees this process of reification at work in the cultural appropriation of Godard's films: 'Even the films of Godard in hindsight seem susceptible to a kind of retroactive canonization-reification in which ostentatious marks of improvisation or editing interventions are frozen over after the fact (and by the sheer familiarity of numerous rescreenings) into the timeless features of the "masterworks".' [p188]

Jameson successfully avoids many of the pitfalls of contemporary film theory because he does not marginalize questions of history. However, as my discussion of the work of Elsaesser, Hansen, and the historians of early cinema indicates, many of Jameson's insights have also been made, with far more historical accuracy and theoretical systematicity, within film studies itself. His occasional essays are too fragmentary to form into any coherent theory (hence my reason for simply listing the main points), and the arguments presented in Part Two may confuse all but those who already have a detailed knowledge of Jameson's previous works. For these reasons *Signatures of the Visible* is not so much a work of film theory but seems more like the testament of a well-known 'outsider' who has become caught up in the imaginary pleasures of film and film theory.

PHILOSOPHY WITHOUT TEARS

Simon Frith

Andrew Benjamin and Peter Osborne (eds), *Thinking Art: Beyond Traditional Aesthetics*, ICA, London 1991; £9.95 paper.

The fourteen essays in this book started as talks at London's Institute of Contemporary Arts in 1990. The speakers were brought together under the auspices of the ICA's Philosophical Forum to consider the relationship of art and philosophy. 'Art has long moved beyond the parameters of its traditional aesthetic idea,' suggest the talks' organisers, Peter Osborne and Andrew Benjamin, and this has had two consequences. First, philosophy now has to engage with individual works and their individual aesthetic claims rather than with the abstract entity 'art': philosophy and criticism are therefore 'inextricably intertwined, and both become bound to art history'. (pxi) Second, as exercises in aesthetic theory, art works have to take account of philosophy, of the possibilities of their own deconstruction. In short, 'if philosophy is to contribute to the deepening of our understanding of art, and art to an increased self-consciousness of the character and limitations of philosophy, each will have to be more open to the other than has hitherto been normal.' (pxv)

Both the words 'normal' and 'hitherto' seem a little lazy. Normal for whom? Normal since when? There's a confusion here about what's at stake – whose aesthetic? Whose history? A confusion that is reflected in the series title. Is the antithesis of 'traditional' aesthetics modernism or postmodernism? And what is meant by 'art'? It is only towards the end of the book that philosophical questions are asked of the performing arts (the book is dominated by fine art criticism); and even then there is only passing mention of popular culture, of the media arts, of the possibility that art might be collective, might not be confined to the West. For a book designed to challenge traditional ways of thinking, this collection remains pragmatically (if not theoretically) faithful to the presentation of art as an autonomous practice, defined by its own history, explicable through close study of individual works. This 'dialogue' between philosophers and artists turns out to be a conversation between philosophers, speaking on the artists' behalf. This is aesthetic theory from the productive point of view – the critic explaining how a work should be read.

But this is to over-generalize. The problem (and stimulus) of a collection like this is that editors can't exercise much control over what is said and written: this is not a coherent account of a coherent position: one paper contradicts another;

the most interesting and fertile ideas tend to lie in throwaway remarks, in passing comments. The pleasure of the book is that it can't be read as a linear argument built up block by block; rather it has to be treated serendipitously, as an awkward moment in one essay resonates with a quite different point in another. Argument here works in echoes and traces; to take the closing essays seriously means reading the opening ones anew. A review can't be a blow-by-blow commentary, a philosophical sportscast, but involves a series of statements (or, rather, restatements) of the issues that, in different but overlapping ways, engage every writer here even when – misled by the starting premise of art *versus* philosophy – they don't know it.

The most obvious account of the problem lies in the recurring reference to the 'autonomy' of art. As Christine Battersby points out in her lucid feminist 'defence' of aesthetics, the British left has long been suspicious of the 'disinterest' that seemed essential to Kantian aesthetic theory and has long sought to rewrite the question of artistic value in terms of a sociology of taste. The problem of this position – in which it is denied that the 'aesthetic' can be described without reference to class or race or gender interests – is laid bare in Margaret Iverson's essay on 'Postmodernism, Feminism and the Anti-aesthetic'. In rejecting Lyotard's apparent return to the 'sublime autonomy' of 1950s art theory (the artist as male hero, expressing his freedom through his alienation), Iverson celebrates those female artists who expose the social construction of their own imagery. But when she writes of Barbara Kruger that 'with her superimposed slogans, she forces out into the open the ideological content latent in the media images she appropriates,' (p87) or suggests that in *Interim* Mary Kelly presents in visual form a position 'similar to the one I have advanced here that Minimalism represented a crucial break in art practice which was to prove fruitful for feminist elaboration and critique', (p92) Iverson seems to describe art as simply an imaginative use of audio-visual teaching aids and artistic skill as the ability to wrap up an argument.

What is left for the aesthetic when art becomes pedagogy? Iverson implies nothing and good riddance, but that doesn't explain the impact of Kruger's or Kelly's work, or why their packaged arguments work on us differently – more pleasantly, more memorably – that in their usual academic setting. Do formal questions have no purchase on artistic value? This is the question that (differently put) dominates most of the essays here. A recurring issue, for example, is whether modern art is associated with abstraction – the refusal of representation – because art can no longer represent anything or because abstraction is, in itself, a way of representing modern experience. Peter Burger suggests this is precisely the problem of modernism, first raised by Hegel: 'Art is the unity of subject and object, of the intellect and the senses, and yet that is exactly what it cannot be since alienation is the fundamental condition of modern life. In a word: art in modernity is forever coming up against the conditions of its impossibility.' (p9) Howard Caygill explores this issue through Beckett's and Heidegger's attempts 'to think of art without aesthetic'. – 'Both writers suggest that the beyond aesthetic cannot be spoken, although it can be not spoken through negation or through excess.' (p27) David Batchelor and Peter Osborne argue that abstraction is not the same thing as non-representation. In Batchelor's words, 'it may be argued that a Mondrian or a Rothko is an image of *something*, but not an image of some *thing*. It seems safer to think of the work as representing, or attempting to express, a kind of conception or understanding of a world, to be *like* that world in an abstract way.' (p55) Osborne similarly understands abstraction as 'both a reflection of the form of social experience in developed capitalist societies and a specific artistic strategy to express such experience (alienation) through its distance from and dissonance with established aesthetic norms'.(p62)

Osborne is taking his argument from Adorno, and Adorno's version of the modernist dilemma is dominant here, even if, as Christa Burger points out, 'the passages in *Aesthetic Theory* which circumscribe the relationship between mimesis and rationality are extraordinarily opaque.' (p135) Adorno can certainly be read as following Kant in treating the aesthetic function as essentially cognitive. Artists represent the world by making an argument about it, know the world by working on it, and the modernist dilemma (the Hegelian issue) is that when subject and object are split – when the world can't be *grasped* – then the aesthetic atrophies. On the other hand, the artist's failure of expression can become, in itself, a way of knowing the world, knowing one's alienation from it. Cultural attention begins to focus on the struggle to express (and its heroics); the artistic process becomes more significant than the artistic object (which is now suspect). As Alistair Williams argues, for Adorno the music critic, modernism begins with Beethoven's 'spiritual isolation from the world' in his late work, and his 'recognition, in musical terms, of the irreconcilability of direct expression and form'.(p145)

Adorno's political concern was, in Osborne's words, how to understand 'the social determinants of artistic practice', without thereby denying its possibilities as a critical practice. What is at issue is not the relationship between expression and construction as such – the fact that what we want to say is always mediated by the forms and objects through which we have to speak – but that 'subjective' expression always involves objectification, means submitting ourselves either to the world of things (and magic) or to the world of reason (and technology). (Adorno, after all, once remarked that ideally Schoenberg's music should be read not heard; once musical instruments, musical bodies, are involved, the sounds become encrusted with extraneous social significance.) Art is, therefore, impossible – the subject can never be expressed through the object – but necessary. Not to try would be to die; death stalks Adorno's pages more poignantly than it does Beckett's.

Adorno's position hardly goes 'beyond' traditional aesthetics; rather, it laments their passing. The lost faculty is our individual ability to grasp the world formally and, indeed, we could say that 'traditional' aesthetics were constructed by modernism in its very frustration. I'm not at all clear that postmodernism goes beyond traditional aesthetics either. We may now pay lip service to the blurring of cultural boundaries, but artistic creativity, the work of the unique, original, 'individual' subject is still contrasted with craft, with the serial, institutional turnover of images. We may now assert that, cognitively, all texts are unstable, but the critical task remains interpretation.

The assumptions here, it seems, only become problematic when attention shifts from high art to the performing arts, to the popular arts, to the collective arts; when we ask not what it means to make art but what it means to respond to it.

To take the last point first, there is a clear belief in this book that the critic's task is to *explain art to its audience*. Michael Newman, for example, questions the value of double mimesis in such postmodern work as Cindy Sherman's not because he thinks viewers might not get the joke but because he thinks they might not get the point. But from a viewer's perspective the pleasure of the *trompe l'oeil*, like the pleasure of Cindy Sherman's photos, is not that we think, even momentarily, that such images are the real thing but that we know immediately that they're not: what we respond to is not the illusion but the creation of an illusion, just as when we're children we enjoy hand shadow rabbits because we know they're hands not rabbits!

This is to come to the problem of interpretation. Benjamin and Osborne agree that the 'crisis' in the aesthetic means that 'the need for interpretation is both intensified and deepened', (pxi) and presumably at least part of the point of this book is to provide examples of good art criticism – such as Howard Caygill on Greg Bright: 'His paintings and sculptures present neither things nor "thingness", but inscribe a route which, refusing to pass through aesthetic oppositions, nevertheless marks the recognition of an obligation. These works offer ways which are both excessive and negative.' (p27) – or Andrew Benjamin on Keifer: 'The approaches taken here to Keifer, while tentative, open up interpretation. Henceforth, interpretation, rather than involving the banality of an opened pluralism, will be linked to the opening of a plurality in which judgment is constrained to act.' (p109)

Says who? In this reader, at least, such authoritarian announcements (about rather indistinct black and white pictorial examples) are unconvincing – that is, they do not account for the artistic experience on offer. By contrast, in his discussion of muscial serialism, Alistair Williams occasionally lets slip a different (and unexplained) sort of descriptive term. 'There is,' he writes of Boulez's *Structures Là*, 'a certain austere beauty in the way certain sonorities or constellations of sonorities gleam through the texture.' (p149) (Note the self-protective use of the word 'certain'.) Boulez's 'extraordinary ear for texture and spacing,' Williams later notes, 'produces moments of sensuous beauty' in the 3rd Piano Sonata, (p152) and what's striking is less the theoretical significance of 'beauty' (for Boulez, as for Adorno, it seems to be defined in terms of a sensual immediacy) than that Williams assumes that his readers (Boulez's listeners) know what moments he's talking about.

The issue is the relevant significance for an aesthetic response of concept and feeling. The philosophers here mostly follow Christine Battersby in rejecting the Kantian notion of 'immediacy' and go beyond her by discounting sensuality too. Now in one respect this way of putting the argument – in terms of immediate response *versus* considered reflection – is mistaken. As Peter Burger elegantly argues, 'aesthetic discourse doesn't attach itself to works of art after the fact but is rather that which makes them possible in the first place,' (p12) and as Georgina Born makes clear in her piece on 'Music, Modernism, and Signification,' 'the core of music as culture is its existence as an organized and meaningful sound, which is already encultured, and which is perceived as "music" only by virtue of its difference from "noise" or "sound-in-general".' (p166) In short, 'immediate' – or sensual – response is already conceptually framed; which is not to say that there isn't an immediate response, even if most of the contributors here do seem peculiarly detached from it.

This is the reason why, for me, the most interesting essays in the book, the ones that do seek to go beyond traditional aesthetics, are those on the performing and 'mass' arts. Born's essay is the most straightforward of these. While still working within the modernist discourse she does question the boundaries of the aesthetic object: the meaning of music (and, by implication, all art) lies in its intertextuality. And the questions this raises about the creative process and the nature of interpretation are taken up, in different ways, in Sandra Kemp's arguments about dance (see pp91-102 in this issue), Jean-Jacques Lecercle's about cinema (again, see pp80-90 in this issue), and Sylviane Agacinski's about architecture.

Kemp addresses an aesthetic object which is unstable, an aesthetic experience which is elusive, an aesthetic material which is literally embodied, an aesthetic text which is both subject (willed movement) and object (of the choreographer, of the spectator, of discourse). Dance is a medium in which Adorno's terms (mimesis *vs* reason, construction *vs* expression) become indistinguishable. Kemp's point (and the argument applies to music too – even serialism) is that in dance aesthetic experience is 'something less than rational cognition; more than sensory awareness'. (p188)

In exploring the meaning of movement, Kemp raises questions about space and time, questions ignored in the fine art focus on the still depiction, in the art music focus on structure, but taken up in Lecercle's witty commentary on Deleuze's *Cinema* and Bergson's theory of the image. For Lecercle the importance of Deleuze's work is that it challenges the primacy of language in aesthetic (and interpretative) theory – the image, in his words, is no utterance; in terms of time and space, what we need to understand is not Freud's unconscious but cinema's – if the cine camera is a metaphor for a body with consciousness then the unconscious is simply that which the camera presently doesn't (but could, and might) see. Agacinski's essay on the monument asks another set of questions, about the purpose of art (putting material rather than perception to the test) and its social basis (a building, unlike a drawing or a blueprint, can only be 'read' as a collaborative act).

All these questions – about performance, about moving imagery, about technology, about collaboration – would have been pushed further if philosophers didn't continue to define art in such conventional terms. There's an irony here. In showing so powerfully the problems of an aesthetic theory dominated by problems of meaning and depiction, of an aesthetic theory which, in the end, equates art with language, Kemp and Lecercle aren't so much going beyond traditional aesthetics as reminding us of alternative philosophies – Bergson, and the eighteenth century rationalists, like Adam Smith, who took for granted music's superiority to the imitative arts. As usual, the way forward turns out to mean retracing the path by which we got here.

BACK ISSUES

1 PETER WOLLEN on fashion and orientalism . . . DENISE RILEY on 'women' and feminism . . . DICK HEBDIGE's sociology of the Sublime . . . LAURA MARCUS on autobiographies . . . JOHN TAGG Should art historians know their place? . . . FRANCO BIANCHINI on the GLC's cultural policies . . . HOMI K. BHABHA, STEPHAN FEUCHTWANG & BARBARA HARLOW on Fanon . . . Reviews by COUSINS on Foucault, MCLENNAN on Norris, SCHWARZ on Englishness and O'PRAY on Powell & Pressburger

2 MARY KELLY, ELIZABETH COWIE & NORMAN BRYSON on Kelly's Interim . . . GREIL MARCUS on subversive entertainment . . . GEORGINA BORN on modern music culture . . . GEOFFREY NOWELL-SMITH on popular culture . . . IEN ANG on 'progressive television'. . . ALAN SINFIELD on modernism and English Studies in the Cold War . . . TONY BENNETT on Eagleton

3 **TRAVELLING THEORY**
JULIA KRISTEVA on the melancholic imaginary . . . DAVID EDGAR on carnival and drama . . . KOBENA MERCER Black hair/style politics . . . JACQUES RANCIÈRE on journeys into new worlds . . . PETER HULME'S Caribbean diary . . . BILL SCHWARZ on travelling stars . . . GINETTE VINCENDEAU on chanteuses réalistes . . . STEVE CONNOR on Springsteen . . . CHRISTOPHER NORRIS on Gasché's Derrida

4 **CULTURAL TECHNOLOGIES**
SIMON FRITH making sense of jazz in Britain . . . GRISELDA POLLOCK on Doré's London . . . COLIN MERCER on entertainment . . . TONY BENNETT's exhibitionary complex . . . IAN HUNTER setting limits to culture . . . DAVID SAUNDERS on copyright and literature . . . JODY BERLAND on television

5 **IDENTITIES**
HOMI K. BHABHA on the commitment to theory . . . PHILIP COHEN on Tarzan and the jungle bunnies . . . GLENN BOWMAN on Palestinian nationalist consciousness . . . KRISTIN ROSS on Rimbaud and spatial history . . . KAJA SILVERMAN on Liberty, maternity, commodification . . . ADRIAN RIFKIN on Carmenology . . . MARGARET SOTAN's epistemology of the wandering woman . . . ANDREW BENJAMIN on psychoanalysis . . . GILL DAVIES on heritage . . . LES BACK on soundsystems

6 **THE BLUES**
JACQUELINE ROSE on Margaret Thatcher and Ruth Ellis . . . JAMES DONALD How English is it? . . . BENITA PARRY on Kipling's imperialism . . . JOHN SILVER on Carpentier . . . MITRA TABRIZIAN & ANDY GOLDING's Blues . . . BARBARA CREED on *Blue Velvet* . . . JOSEPH BRISTOW on masculinity . . . GRAHAM MURDOCK on Moretti's *Bildungsroman* . . . EDMOND WRIGHT on post-Humptydumptyism

7 **MODERNISM/MASOCHISM**
VICTOR BURGIN's Tokyo . . . LINDA WILLIAMS on feminine masochism and feminist criticism . . . JOHN TAGG on criticism, photography and technological change . . . GEOFF BENNINGTON: L'arroseur arrosé(e) . . . EMILIA STEUERMAN on Habermas vs Lyotard . . . PAUL CROWTHER on the Kantian sublime, the avant-garde and the postmodern . . . MARK COUSINS on Lévi Strauss on Mauss . . . IAIN CHAMBERS being 'British' . . . ADRIAN FORTY on lofts and gardens . . . LISA TICKNER on Griselda Pollock

8 **TECHNO-ECOLOGIES**
PETER WOLLEN Cinema/Americanism and the robot . . . JOHN KEANE on the liberty of the press . . . S.P. MOHANTY on the philosophical basis of political criticism . . . DAVID KAZANJIAN & ANAHID KASSABIAN Naming the Armenian Genocide . . . PAUL THÉBERGE The 'sound' of music . . . DAVID TOMAS The technophilic body . . . FÉLIX GUATTARI The three ecologies . . . MARGARET WHITFORD on Sartre

9 **ON ENJOYMENT**
SLAVOJ ŽIŽEK The undergrowth of enjoyment . . . PETER OSBORNE Aesthetic autonomy and the crisis of theory . . . RACHEL BOWLBY The judgement of Paris (and the choice of Kristeva) . . . JOSEPH BRISTOW Being gay: politics, identity, pleasure . . . GAIL CHING-LIANG LOW White skins black masks . . . CHRISTINE HOLMLUND I Love Luce . . . LINE GRENIER From diversity to indifference . . . MARK COUSINS Is chastity a perversion? . . . SIMON CRITCHLEY Review of Christopher Norris

Back issues cost £12.99 each
Make cheque or money order payable to Lawrence & Wishart and send to:
Lawrence & Wishart, 144a Old South Lambeth Road, London SW8 1XX

NEW FORMATIONS

Now in its sixth year, *New Formations* has established a reputation nationally and internationally as one of Britain's most significant journals of cultural debate, history and theory. *New Formations* brings new and challenging perspectives to bear on the categories that frame cultural analysis and political action; as one reviewer writes, the journal has become 'a vital tool in honing an awareness of the politics of culture'.

WHY NOT SUBSCRIBE?
MAKE SURE OF YOUR COPY

The issues for 1992 are Nos. 16, 17 and 18.

Subscription rates, 1992 (3 issues)

Individual Subscriptions

UK	£28.00
USA	$50.00
Rest of World	£30.00

Institutional Subscriptions

UK	£45.00
USA	$74.00
Rest of World	£46.00

Please send one year's subscription starting with Issue Number ____________

I enclose payment of ____________________________

Please send me ________________ copies of back issue no. ____________

I enclose total payment of ____________________________

Name: ____________________________

Address: ____________________________

____

Please return this form with cheque or money order payable to Lawrence & Wishart and send to:
Lawrence & Wishart, 144a Old South Lambeth Road, London SW8 1XX

OXFORD ART JOURNAL

Edited by: Annie E. Coombes, Tamar Garb, Andrew Hemingway, Fred Orton, Deborah Philips, and Richard Wrigley

The OXFORD ART JOURNAL holds an international reputation for publishing innovative critical work in art history, with a strong emphasis on the political analysis of visual art and material culture.

AMERICAN ART AND LATIN AMERICAN ART

OXFORD ART JOURNAL *Volume 15 Number 1, 1992*

The new issue focuses on North American Art

Angela Miller on the mechanisms of the market and the invention of western regionalism; **Michael Hatt** on masculinity and the black body in mid-nineteenth-century American sculpture; **Sarah Burns** on gender politics in the criticism of Cecilia Beaux; **Timothy R. Rodgers** on Alfred Stieglitz, Duncan Phillips, and the '$6000 Marin'; **J. Gray Sweeney** on racism, nationalism, and nostalgia in cowboy art; **Shulamith Behr** on Kandinsky, Mitrinovic, and Pan-Christian Universalism; **Anthony Hughes** on the connoisseur of industry; **Richard Wrigley** on Apelles in Bohemia; and **Terry Atkinson** beholding Courbet from the side.

OXFORD ART JOURNAL *Volume 14 Number 1, 1991*

From a recent issue centred on Latin American Art

Being Drawn to an Image by **Guy Brett**

'Her Dress Hangs Here': De-Frocking the Kahlo Cult by **Oriana Baddeley**

Revolution as Ritual: Diego Rivera's National Palace Mural by **Leonard Folgarait**

Surrealising the Baroque: Mexico's Spanish Heritage and the work of Alberto Gironella by **Valerie Fraser**

Abstract Expressionism and Third World Art: A Post-Colonial Approach to 'American' Art by **David Craven**

Géricault and Georget: Portraying Monomaniacs to service the Alienist's Monomania by **Albert Boime**

Fictional Unities: 'Antifascism' and 'Antifascist Art' in 30s America by **Andrew Hemingway**

Subscription rates Volume 15 1992, 2 issues

Institutions: Europe £33.00, elsewhere US$69.00

Individuals: Europe £19.00, elsewhere US$42.00

Please note that subscriptions are for complete volumes only. Individual rates apply only when subscriptions are paid for with a personal cheque or credit card and delivered to a private address.

To subscribe, obtain further information or a *free sample copy* please return to Journals Marketing Department (X), Oxford University Press, Pinkhill House, Southfield Road, Eynsham, Oxford OX8 1JJ, UK

PUBLISHED BY OXFORD UNIVERSITY PRESS